# NASCAR NEXTEL CUP SERIES 2004

## 2004 NASCAR NEXTEL CUP SERIES AWARDS CEREMONY

Waldorf=Astoria, New York, N.Y.
December 3, 2004

# Acknowledgements
## NASCAR NEXTEL Cup Series 2004

Since 1988, UMI has chronicled each racing season by publishing the NASCAR Cup Series Yearbooks, which are presented annually at the NASCAR Awards Ceremony in New York City. Beginning in 1993, we also undertook the task of "filling in" the seasons from 1972, the beginning of the sport's "Modern Era," through 1998, the year the first book was published. With that completed, UMI then produced two additional volumes that recorded the sport's history from its inception in the late 1940s through the 1971 season.

This year we are pleased to introduce "NASCAR NEXTEL Cup Series 2004," the first yearbook to bear the name of new series sponsor Nextel Communications, Inc. In some ways, this is a continuation of the line of books that now spans the entire history of NASCAR Cup Series competition. On the other hand, the story of the 2004 season represents a new age in the sport, highlighted by the inaugural Chase for the NASCAR NEXTEL Cup, the exciting 10-race conclusion to the season that pitted the year's 10 best drivers against each other to compete for the privilege of being crowned the first NASCAR NEXTEL Cup Series champion.

Just as NASCAR, in conjunction with its many partners and sponsors, has continually strived to present the very best in motorsports competition, we at UMI Publications have been diligent in producing the highest quality products for you to enjoy.

But we could never do it alone. Without the assistance of many talented and dedicated people, this book simply would not be possible. Therefore, we would like to recognize those who helped bring it all about.

To our longtime friends at NASCAR, we once again offer our heartfelt appreciation. Thanks especially to Brian France, Mike Helton, George Pyne, Jim Hunter, Mark Dyer, Jennifer White, Paul Schaefer and Catherine McNeill, for their help and guidance throughout the year.

We would also like to express our gratitude and appreciation to our new friends at Nextel Communications, Inc. To Michael Robichaud, Mike Mooney, Jill Gregory and Becky Cox, we welcome you and thank you for your support and outstanding service to this effort.

We are pleased to have veteran motorsports journalist Gary McCredie document the story of the 2004 NASCAR NEXTEL Cup Series season. Gary's extensive knowledge of the sport combined with his stylistic portrayal of the year's events is a true asset, and we thank him for his outstanding work.

No book such as this one would be worth having if it were not for the captivating imagery that brings the story to life. Therefore, we would like to recognize the hard-working and very gifted photographers who make it possible. Again this year, the staff of CIA Stock Photography — Don Grassman, Ernie Masche, Gary Eller, Tom Copeland and Andrew Copley — contributed their finest work, and we thank them for their dedication.

We would also like to welcome Action Sports Photography to the Yearbook staff. To Walter Arce, Phil Cavali, Matt Thacker, Russell LaBounty and Tina Snyder, we say thank you for your outstanding contributions.

Sadly UMI, along with the entire racing community, lost veteran photographer David Chobat midway through the season. For 25 years, David captured nearly every defining moment in this sport's history and recorded them on film for us to enjoy and remember. He contributed heavily to almost every racing-related publication we produced over the years. But more than that, he was a good fiend to us all, and he is sorely missed.

Most of all, we'd like to thank you, the fans of NASCAR NEXTEL Cup Series racing, for your support over the years. We're proud to say that NASCAR has the greatest fans anywhere, period. This book is for you, and we hope you enjoy it as much as we enjoyed bringing it to you.

### UMI Publications, Inc. Staff

President and Publisher:
**Ivan Mothershead**

Vice President and Associate Publisher:
**Rick Peters**

Controller:
**Lewis Patton**

COO & VP and National Advertising Manager:
**Mark Cantey**

Advertising Executive:
**Paul Kaperonis**

Managing Editor:
**Ward Woodbury**

Associate Editor:
**Ritchie Hallman**

Art Direction/Publication Design:
**Brett Shippy**

Manager of Information Systems/ Publication Design:
**Mike McBride**

Administrative Staff:
**Stephanie Cook, Mary Flowe, Renee Wedvick**

Color Proofing provided by Gray Graphics. Proudly produced and printed in the U.S.A.

ISBN#0-943860-35-0

The NASCAR NEXTEL Cup Series marks are used under license by NASCAR, Inc. and NEXTEL Communications, Inc.

# Foreword

## NASCAR NEXTEL Cup Series 2004

"Every driver, crewman, sponsor and car owner has you in mind in everything they do. You expect the best in competition, and we're here to exceed your expectations."

NASCAR made a commitment to take bold new steps to enhance our core brand of competition. We made a fresh start this year on several fronts, and the results exceeded our highest expectations.

We introduced the Chase for the NASCAR NEXTEL Cup this year to achieve the goals of delivering a new excitement to our fans, and new value to corporate America.

By any standard, there was a sense of added drama in the achievements of NASCAR NEXTEL Cup Series drivers and teams in 2004. We believe that the Chase for the NASCAR NEXTEL Cup is the perfect package to compliment superior performance under intense pressure.

The Chase proved to be a meaningful stage for the best race car drivers to showcase their talent, determination and instinct. They produced a season-long storyline that led to the closest points finish in NASCAR NEXTEL Cup Series history, which boiled down to the last lap of the last race of the season. That's the door-to-door drama that built NASCAR racing into one of the most popular sports in America.

We salute Kurt Busch, Jack Roush and the IRWIN/Sharpie Ford team on their 2004 NASCAR NEXTEL Cup Series championship. We salute the rest of the Chase drivers for showing their own championship traits: Jimmie Johnson, Jeff Gordon, Mark Martin, Dale Earnhardt Jr., Tony Stewart, Ryan Newman, Matt Kenseth, Elliott Sadler and Jeremy Mayfield.

We want to congratulate our friends at Nextel Communications on their major contributions to our drivers, teams and tracks in their first year as a title sponsor. We also want to thank Sunoco for a great first year as well. We look forward to sharing greater successes as we move forward.

Finally, to our fans: Thank you for being the greatest, most passionate fans in American sports. Every driver, crewman, sponsor and car owner has you in mind in everything they do. You expect the best in competition, and we're here to exceed your expectations.

Sincerely,

Brian Z. France

# Contents

## NASCAR NEXTEL Cup Series 2004

# Preface
## NASCAR NEXTEL Cup Series 2004

NASCAR-sanctioned stock car competition — especially its top division which traces its roots back to a race run on a dusty dirt track in Charlotte, N.C., in June 1949 — has always been fluid, flowing and ever changing.

*(Above) Roush Racing fields one of the more formidable stables of drivers for the 2004 NASCAR NEXTEL Cup Series season, including (from left) Jeff Burton, defending champion Matt Kenseth, Mark Martin, Kurt Busch and Greg Biffle.*

*(Right, Above) Felix Sabates (left) and Kevin Harvick approach the 2004 season in the usual manner: happily. Sabates, along with partner Chip Ganassi, fields three Dodge teams, while Harvick, one of three drivers employed by Richard Childress Racing, looks to improve on his fifth-place finish in last year's standings.*

*(Right, Below) Reigning NASCAR Busch Series champion Brian Vickers enters NASCAR's top series full-time this year, driving the No. 25 Chevrolet fielded by Hendrick Motorsports in a bid for Raybestos Rookie of the Year honors.*

Sometimes those changes were subtle and somewhat invisible to all those but the sport's most directly involved participants. At other times, they were so evident that they caught the attention of much of the entire sporting world.

Such was the case when NASCAR's premier series put 2003 firmly in the past and hit the ground running at Daytona Beach, Fla., the following February. For one, it had a new name: the NASCAR NEXTEL Cup Series. The series' prime sponsor of 33 years, R.J. Reynolds' Winston brand, had bowed out at the end of 2003 and Reston, Va.-based Nextel Communications had stepped in to take its place. A leading company in wireless communications, Nextel had agreed to back the series through the 2013 season.

"Realignment 2004 and beyond," as announced by NASCAR Chairman Bill France Jr. at the start of the 2003 season, went into effect. North Carolina Speedway, in Rockingham, found itself with one NASCAR NEXTEL Cup Series race instead of two, California Speedway, in Fontana, would now host two races instead of one, and the date of the legendary Southern 500 at Darlington (S.C.) Raceway had been switched from the first week in September to the second week in November.

Another surprise came in mid-September when France, 70, announced he was retiring immediately as the sanctioning body's chief executive officer, a post he'd inherited from his dad, Bill France Sr., in 1972. Replacing him would be his son, Brian Z. France, 41, who had spent years learning the business of NASCAR from the ground up, and he wasted no time in taking the reins. By the end of the year, Unocal had bid adieu as NASCAR's official fuel supplier, making the way for Sunoco in 2004, while "racing back to the caution" had also been abandoned.

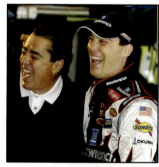

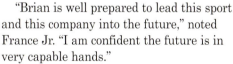

"Brian is well prepared to lead this sport and this company into the future," noted France Jr. "I am confident the future is in very capable hands."

By the time the competitors of the newly-named NASCAR NEXTEL Cup Series were gearing up for testing sessions at Daytona International Speedway in January, about all had been settled and committed to paper. Drivers and teams that elected to stay intact had inked updated contracts, while some organizations had elected to make extensive changes. Sponsorship questions had been settled, 2003 series champion Matt Kenseth was prepared to defend his title, and a strong group of newcomers was ready to duke it out for the series' Raybestos Rookie of the Year title.

Then came the biggest change of all. Formally announced in mid-January 2004, the points system used to determine the overall series champion since 1975 had been modified. Brian France and NASCAR president Mike Helton, in making the announcement, labeled the biggest change in NASCAR competition in 30 years the "Chase for the NASCAR NEXTEL Cup."

"The Chase for the NASCAR NEXTEL Cup will provide a better opportunity for more drivers to win the championship, creating excitement and drama throughout the entire (36-race) season," Helton said. "In addition, the Chase will showcase our drivers' talents, increasing the value for all teams and their sponsors.

*(Above Left) Jeremy Mayfield (left) and Kasey Kahne take the wheels of Ray Evernham's Dodges in 2004. With Bill Elliott cutting back to a part-time effort, Mayfield becomes the team's veteran, while Kahne focuses on becoming the series' top rookie.*

*(Above Right) While the NASCAR trailer sports the new look of first-year title sponsor Nextel, Jamie McMurray's Ford wears a paint scheme reminiscent of old, when drivers such as Davey Allison, Ernie Irvan and Ricky Rudd piloted the cars bearing the Texaco/Havoline name.*

*(Below Left) Also new for 2004 is the SUNOCO brand of racing fuel, this year carried in 12-gallon cans, one up from the traditional 11-gallon containers used for years.*

*(Below Right) Goodyear returns for another season as the series' exclusive tire supplier, but this year with new rubber compounds designed to increase safety and competition.*

"This new approach to determining our champion has both the drivers and the fans in mind."

For the 43 competitors in the year's first 26 (of 36) events, the points system would remain the same as it had been since 1975 with one exception. The race winner would now receive 180 points instead of 175, thus assuring he would get at least five more points than the runner-up. Five-point bonuses for leading at least one lap and the most laps would remain in effect.

After the completion of the 26th race, the top 10 drivers in points, plus any other driver within 400 points of the leader, would earn a berth in the Chase for the NASCAR NEXTEL Cup and have their points adjusted. The first-place driver would start anew with 5,050 points, the second-place driver would begin with 5,045,

with incremental five-point drops continuing through the list of contenders. The remaining drivers would keep the points they'd earned and continue to accrue as many more as possible.

At the end of the 2004 season, the NASCAR NEXTEL Cup Series champion would receive more than $5 million, while drivers finishing second through 10th in points were guaranteed at least $1 million.

"The Chase for the NASCAR NEXTEL Cup will be a continuation of our season, with heightened drama," Helton said. "It will increase the spotlight on all competitors and increase the value of being in the series for all teams.

"This will be exciting and fair."

Helton also pointed out that since 1975, no driver lower than 10th in points with 10 races left in the season had ever managed to recover and win the championship. Yet to be as fair as possible the 400-point cutoff was added to include drivers outside the top 10 in the final Chase.

The Chase was set to begin on Sept. 19 with the Sylvania 300 at the 1.058-mile New Hampshire International Speedway in Loudon, and would end Nov. 21 in Florida with the Ford 400 on the 1.5-mile Homestead-Miami Speedway. In between were a mixture of events on short and intermediate tracks and the 2.66-mile Talladega (Ala.) Superspeedway.

The competitors faced changes in racing procedures and technical rules, as well, at the start of the 2004 NASCAR NEXTEL Cup Series season. For example, Goodyear, the series' official tire supplier, came up with a new, softer tire compound designed to wear more evenly at racing speeds. The new compound could also reduce tire failure, but it would also affect pit strategy by encouraging more four-tire pit stops.

Spoiler heights and restrictor-plate sizes had also been changed. With the exception of packages for Daytona and Talladega, the two restrictor-plate tracks, spoiler heights had been reduced 3/4-inch to 5-1/2 inches, while they were increased 1/2-inch to 6-3/4 inches at the two "plate" venues. The plate openings had been increased slightly from 7/8-inch to 29/32-inch.

Also, the gas or "dump" can capacity had been increased from 11 to 12 gallons. And, too, the twin ignition-system units now had to be mounted on the car's dashboard to facilitate inspection procedures.

Yet another big change facing the teams as they readied for 2004 was the system of award-

ing provisional starts. Most significantly was the change from 36 to 38 in the number of cars making the 43-car field via qualifying. That reduced the number of available provisional starts from seven to five, while the "champion's provisional" for the 43rd spot was retained when applicable.

NASCAR's previously more conservative policy concerning pre-event testing was liberalized a bit for 2004. Teams now could avail themselves of five two-day private-car tests and four single-day tests at tracks hosting series events. Teams with drivers running for the Raybestos Rookie of the Year Award would be allowed seven two-day and five single-day tests for a total of 19 days. Previously, teams were allowed

five two-day tests while that number was nine for rookies.

Usually, drivers, crew chiefs and leading mechanics who move from one team to another highlight a new season. While that happened to some degree as 2003 came to an end, the big news of the off-season was the number of changes occurring within the teams themselves.

Going into 2004, Bobby Labonte and Tony Stewart were set for another year with Joe Gibbs Racing and their team sponsors, Interstate Batteries and The Home Depot. They'd have to approach the new season, though, without the guiding hand of the "boss," as team owner Gibbs had decided to "return home" to the NFL and the team he'd led to three Super Bowl victories, the Washington

Redskins. Gibbs left professional football at the end of 1992 to fully oversee the NASCAR NEXTEL Cup Series team he'd formed that year.

Since that time, while Gibbs' race team had prospered, winning championships in 2000 and 2002, the "Skins" had sunk into mediocrity. Gibbs got the call from the team's owner to come back; he accepted and left most of the race team's administration in the hands of his 34-year-old son, J.D. Gibbs.

"If this were five or seven years ago, he wouldn't do this," Labonte noted. "But he feels the timing is right for him to go coach."

"I know his commitment to winning is unmatched. He's always been a coach, and football has always been very close to him," Stewart said. "Fans of the Redskins should be very happy."

(Top) Jimmie Johnson (left) gets some friendly words of advice from Jeff Gordon. Johnson enters the season as a championship contender after finishing second in 2003 and fifth the year before that, but he'll surely have to beat his teammate and co-owner, who is intent on capturing title No. 5.

(Above) Penske driver Ryan Newman led all competitors with eight wins and a gaudy 11 Bud Poles in 2003. Adding consistency to the mix is his plan for improving on a sixth-place finish in last year's standings.

(Left) An unlikely scenario for the 2004 season is that Jack Roush's Ford with driver Jeff Burton will remain without a primary sponsor on its quarter panels for very long. Over eight seasons, Burton put the No. 99 in victory lane 17 times.

*Joe Gibbs (above) began fielding his team in 1992 and developed it into a powerhouse, winning the championship in 2000 with driver Bobby Labonte (top right) followed by rookie honors in 2001 and another championship in 2002 with Tony Stewart, pictured at top with 2003 champion Matt Kenseth. Before the start of the current season, Gibbs was offered and accepted the head coaching position with the Washington Redskins, the NFL team he previously led to three Super Bowl wins.*

*(Right) Dale Earnhardt Jr. is set to begin his fifth full season of competition, again led by crew chief Tony Eury Sr. (right), riding the momentum of a 2003 season that yielded two wins, 13 top fives, 21 top 10s and a third-place finish in the championship standings.*

Roush Racing and Robert Yates Racing had long been considered Ford Motor Co.'s flagship NASCAR NEXTEL Cup Series operations, and when they decided to meet the challenge presented by Chevrolet and Dodge by combining resources, it was, indeed, a newsworthy event. The two owners created a separate engine-building facility in Mooresville, N.C., and all powerplants developed and built there would go into the cars of both teams. Also, the agreement to cooperate would include Wood Brothers Racing and its driver, Ricky Rudd, who had been getting engines from Roush.

"Robert Yates has always had great horsepower and Jack Roush has always had great fuel mileage," said Yates driver Elliott Sadler. "You put those two together ..."

"I think we'll be much stronger (and) lead more laps ... win more races," added Roush's Matt Kenseth. Roush himself noted that the move put his massive operation "ahead of where we were last year."

Both teams suffered in 2003. Sadler won no races and was 22nd in points, while his teammate, Dale Jarrett, won one event and was 26th in the standings. In the Roush sta-

ble, titlist Kenseth also won just one race. Of his teammates, Kurt Busch scored four wins and Greg Biffle, one, while Mark Martin and Jeff Burton went winless. None of the four cracked the top 10 in points, and Burton faced 2004 without a sponsor.

On the move: The Wood Brothers team went winless again in 2003, which prompted a radical solution. Based in rural Stuart, Va., since its inception in the early 1950s, the team relocated to Mooresville, N.C., during the off-season. The Woods leased Yates' shop after his teams moved into a new complex in the same town.

The Chip Ganassi Racing with Felix Sabates team also had a less-than-stellar season with its drivers, Jamie McMurray, Sterling Marlin, and Casey Mears, all going without victories

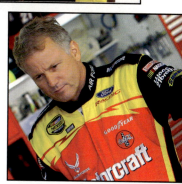

and finishing out of the hunt. Ganassi decided a "fix" was in order and, going into the 2004 season, was readying to move his operation from Mooresville to Concord, N.C., near Roush's complex.

Bill Elliott's future in racing, a subject of discussion late 2003, was finally determined when Elliott, who ran his first series race in 1976, announced his semi-retirement. He would remain with Dodge owner Ray Evernham and would help new team driver Kasey Kahne through his rookie season. Elliott said he would run a few selected races in 2004, and that moved Jeremy Mayfield up a notch as Evernham's No. 1 driver.

At Penske Racing, driver Rusty Wallace hoped to end an almost-three-year losing streak by appointing a new crew chief, Larry Carter. Fellow Penske driver Ryan Newman (2003's leading race winner) anticipated no changes in his team, but Penske himself made a big move when he acquired a major stake in the neighboring Jasper Motorsports team. Driver Dave Blaney left the team and was replaced by promising rookie contender Brendan Gaughan.

Going into Daytona there was a shuffle of sorts at Dale Earnhardt, Inc. The organization "downsized" from three drivers to two, retaining Dale Earnhardt Jr. and Michael Waltrip. Also, Ty Norris, DEI's executive vice presi-

dent of motorsports, resigned after eight years and was replaced by former chief engine builder Richie Gilmore.

Richard Childress Racing remained committed to a three-team effort. Driver Kevin Harvick was again paired with crew chief Todd Berrier. Rookie driver Johnny Sauter was teamed with crew chief Kevin Hamlin, while Chris Andrews was named to oversee Robby Gordon's Chevrolet.

Several drivers found themselves without rides going into 2004, a few sported new sponsors or signed with new teams, and the 2004 roster of drivers seeking the NASCAR NEXTEL Cup Series Raybestos Rookie of the Year Award was strong and promising. Joining Gaughan, Kahne and Sauter were Scott Riggs (MBV Motorsports), Scott Wimmer (Bill Davis Racing) and 2003 NASCAR Busch Series champion Brian Vickers (Hendrick Motorsports).

*(Top Left)* Team owners and recognized engine-building experts Robert Yates (left) and Jack Roush decided to combine forces to produce powerplants for their teams.

*(Top Right)* Beneficiaries of the arrangement include Yates teammates Elliott Sadler (left) and Dale Jarrett, both of whom start the season hoping to rebound from sub-par years in 2003.

*(Above)* Also applying Yates/Roush power in 2004 is veteran driver Ricky Rudd, who starts his second season behind the wheel for the Wood Brothers.

*(Far Left)* After three full seasons in the NASCAR Busch Series, Scott Wimmer takes over the No. 22 Caterpillar Dodge at Bill Davis Racing, another member of a strong freshman class in 2004.

*(Left)* With one complete season of experience under his belt, Casey Mears returns to the seat of the Target Dodge fielded by Chip Ganassi Racing with Felix Sabates.

# 2004 NASCAR NEXTEL Cup Series
# CHAMPION

## KURT BUSCH

"I want to dedicate this championship to Jimmy Fennig because of the knowledge he's given me in learning how to drive these race cars. That's what helped us to win."

*(Opposite Page) 2004 NASCAR NEXTEL Cup Series Champion Kurt Busch. In his fourth full year of competition, Busch, a native of Las Vegas, Nev., collected career wins number 9, 10 and 11, and combined them with remarkable reliability to take the coveted crown.*

Knowing we had such a small cushion in points going into the last race at Homestead, Fla., I was just very, very anxious to get the race started. But it felt like it was "zero-zero" again. After the race was over, I thought this had to be anything and everything people imagined the Chase for the NASCAR NEXTEL Cup could be.

I was in favor of the new change in determining points because of the way it gave our team a new outlook in how to approach the championship. And that was to create a 26-race "regular season" with a 10-race "playoff." So we definitely liked the new format because we found the correct frame of mind to approach specific races that led up to the final 10. And, of course, when we did get into the final 10, it was how aggressively we would race at each track. The idea was to get as many bonus points as we could and, of course, get the best finish.

It's an unbelievable experience to be able to put together a championship effort considering the caliber of racing NASCAR offers us. It's like it's every child's dream to grow up and be able to drive race cars and to do it at this level. To be as competitive as we've been, it's very satisfying to be able to obtain what really is the first NASCAR NEXTEL Cup Series championship. There was a new format, it took a whole new outlook, and it's a testament to what our team is capable of, as well as me being able to persevere out on the race track.

(Above) Time and again, the Sharpie Ford crew stepped up at critical moments and provided excellent, lighting-fast stops for their driver. Even in times of adversity, they managed to service, fix and adjust the race car well enough to allow Busch to maximize the situation and gather the most points possible.

(Right) Eighteen-year veteran crew chief Jimmy Fennig (left) served as leader, coach and mentor to Busch and the entire "97" team in their championship quest. Over the 36-race season, the team exhibited superb preparation, evidenced by their 21 top-10 finishes and the fact that Busch failed to complete just three events.

I think for Jack Roush, our team owner, doing this almost makes winning the final NASCAR Winston Cup championship last year with Matt Kenseth, so much sweeter. Being able to back that up with the first NASCAR NEXTEL Cup championship — it just blends together. It's the old era meeting the new era. Jack jokes about it and says he's now two for 18 in championships. But it's really a tremendous opportunity for Roush Racing to be known as a company that fields competitive race teams with the best equipment you can have. Jack gives us that. He's also helped me to understand just how much work is involved and how to see the bigger picture in life. Jack is somebody I try and model myself after.

Homestead-Miami Speedway has gone through two facelifts and that's good. The track itself has definitely increased interest in racing, and it has created a platform for us to have the final race of the year. It's not quite the equivalent of Daytona or Indianapolis just yet. But with the final event being there, and the way the points system is now structured, it comes down to that one single race. Before long, Homestead-Miami Speedway will have the reputation of being a championship race track where everything is decided. It will have so much of an impact on our sport in the next couple of years that it will be right up there with Daytona and Indy.

At Homestead, after the wheel came off my car and we had a bad pit stop, I wanted to impress on the team that it was now our final opportunity to win the championship. We needed things to go correctly with no more mistakes from there on out. I wasn't trying to get on crew chief Jimmy Fennig's case; really, I was trying to be a cheerleader at that time. I wanted to get everybody pumped up and focused. I guess it worked.

*(Left) Team owner Jack Roush, who began fielding a single team in 1988 with driver Mark Martin, has continually built his organization, which now supports five full-time teams. Over that 17-year span, Roush-owned cars have gone to victory lane 74 times and now account for back-to-back NASCAR Cup Series championships.*

*(Below) At just 26 years of age, Kurt Busch displays focus and intensity beyond his years, something he credits to his relationship with Jack Roush.*

*Kurt Busch lights up the tires to the delight of his crew after scoring the win at New Hampshire International Speedway in September. The victory, his third of the season, not only completed a season sweep in Loudon, N.H., as the first race in the Chase for the NASCAR NEXTEL Cup, it also got his drive toward the championship started on the right foot.*

I've seen things go wrong before and have tried to understand that what I need to do as a driver is persevere and stay focused on the task at hand. In the last 10 races, the race tracks challenged every team. I was exhausted when it all ended.

I have a lot to be thankful for and a lot of people to thank. That includes, Jack, Jimmy, everyone on our team, the other Roush teams, Sharpie and IRWIN, Ford Motor Co. and all of our sponsors. They make it possible for me to do what I love.

When I started racing I was working full-time for the Las Vegas Valley Water District. I was on the construction crew. We would fix pipelines that had broken under the street and were creating floods. It was fun, and it helped me to understand that kind of work and life. It was entirely different from racing and gave me a wealth of knowledge about the potable supply of water for the Las Vegas valley, but it especially taught me about what hard work is all about.

Racing with NASCAR and winning this championship is certainly an exciting time in my life. But winning the NASCAR NEXTEL Cup Series championship means there's still quite a bit of work to do. That includes anything we can do to help NASCAR and Nextel propel our sport forward. The time we do get off will give us a chance to reflect on this season and prepare for the season to come, as well as just relish winning the championship. Celebrations like this don't come very often. It takes a full year of work and sacrifice to have things go your way, and yet Jimmy Fennig has done this for 18 years and now has his first title. I want to dedicate this championship to him because of the knowledge he's given me in learning how to drive these race cars. That's what helped us to win.

Being the NASCAR NEXTEL Cup Series champion carries responsibilities. I'm going to try to help both NASCAR and Nextel by doing anything I can. Anything they request me to do, I'll do as long as I'm up to the task. I guess I'm more or less a traditionalist. I like the history of our sport — the past champions, the tracks that helped make NASCAR what it is today. Being the first NASCAR NEXTEL Cup Series champion is being part of a new era as far as sponsorship and marketing goes. I hope I can be a bridge that connects the past with the future and help NASCAR and Nextel advance our sport.

I also really owe a lot to my dad, Tom, and my mother, Gaye. They were there for me all the way. My father was always there. He was the first one I'd go to following a race. I would ask him questions about what I did wrong and how I could do better.

And there's my little brother, Kyle. He'll be coming into the NASCAR NEXTEL Cup Series in 2005. He made his first start in our series this year at Las Vegas, which was kind of cool. It was in the town where we grew up and at a track we watched being built. He made his first start with me there, and he'll be full-time in the series next year in the Kellogg's car. He did a phenomenal job learning about NASCAR Busch Series cars and what they demand of a driver, as well as on the media relations side of things. He's done a tremendous job in a very short time, and that will make him a great racer down the road.

Finally, I want to thank all of the great fans of NASCAR racing. Whether you cheer for me or for some other driver, what's really important is

your support of the sport, its competitors and its sponsors. Without that, none of this would be possible, and all of us know and appreciate what you do.

I hope to see you at the track in 2005.

Kurt Busch
2004 NASCAR NEXTEL Cup Series Champion

*(Above) Kurt Busch rides ahead of Roush Racing teammate and outgoing champion, Matt Kenseth. Undoubtedly, lessons learned by the DeWalt team in last season's campaign to the title paid huge dividends for the IRWIN/Sharpie team in this year's championship battle.*

*(Left) The entire 2004 NASCAR NEXTEL Cup Series championship team assembles on stage at Homestead-Miami Speedway to take one for the history book.*

# DAYTONA 500

## DAYTONA INTERNATIONAL SPEEDWAY
### FEBRUARY 15, 2004

*"Year after year after year. There were not many things that ate the man's insides out, but losing this race over and over, you could see it on his face ... Inside of me, that started the desire to win this race."*

— Dale Earnhardt Jr.

Ask any fan of Major League Baseball to describe the most exciting moment of the start of the regular season and the answer most likely would be the "crack of the bat" as ash meets rawhide when the batter connects with the first pitch of the first game.

For the fan of NASCAR NEXTEL Cup Series racing, the "crack" has to be the sound made by 43 engines all roaring at once immediately after the grand marshal for the Daytona 500 gives the traditional command, "Drivers, start your engines!"

While the Daytona 500 is still the most famous and prestigious points-paying race of 36 that make up the series, it's also the last of a string of February events at the famed Daytona track that comprise Speedweeks. The NASCAR NEXTEL Cup Series portion of this festival begins with the annual non-points Budweiser Shootout for the previous season's series pole winners and past winners of the event itself. It's followed by Bud Pole qualifying, which determines just the pole winner and second-place starter for the 500 and then the Gatorade Twin 125s, two 125-mile qualifying races (always run on the Thursday before the Sunday race), which fill in starting spots three through 30.

*A triumphant Dale Earnhardt Jr. climbs from the No.8 Budweiser Chevrolet after prevailing in the Daytona 500. It was his fifth career appearance in "The Great American Race."*

*(Above) Dale Jarrett (88) gets some drafting help from Dale Earnhardt Jr. (8) as the pair slips past Ryan Newman's Penske Dodge during Bud Shootout action on Saturday night. Later, Earnhardt would again provide a push for Jarrett that carried both drivers past leader Kevin Harvick and into the top two finishing positions.*

*(Right) Reporters surround Greg Biffle after a fast lap at 188.387 miles per hour during Bud Pole qualifying landed him in the No. 1 starting position for the Daytona 500. Unfortunately, his crew was forced to swap engines before the big race, which dropped Biffle to the rear of the field at the start.*

The remainder of the 43-car field is set by time trials and provisional starts based the previous year's car-owner points.

Though it has no direct bearing on the 500-mile race itself, Dale Jarrett's victory in the 70-lap Shootout, on Feb. 7, provided a boost to both his Robert Yates Racing team and the new engine-building alliance forged by Yates and fellow Ford team owner Jack Roush. Now working out of a common engine-building facility in Mooresville, N.C., the two were pooling their extensive expertise and technology.

The Shootout was, as in 2003, divided into two segments of 20 and 50 laps with a 10-

minute break in between. Jeff Gordon and Jamie McMurray were strong in the first segment, and the race got serious in the second. Jeremy Mayfield put his Dodge into the lead on the 51st lap and nine laps later was fending off a challenge from Dave Blaney when the two drivers collided.

The incident allowed Jarrett to charge forward with just 10 laps left. At the end, he caught up with Dale Earnhardt Jr.'s Budweiser Chevrolet, passed it, and then got a "push" from Earnhardt as both drivers passed race leader Kevin Harvick on the final lap. Jarrett beat last year's winner, Earnhardt, by just 0.157-second to win the event for the third time. Harvick was third, Roush driver Mark Martin took fourth and Gordon was fifth.

"I've got to thank my buddy, Dale Jr.," Jarrett said. "He was knocking the devil out of my (rear) bumper, and that's probably what I needed to get up there. The last two times we won this thing (1996; 2000), we won the Daytona 500. So I'm really looking forward to next Sunday."

Bud Pole qualifying the day after the Shootout was also a vindication of sorts for the Roush-Yates "grand experiment." Greg Biffle went out and, in Roush's No. 16 National Guard Ford, ran around the 2.5-mile tri-oval in 47.774 seconds at a speed of 188.387 mph. He then had to wait for most everyone else to make their attempts and was as nervous as a kitten in a

room with a pit bull toward the conclusion of the session. Yet in the end, the pole was his. The closest anyone could come to besting him was Yates' driver, Elliott Sadler, who notched the outside front-row spot in the M&M's Ford with a lap at 188.355 mph.

(Left) Dale Earnhardt Jr. notches his first win of the weekend with a triumph in the first Gatorade Twin 125.

(Below) Earnhardt Jr. (8) leads Jeff Burton (99), Jamie McMurray (42) and John Andretti (1) during the first Twin. Earnhardt started second and took the lead with 14 laps to go on the way to the win. McMurray took third at the finish with Burton in fifth.

(Bottom Left) Elliott Sadler makes a joyful appearance in victory lane following his win in the second Gatorade Twin 125.

(Bottom) Sadler (38) duels for the lead with Ricky Rudd (21) during their 125-mile qualifier. Sadler led three times for 26 laps, including the last 18, while Rudd faded to eighth place at the end.

Roush teammates Kurt Busch (97) and Greg Biffle (16) run together under Jimmy Spencer (7) along Daytona's frontstretch. Biffle, after starting from the rear of the field under penalty, never made it to the front, but still managed a strong showing and finished 12th, four spots ahead of Busch.

"I was sweating it out. I'm still half-sick to my stomach from watching the rest of those cars go," Biffle admitted. "Winning this pole is more prestigious than anywhere else throughout the season. I really wanted to start our season out this way. Having an opportunity to be there, I was just sweating it even worse.

"Everything is going good for us right now. I never thought we'd be on the pole for the Daytona 500."

"(This) means a lot. Daytona has not been our best place," Roush added. "Greg has brought Roush Racing the NASCAR Craftsman Truck Series championship and the NASCAR Busch Series championship, which were the first two championships we've had, and Ford gave us all the technical support we could have asked for this winter.

"I hadn't expected to be under the limelight here with Greg a week before the race. The idea of having the pole, I'd never given it a consideration."

The Twin 125s not only provide race-hungry fans the excitement they'd missed since the circuit's final race in November, they also give the drivers and teams 50 additional laps of "practice" to see how their cars are stacking up and what setup changes, if any, might need to be made. This year's events did two things: They further added to the credibility of the new Roush-Yates spirit of cooperation in Ford's ongoing battle with Chevrolet, and they had about everyone casting a wary eye on the team that had so thoroughly dominated the restrictor-plate tracks at Daytona and Talladega, Ala., in past years – Dale Earnhardt Inc.

(Left) Joe Nemechek pits for four fresh tires and 13 gallons of fuel. With the Commander in Chief on hand at Daytona, Joe Nemechek gave the Army great representation by taking his MB2 Monte Carlo to sixth place in the race.

(Below) Michael Waltrip's thoughts of repeating as Daytona 500 champion came to an abrupt end along the backstretch in a multicar accident before the halfway point. Safety crews righted the NAPA Chevrolet and Waltrip climbed out with minimal bumps and bruises.

Dale Earnhardt Jr. handily won the first twin, while Sadler came home first in the second. Other than that, the events were almost trouble free with just one yellow flag slowing race No. 1 for six laps. The caution, however, did ruin the day for Biffle and four-time series champion Jeff Gordon. Biffle led the race's first 22 laps but lost 13 places while pitting under yellow and finished 14th.

Gordon started 20th and was working his way toward the front. When the caution came out on lap 21, he became part of it when he slammed into the rear of another car, which damaged his Chevrolet's front end. He finished the race in 21st, a lap down, and was forced to take a provisional start to get into the 500. It was only the second time in his career (366 races) he'd been forced to do so.

Gordon also had to make a second pit stop and thereby inadvertently became a "pick" for Earnhardt Jr. When Gordon reentered the event, the lead pack, with Michael Waltrip in front and Earnhardt running second, caught up to him. On lap 37, Earnhardt swept past his DEI teammate and went on to win. Tony Stewart and Jamie McMurray went by, as well, and Waltrip finished fourth.

In the second event, Sadler led the first two laps, laps 24-29 and took the lead for good on lap 31 when he got back onto the track first after a pit stop.

For a while, anyway, on the day of the 500, the drivers had to take a back seat to the sea of celebrities who turned pit road into a "happening." In attendance were country music artists Lee Greenwood and LeeAnn Rimes; Boston Red Sox pitchers Derek Lowe and Tim Wakefield;

(Above) Rookie Scott Wimmer prepares to take the Caterpillar Dodge back into action after a quick stop for two tires and a load of fuel. In his 10th career NASCAR NEXTEL Cup Series start, Wimmer was perhaps the surprise of the race, posting a personal best third place.

(Right) Kevin Harvick (29) is hounded from behind by Jeff Gordon (24) as the two Chevrolets work to the outside of Jeff Burton's Ford (99). Harvick led early in the event and stayed in the hunt most of the day before finishing fourth, while Gordon worked his way into the top 10 after having to use a provisional to make the field. Burton's day was cut short when his engine expired on lap 25.

former world heavyweight champion Evander Holyfield; actor James Cavielzel and Miss America Ericka Dunlap. Actress Whoopi Goldberg was the event's official starter and Hollywood idol Ben Affleck was scheduled to give the command to start engines.

Affleck, however, was "bumped" aside by a bigger celebrity – perhaps the biggest of all – who flew in to get the field underway. George W. Bush was just the third sitting U.S. president to visit the Daytona facility for an event.

His dad, George H.W. Bush, visited in 1992 and Ronald Reagan was on hand to watch Richard Petty win his 200th race in July 1984.

After the president gave the traditional order and Goldberg waved the green flag, the drivers got down to business – especially Earnhardt Jr., who turned the predictions of more than a few into reality.

Earnhardt Jr. led six times for 58 laps – including the final 20 – and beat the No. 20 Chevrolet of Tony Stewart to the checkered flag by 0.273-second. In taking his first Daytona 500 victory (but his eighth win at the track), "Junior" had to race smart and fend off a feisty Stewart. The win, however, was his to keep and it came six years to the day after his dad won it on his 20th try.

"Year after year after year. There were not many things that ate the man's insides out, but losing this race over and over, you could see it on his face," the son said of his late father's frustration. "Inside of me, that started the desire to win this race."

Earnhardt Jr. led the first 29 laps before giving way to Kevin Harvick. He remained in contention but raced the track and avoided trouble. One mishap – a 12-car incident on the 71st lap – saw his teammate, Waltrip (the winner two of past three 500s) roll three times.

Following a two-tire pit stop late in the event, rookie Scott Wimmer took the lead on

lap 171. The move put him up front and ultimately gave the Caterpillar Dodge driver a third-place finish. Stewart and Earnhardt left the pits with four fresh Goodyears, though, and that made the difference. Coming off the fourth corner on the 181st circuit, Earnhardt ducked under Stewart, who was trying his best to block the move, dove underneath the Home Depot Chevrolet and was on his way to the win.

"I tried and tried to figure out how to pass him," Earnhardt said. "I got a run on him and ... I made it happen somehow."

Earnhardt Jr. completed the race in 3 hours, 11 minutes and 53 seconds at an average speed of 156.345 mph and won $1,495,070. Harvick and Jimmie Johnson finished fourth and fifth, respectively, Gordon salvaged an eighth-place finish and Biffle, who was forced to start at the rear of the field after his crew changed engines before the race, was 12th.

*Dale Earnhardt Jr. (8) stalks Tony Stewart (20) at the front of the field with Jimmie Johnson (48) alongside. Stewart led seven times for an event-leading 97 laps, but he couldn't hold off Earnhardt, who took the lead for the last time with 19 laps remaining.*

## Daytona 500 *final race results*

| Fin. Pos. | Start Pos. | Car No. | Driver | Team | Fin. Pos. | Start Pos. | Car No. | Driver | Team |
|---|---|---|---|---|---|---|---|---|---|
| 1 | 3 | 8 | Dale Earnhardt Jr. | Budweiser Chevrolet | 23 | 28 | 32 | Ricky Craven | Tide/Mr. Clean AutoDry Chevrolet |
| 2 | 5 | 20 | Tony Stewart | Home Depot Chevrolet | 24 | 40 | 7 | Jimmy Spencer | Johnny Cat Dodge |
| 3 | 26 | 22 | Scott Wimmer | Caterpillar Dodge | 25 | 22 | 19 | Jeremy Mayfield | Dodge Dealers/UAW Dodge |
| 4 | 10 | 29 | Kevin Harvick | GM Goodwrench Chevrolet | 26 | 21 | 30 | Johnny Sauter | America Online Chevrolet |
| 5 | 6 | 48 | Jimmie Johnson | Lowe's Chevrolet | 27 | 24 | 09 | Johnny Benson | Miccosukee Resort Dodge |
| 6 | 14 | 01 | Joe Nemechek | U.S. Army Chevrolet | 28 | 41 | 14 | Larry Foyt | LPGA Dodge |
| 7 | 2 | 38 | Elliott Sadler | M&M's Ford | 29 | 18 | 2 | Rusty Wallace | Miller Lite Dodge |
| 8 | 39 | 24 | Jeff Gordon | DuPont Chevrolet | 30 | 42 | 50 | Derrike Cope | Thrifty/Melling Engine Parts Dodge |
| 9 | 12 | 17 | Matt Kenseth | DeWalt Power Tools Ford | 31 | 20 | 12 | Ryan Newman | ALLTEL Dodge |
| 10 | 31 | 88 | Dale Jarrett | UPS Ford | 32 | 32 | 4 | Kevin Lepage | YOKE TV.com Chevrolet |
| 11 | 13 | 18 | Bobby Labonte | Passion of the Christ/Interstate Chev. | 33 | 34 | 43 | Jeff Green | Cheerios/Betty Crocker Dodge |
| 12 | 1 | 16 | Greg Biffle | U.S. Army National Guard Ford | 34 | 36 | 10 | Scott Riggs | Valvoline Chevrolet |
| 13 | 29 | 1 | John Andretti | Post/Maxwell House Coffee Chevrolet | 35 | 30 | 31 | Robby Gordon | Cingular Wireless Chevrolet |
| 14 | 25 | 41 | Casey Mears | Target Dodge | 36 | 7 | 42 | Jamie McMurray | Texaco/Havoline Dodge |
| 15 | 23 | 23 | Dave Blaney | Whelen Dodge | 37 | 4 | 40 | Sterling Marlin | Coors Light Dodge |
| 16 | 15 | 97 | Kurt Busch | Sharpie Ford | 38 | 9 | 15 | Michael Waltrip | NAPA Chevrolet |
| 17 | 19 | 0 | Ward Burton | NetZero Hi-Speed Chevrolet | 39 | 35 | 25 | Brian Vickers | GMAC Financial Services Chevrolet |
| 18 | 16 | 21 | Ricky Rudd | Motorcraft Ford | 40 | 37 | 49 | Ken Schrader | Schwan's Home Service Dodge |
| 19 | 17 | 77 | Brendan Gaughan | Kodak Easy Share/Eckerd Drugs Dodge | 41 | 27 | 9 | Kasey Kahne | Dodge Dealers/UAW Dodge |
| 20 | 38 | 5 | Terry Labonte | Kellogg's Chevrolet | 42 | 11 | 99 | Jeff Burton | NBA All-Star Game on TNT Ford |
| 21 | 33 | 45 | Kyle Petty | Georgia-Pacific/Brawny Dodge | 43 | 8 | 6 | Mark Martin | Viagra Ford |
| 22 | 43 | 33 | Mike Skinner | Bass Pro Shops/Tracker Boats Chevrolet | | | | | |

# SUBWAY 400

## NORTH CAROLINA SPEEDWAY
### FEBRUARY 22, 2004

*"It feels good to come out of the box and win right away."*

— *Matt Kenseth*

It's been said that, in life, timing is everything, and going into the season's second NASCAR NEXTEL Cup Series race at North Carolina Speedway timing appeared to be right for Dale Jarrett.

Jarrett arrived at "The Rock" with a bit of a spring in his step — and for good reason. First, he was the event's defending champion, but more important, following Speedweeks at Daytona International Speedway, the driver of Robert Yates Racing's No. 88 UPS Ford seemed to have put a dismal 2003 season well behind him. Jarrett got off to a roaring start by winning the Budweiser Shootout — the non-points dash for the previous year's Bud Pole winners and former winners of the event itself — and followed that up with a solid 10th-place finish in the 500, which put him 10th in NASCAR NEXTEL Cup Series points, 51 behind leader Dale Earnhardt Jr.

Now with a fresh season featuring a new series sponsor and a revised points system, Jarrett faced the 1.017-mile Sandhills oval with optimism.

"Rockingham is a driver's track," Jarrett noted. "It has a lot of different elements that you have to learn to cope with. It's up to the driver and crew to make a good-handling race car."

Matt Kenseth (17) and rookie Kasey Kahne (9) flash under the checkered flag side by side at the conclusion of the Subway 400 at Rockingham. Kenseth dominated the event by leading five times for 259 laps, but eked out the win by a scant 0.01 second in one of the closest finishes on record.

*(Above) Ryan Newman is all smiles as he prepares for 393 laps on the North Carolina oval. To the surprise of none but the chagrin of many, Newman grabbed his first Bud Pole of the year, raising his ratio of poles to starts to 23 percent in his brief NASCAR NEXTEL Cup Series career.*

*(Right) Jeff Gordon sits at the ready in his DuPont Monte Carlo, slotted in the fifth starting spot for the Subway 400. Gordon was able to lead twice in the first 100 laps before settling in for a 10th-place finish.*

Jarrett, the 1999 series champion, had to consider Rockingham one of his better venues. His record at the track encompassed 12 top-five finishes in his last 16 starts, and that included six second-place showings in eight starts from February 1996 through the same month in 1999.

Earnhardt Jr., of course, showed up at Rockingham in the catbird's seat. The driver of the No. 8 Budweiser Chevrolet had captured the Daytona 500 in just his fifth try (it took his dad, the late Dale Earnhardt, 20 years to win it), and for the first time in his career he found himself leading the series standings. With 185 points, he was five in front of runner-up Tony Stewart, who had finished second at Daytona in the No. 20 Home Depot Chevrolet.

Under the old points system, the two drivers would have been tied in markers with 180 each (Stewart had picked up 10 bonus points at Daytona for leading the most laps). But now

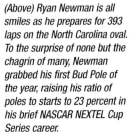

the race winner was guaranteed 185 points, 180 for winning and five more for leading at least one lap.

The surprise driver in the Daytona 500 had to be Bill Davis Racing's Scott Wimmer, who, on the strength of a gutsy pit-stop call by his crew chief, finished third. Not only did Dodge-driving Wimmer jump out front in Raybestos Rookie of the Year points, he was also solidly in third in overall points behind Earnhardt Jr. and Stewart. Wimmer's finish at Daytona was the best by a rookie since Jeff Gordon came home fifth in 1993.

"Dodge Boys" Ryan Newman (12), Jamie McMurray (42), Kasey Kahne (9) and Rusty Wallace (2) pace the starting field through Rockingham's high banks on the way to the initial green flag. Six of the first eight starters, including Jeremy Mayfield (19) and Jeff Green (43), drove Dodges, with Jeff Gordon (24) and Dale Earnhardt Jr. (8) representing the "Bowtie Brigade."

(Above) Driver Kirk Shelmerdine was on hand at Rockingham to make his third career start in NASCAR's top series. As a crew chief in the late 1980s and early 1990s, Shelmerdine helped Dale Earnhardt to four series titles, in 1986-87 and 1990-91.

(Left) Defending race champion Dale Jarrett (88) and rookie Scott Wimmer (22) run together on Rockingham's frontstretch. Wimmer, who posted an outstanding third place the week before at Daytona, drove from 31st to 15th in the race, while Jarrett suffered engine problems.

Chevrolet drivers did exceedingly well at Daytona, with Kevin Harvick, Jimmie Johnson, Joe Nemechek and Gordon finishing fourth, fifth, sixth and eighth, respectively, and except for Gordon the points standings going into Rockingham reflected this. Gordon, in the No. 24 DuPont Chevrolet, picked up five bonus points by leading a lap at Daytona, and this put him one spot up on Elliott Sadler, who finished seventh in the 500 but entered Rockingham eighth in points.

Matt Kenseth, the defending series champion who had a series-high 25 top-10 finishes in 2003, collected his first of the new season with a ninth-place effort at Daytona. Dating back to the 2003 season, he now had been in the top 10 for 36 consecutive weeks. The only time he'd been out of the front 10 in points last year was, ironically, after the Daytona 500 when he was 19th, but he quickly moved up to sixth following Rockingham.

"Rockingham is always going to be a special place for me," noted Roush Racing's Kenseth. "My first NASCAR Busch Series win was there (1998), and I also clinched the (NASCAR) championship there in November."

(Right) Jeremy Mayfield brings his Evernham Motorsports Dodge in for fresh rubber and a load of fuel. Unfortunately, penalties for pit-road infractions combined with overheating problems took Mayfield out of contention and dropped him to an 11th-place finish, two laps down.

(Below) Matt Kenseth (17) finds the low groove to his liking as he makes a bid on Jamie McMurray (42) with Ken Schrader on the outside. Kenseth spent the first 89 laps of the event moving through the field from his 23rd-place starting slot before taking the lead for the first of five times during the day.

156.475 mph in winning his 19th career Bud Pole Award in 82 races. For Newman, last year's leading pole (and race) winner, it was his second straight No. 1 start at the Rockingham track and his third in five races.

Jamie McMurray, also in a Dodge, was second fastest with a lap time and speed of 23.563 seconds at 155.379 mph, making it his third top-10 start in four races at Rockingham and his second on the front row. Rookie contender Kasey Kahne posted his first top-10 start in just his second NASCAR NEXTEL Cup Series event, and Newman's Penske teammate, Rusty Wallace (the Rockingham qualifying record holder), was fourth fastest. Rounding out the top five in time trials was Gordon, who landed in the top five at Rockingham for the first time since November 2001.

Forty-five drivers showed up for the event, and Morgan Shepherd and Andy Belmont, neither of who took qualifying laps, were bumped from the field.

Kenseth had finished in the top 10 in his previous five races at The Rock, and this race would also be his 150th career series start.

Qualifying for the Subway 400 got underway two days before the race. After it was over, the only guy who (aside from his teammates) might have offered the Bud Pole winner his heartfelt congratulations was Jared Fogle, the race sponsor's TV spokesman.

Ryan Newman had done it again. The Penske Racing South Dodge driver lapped the 1.017-mile oval in 23.398 seconds at a speed of

Rockingham ... a "special place" for Matt Kenseth? It would seem the defending series champion took his own words to heart — and quite seriously. The Cambridge, Wis., native wasted little time in deciding to show everyone his championship was not a fluke.

Starting 23rd, the "champ" ended up leading five times for 259 of the event's 393 laps. The hooker, though, was the finish. In a word, it was a thriller.

Late in the event (lap 351) Kenseth and Kahne were en route back onto the speedway after completing crucial pit stops, when the last of seven caution flags slowed the race.

Under rules that went into effect in 2003, NASCAR officials had "frozen" the field. Kenseth and Kahne both got back onto the track, and while some couldn't initially see how it happened, they ended up keeping first and second place when the race went green for the final time on lap 364. It shook out that Kenseth and Kahne remained on the track while other leading drivers pitted during the caution, giving Kenseth the lead for the last time on lap 359 with Kahne in second.

The result was the fourth-closest finish in series history since NASCAR instituted electronic scoring in 1993. Kenseth's No. 17 DeWalt Tools Ford was just 0.010-second in front of Kahne's No. 9 Evernham Motorsports Dodge at the finish.

It was so close that Kahne's crew started doing a victory dance before they found out their man was the runner-up.

"That didn't look like us," Kenseth said. Usually, we don't lead all those laps. Even if we win, we usually kind of sneak up at the end.

"It feels good to come out of the box and win right away."

Although McMurray's car owners, Chip Ganassi and Felix Sabates, at first disputed the finish, the driver had no problem accepting third place. His teammate, Sterling Marlin, was fourth, and Earnhardt Jr. took fifth.

Kenseth completed the event in 3 hours, 34 minutes and 5 seconds at an average speed of 112.016 mph and won $222,303.

Johnson was eliminated by an accident, and a blown engine got the better of Jarrett.

*Matt Kenseth celebrates the victory, his first in nearly a year and the eighth of his career in 150 starts. The win moved the defending series champion up seven positions in the standings, from ninth to second, just seven points behind leader Dale Earnhardt Jr.*

## Subway 400 *final race results*

| Fin. Pos. | Start Pos. | Car No. | Driver | Team | Fin. Pos. | Start Pos. | Car No. | Driver | Team |
|---|---|---|---|---|---|---|---|---|---|
| 1 | 23 | 17 | Matt Kenseth | DeWalt Power Tools Ford | 23 | 10 | 16 | Greg Biffle | Subway/National Guard Ford |
| 2 | 3 | 9 | Kasey Kahne | Dodge Dealers/UAW Dodge | 24 | 12 | 01 | Joe Nemechek | U.S. Army Chevrolet |
| 3 | 2 | 42 | Jamie McMurray | Texaco/Havoline Dodge | 25 | 11 | 18 | Bobby Labonte | Interstate Batteries Chevrolet |
| 4 | 13 | 40 | Sterling Marlin | Coors Light Dodge | 26 | 24 | 20 | Tony Stewart | Home Depot Chevrolet |
| 5 | 7 | 8 | Dale Earnhardt Jr. | Budweiser Chevrolet | 27 | 18 | 49 | Ken Schrader | Schwan's Home Service Dodge |
| 6 | 1 | 12 | Ryan Newman | ALLTEL Dodge | 28 | 8 | 43 | Jeff Green | STP/Cheerios/Betty Crocker Dodge |
| 7 | 4 | 2 | Rusty Wallace | Miller Lite Dodge | 29 | 39 | 1 | John Andretti | DEI/Snap-On Chevrolet |
| 8 | 27 | 97 | Kurt Busch | Sharpie IRWIN Ford | 30 | 37 | 50 | Derrike Cope | Matrix Systems Dodge |
| 9 | 16 | 0 | Ward Burton | NetZero Hi-Speed Chevrolet | 31 | 19 | 10 | Scott Riggs | Valvoline Chevrolet |
| 10 | 5 | 24 | Jeff Gordon | DuPont Chevrolet | 32 | 38 | 14 | Larry Foyt | A.J. Foyt Racing Dodge |
| 11 | 6 | 19 | Jeremy Mayfield | Dodge Dealers/UAW Dodge | 33 | 33 | 15 | Michael Waltrip | NAPA Chevrolet |
| 12 | 21 | 6 | Mark Martin | Viagra Ford | 34 | 43 | 80 | Andy Hillenburg | Commercial Truck & Trailer Ford |
| 13 | 32 | 29 | Kevin Harvick | GM Goodwrench Chevrolet | 35 | 17 | 32 | Ricky Craven | Tide Chevrolet |
| 14 | 36 | 30 | Johnny Sauter | America Online Chevrolet | 36 | 34 | 31 | Robby Gordon | Cingular Wireless Chevrolet |
| 15 | 31 | 22 | Scott Wimmer | Caterpillar Dodge | 37 | 28 | 99 | Jeff Burton | SKF Ford |
| 16 | 20 | 25 | Brian Vickers | GMAC Financial Services Chevrolet | 38 | 42 | 46 | Carl Long | Al Smith Dodge Dodge |
| 17 | 35 | 5 | Terry Labonte | Kellogg's Chevrolet | 39 | 30 | 45 | Kyle Petty | Georgia-Pacific/Brawny Dodge |
| 18 | 25 | 38 | Elliott Sadler | M&M's Ford | 40 | 9 | 88 | Dale Jarrett | UPS Ford |
| 19 | 22 | 21 | Ricky Rudd | Motorcraft Ford | 41 | 29 | 48 | Jimmie Johnson | Lowe's Chevrolet |
| 20 | 15 | 77 | Brendan Gaughan | Kodak Easy Share Dodge | 42 | 41 | 72 | Kirk Shelmerdine | Freddie B's/Tucson Ford |
| 21 | 14 | 41 | Casey Mears | Target Dodge | 43 | 40 | 09 | Joe Ruttman | Miccosukee Resort Dodge |
| 22 | 26 | 4 | Kevin Lepage | YOKE TV.com Chevrolet | | | | | |

# UAW-DAIMLERCHRYSLER 400

## LAS VEGAS MOTOR SPEEDWAY
### MARCH 7, 2004

*"It's great to come to Vegas ... you don't always leave here a winner, so this was fun."*

— *Matt Kenseth*

A fter a rare week off between events on a 36-race NASCAR NEXTEL Cup Series schedule, the tour's teams journeyed from the Sandhills region of North Carolina to an equally sandy locale, the 1.5-mile Las Vegas Motor Speedway in the nation's gaming Mecca long ago carved out of the Nevada desert.

And after Bud Pole qualifying had been completed two days before the 400-mile event, it was apparent that all bets were off. NASCAR Raybestos Rookie of the Year contenders notched three of the top eight starting spots for the UAW-DaimlerChrysler 400, and, perhaps fittingly (at least for the event's co-sponsor), Dodge drivers landed in six of the first 10 starting positions.

With just two races in the books, one of the circuit's hottest drivers appeared to be rookie Kasey Kahne. Fresh off an incredibly close second-place finish at "The Rock," the pilot of Evernham Motorsports' No. 9 Intrepid toured the Las Vegas oval at 174.904 mph to capture the pole and set a track record in the process. While the top six qualifiers all exceeded the 174 mph mark, Kahne's speed was comfortably quicker than the lap at 174.548 mph posted by No. 2 starter – and hometown driver – Kurt Busch, in the No. 97 Roush Racing/IRWIN Tools Ford.

*Las Vegas native Kurt Busch waits for adjustments to his IRWIN Industrial Tools Ford in the LVMS garage. The Roush Racing driver turned his luck around at the Nevada track and posted a top-10 finish from a front-row start, which moved him into fifth in points at the end of the event.*

*(Right) Mark Martin quietly bides his time along pit road before Las Vegas qualifying. Martin, winner of the inaugural event at LVMS in 1998, stumbled a bit in time trials and started 27th but made up for it with a fifth-place finish in Sunday's race.*

*(Below) Kasey Kahne (9), who notched his first Bud Pole in just his third career NASCAR NEXTEL Cup Series start, leads the field under green to begin the UAW-DaimlerChrysler 400. Kahne nearly won the race as well, but wound up in the runner-up spot for the second consecutive event.*

"We tested the three days after (Rockingham), and I was really tired," Kahne said. "I didn't get much sleep because I kept trying to finish better."

First-year driver Brian Vickers secured the No. 3 spot, in the Hendrick Motorsports/GMAC Financial Services Chevrolet (174.537 mph), Dodge-driving Jamie McMurray was fourth quickest at 174.436 mph and Ryan Newman, also in a Dodge, took the fifth starting position at 174.340 mph.

Jeremy Mayfield (Dodge), Bobby Labonte (Chevrolet), Brendan Gaughan (Dodge), Greg Biffle (Ford) and Bill Elliott (Dodge) completed the top 10 qualifiers. Scott Wimmer, Derrike Cope, Carl Long and Kirk Shelmerdine used provisional starts to complete the 43-car field, while only one driver, Larry Gunselman, was eliminated.

The "reverse surprise" in qualifying turned out to be Jeff Gordon, who arrived at Las Vegas with three straight top-10 finishes at the Nevada track, but hit the wall and ended up 20th on the speed chart when time trials were completed.

"I went down into turns one and two on the second lap, and the car got loose," Gordon explained. "I came through (turns) three and

four trying to make up a little bit of time. But I got loose and hurt the car pretty bad."

Had Dale Earnhardt Jr. and his DEI/Budweiser Chevrolet team been able to peer into the future, they may have decided to bring a pair of "loaded" dice to the track. But rough times were still a few days away, as coming into the 400-miler at Las Vegas, he believed he was in the catbird's seat.

Earnhardt Jr. finished fifth at Rockingham – his second straight top-five finish of the young season – and remained first in points. But not by much. He was only seven markers in front of Matt Kenseth (340-333), who edged out Kahne to win at Rockingham. At this point a year ago, Earnhardt was 38th in points.

Kenseth's stirring victory at Rockingham moved him from ninth to second in the standings, where he was 39 points ahead of Richard Childress Racing's Kevin Harvick. A 13th-place finish at Rockingham allowed Harvick to move up one spot in points, and he entered the Las Vegas event hoping to do better than the 13th-place finish he posted in last year's version of the race.

Bill Davis Racing's rookie driver, Scott Wimmer, finished 15th in the Subway 400 at North Carolina Speedway and dropped from third to fourth in NASCAR NEXTEL Cup Series points. With just 11 series races under his belt, Wimmer, with 288 points, was making his "maiden voyage" to Las Vegas.

By finishing 10th in the Subway 400, Gordon moved from seventh to fifth in points and was just two behind Wimmer (288-286). Gordon had competed in all six events contested at Las Vegas with three top-10 finishes, including a win in 2001. Yet he'd failed to crack the top 15 in the last two events there, and hitting the wall in qualifying certainly did his morale little good.

Tony Stewart had less than a great day in the Subway 400 – he finished 26th – and that caused him to fall from second place to sixth in points, 75 behind leader Earnhardt Jr. and just eight in front of seventh-place Busch. Stewart had competed in five races at LVMS, scoring three top-five finishes. His best showing was second place in the 2000 version of the event.

Busch did Roush Racing proud at Rockingham. He finished eighth in the 400-miler there and leaped from 16th to seventh in points with 257. Although he could loosely call LVMS his "home track," Busch, with three starts there, had yet to finish a race in the top 10.

*(Above) Kevin Harvick (29) takes a peek on the outside of Bobby Labonte's Interstate Batteries Chevrolet at the entrance to turn one. Harvick led twice for 43 laps in the second half of the race and looked like a sure top-five bet, but his Chevrolet's fuel cell ran dry with a handful of laps remaining.*

*(Below) Tony Stewart (20) leads the way for Michael Waltrip (15) and Ryan Newman (12). Stewart surged to the front on four occasions after starting 19th and took home a third-place finish – good enough to move into second in points behind Kenseth.*

*(Below) Matt Kenseth (17) takes the green flag for the lap-143 restart following the third of six cautions during the race. Behind Kenseth on the outside are Kevin Harvick (29) in second, Bobby Labonte (18) third, Tony Stewart (20) fourth and Kasey Kahne (9) in fifth.*

*(Right) The DeWalt Tools team celebrates its second straight tri-umph after Kenseth led the final 38 laps of the race. The wins, combined with a ninth-place fin-ish in the Daytona 500, moved the defending champion to the top of the standings, 88 points ahead of Dale Earnhardt Jr.*

Just two points behind Busch was Elliott Sadler. The driver of the No. 38 Robert Yates Racing/M&M's Ford finished 18th at Rockingham and remained eighth in points. Going into the UAW-DaimlerChrysler 400, he was obviously hoping for a better roll of the dice than in years past. In five races at Vegas he'd finished 20th or worse.

Ward Burton was grinning after he finished ninth at Rockingham, mainly because the effort moved him from 17th to ninth in the series standings. He now was just five points behind Sadler (255-250) and nine in front of 10th-place Joe Nemechek.

When the flagman dropped the checkered banner on the UAW-DaimlerChrysler 400, 3 hours, 6 minutes and 35 seconds after he'd dropped the initial green flag, it was hard to figure out who had more reason to whoop it up in victory lane – Kenseth, who'd led almost half the event, or his boss, Jack Roush.

Roush and his employees certainly have the track figured out, as this was their fifth trip to victory lane in the seven races contested there. Kenseth notched his second straight race of the young season – as well as his second in a row

at LVMS – and ended up as the dominator by leading over 46 percent of the race – 123 of 267 laps.

And true to his laid-back personality, he did it on the sly. He started 25th and waited until lap 95 to go to the front for the first of four times. He stayed at the point for 85 of the next 90 laps, giving up the lead only briefly during the event's third and fourth caution periods. But when the yellow flag flew for the fifth time, a stuck lug nut slowed his stop, and he returned to the race running eighth.

Kenseth, however, methodically began pick-ing his way through the field, and when the final caution appeared for debris on lap 202, the DeWalt crew took the opportunity to redeem themselves with a lightning-quick stop, returning their driver to the track in fourth place.

Lap 207 brought the final green flag and, 24 circuits later, Kenseth found himself on the rear bumper of race-leader Kevin Harvick. Clearly with the stronger car, the Wisconsin native moved past the GM Goodwrench Chevrolet and motored on to lead the final 38 laps.

Harvick's Monte Carlo ran out of gas with five laps left (he finished 21st) and that paved the way for Kahne to again grab the runner-up spot. But while the Rockingham event ended as a near-photo finish, this time Kahne was 3.426 seconds behind the winner.

"It's great to come to Vegas," Kenseth said. "You don't always leave here a winner, so this is fun."

"Running second is fine with me right now, (but) we want to win," Kahne added. "We're going to win sometime."

Tony Stewart, Jamie McMurray and Kenseth's teammate, Mark Martin, completed the top five finishers, while Earnhardt Jr. finished 35th and dropped from first to seventh in points after suffering through a miserable day. He made several trips into the pits and behind the wall, but he and his crew were simply unable to figure out why their car handled so terribly.

The day, however, was anything but miserable for Kenseth, who averaged 128.790 mph and won $458,828.

(Top) Kasey Kahne (9) slips past Dale Earnhardt Jr. (8) on the inside. The drivers had completely different experiences over the weekend as Kahne's Dodge was one of the strongest cars on the track, while Earnhardt's Chevrolet never got up to speed and finished in 35th place, 71 laps off the winning pace.

(Above) Elliott Sadler prepares to return to action with fresh Goodyear's and a full load of fuel. Although he did not lead in the race, Sadler's sixth place, his second top 10 in three events, boosted him from eighth to third in points.

## UAW-DaimlerChrysler 400 *final race results*

| Fin. Pos. | Start Pos. | Car No. | Driver | Team | Fin. Pos. | Start Pos. | Car No. | Driver | Team |
|---|---|---|---|---|---|---|---|---|---|
| 1 | 25 | 17 | Matt Kenseth | DeWalt Power Tools Ford | 23 | 3 | 25 | Brian Vickers | GMAC Financial Services Chevrolet |
| 2 | 1 | 9 | Kasey Kahne | Dodge Dealers/UAW Dodge | 24 | 30 | 30 | Johnny Sauter | AOL/IMAX NASCAR 3D Chevrolet |
| 3 | 19 | 20 | Tony Stewart | Home Depot Chevrolet | 25 | 17 | 32 | Ricky Craven | Tide Chevrolet |
| 4 | 4 | 42 | Jamie McMurray | Texaco/Havoline Dodge | 26 | 34 | 0 | Ward Burton | NetZero Hi-Speed Chevrolet |
| 5 | 27 | 6 | Mark Martin | Viagra Ford | 27 | 5 | 12 | Ryan Newman | ALLTEL Dodge |
| 6 | 11 | 38 | Elliott Sadler | M&M's Ford | 28 | 33 | 21 | Ricky Rudd | Motorcraft Ford |
| 7 | 13 | 41 | Casey Mears | Target Dodge | 29 | 15 | 10 | Scott Riggs | Valvoline Chevrolet |
| 8 | 7 | 18 | Bobby Labonte | Interstate Batteries Chevrolet | 30 | 22 | 31 | Robby Gordon | Cingular Wireless Chevrolet |
| 9 | 2 | 97 | Kurt Busch | IRWIN Industrial Tools Ford | 31 | 36 | 09 | Johnny Benson | Miccosukee Resorts Dodge |
| 10 | 21 | 2 | Rusty Wallace | Miller Lite Dodge | 32 | 31 | 49 | Ken Schrader | Schwan's Home Service Dodge |
| 11 | 29 | 88 | Dale Jarrett | UPS Ford | 33 | 40 | 50 | Derrike Cope | redneckjunk.com Dodge |
| 12 | 32 | 45 | Kyle Petty | Georgia-Pacific/Brawny Dodge | 34 | 24 | 43 | Jeff Green | Lucky Charms Dodge |
| 13 | 28 | 99 | Jeff Burton | Pennzoil Ford | 35 | 26 | 8 | Dale Earnhardt Jr. | Budweiser Chevrolet |
| 14 | 6 | 19 | Jeremy Mayfield | Dodge Dealers/UAW Dodge | 36 | 35 | 4 | Kevin Lepage | YOKE TV.com Chevrolet |
| 15 | 20 | 24 | Jeff Gordon | DuPont Chevrolet | 37 | 14 | 15 | Michael Waltrip | NAPA Chevrolet |
| 16 | 12 | 48 | Jimmie Johnson | Lowe's Chevrolet | 38 | 41 | 02 | Carl Long | RacingJunk.com Pontiac |
| 17 | 37 | 5 | Terry Labonte | Kellogg's Chevrolet | 39 | 39 | 22 | Scott Wimmer | Caterpillar Dodge |
| 18 | 23 | 40 | Sterling Marlin | Coors Light Dodge | 40 | 9 | 16 | Greg Biffle | National Guard/Subway Ford |
| 19 | 38 | 01 | Joe Nemechek | USG Sheetrock Chevrolet | 41 | 18 | 84 | Kyle Busch | CarQuest Chevrolet |
| 20 | 10 | 91 | Bill Elliott | UAW/DaimlerChrysler/NTC Dodge | 42 | 43 | 89 | Morgan Shepherd | Voyles/Carter's Royal Disposal Dodge |
| 21 | 16 | 29 | Kevin Harvick | GM Goodwrench Chevrolet | 43 | 42 | 72 | Kirk Shelmerdine | TUCSON/Freddie B's Ford |
| 22 | 8 | 77 | Brendan Gaughan | Kodak Easy Share Dodge | | | | | |

# GOLDEN CORRAL 500

## ATLANTA MOTOR SPEEDWAY
### MARCH 14, 2004

*"Talk about zero to hero; that was awesome. Last week was as bad as it gets."*

— *Dale Earnhardt Jr.*

O ne reason some people love to roll the dice is the thought that they can beat the element of chance. As much as they might fail, they keep trying, hoping for the big score.

Race drivers are the same way. If something goes wrong one week, they don't quit. They keep trying and, sooner or later, the right combination will result in victory.

Not true, you say? Don't tell that to Dale Earnhardt Jr. On March 7 at Las Vegas Motor Speedway, the DEI driver couldn't get out of his own way. His No. 8 Budweiser Chevrolet was beset by one problem after another. He was behind the wall or in the garage almost as much as he was in the race itself, and he ended up rolling "snake eyes."

What a difference a week makes. Seven days later at Atlanta Motor Speedway, the third-generation driver could do no wrong. He led three times for 55 of 325 laps and was 4.584 seconds in front of runner-up Jeremy Mayfield's Evernham Motorsports Dodge at the conclusion of the Golden Corral 500.

"Talk about zero to hero; that was awesome," said the winner in victory lane. "Last week was as bad as it ever gets. We had a terrible, terrible, terrible race at Vegas. We walked out of there beaten up and with our heads down. I lost a ton of confidence."

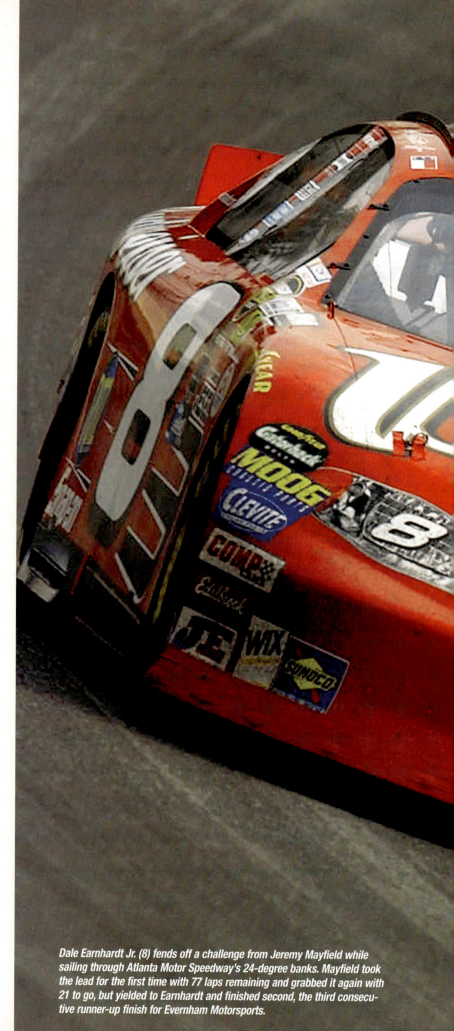

Dale Earnhardt Jr. (8) fends off a challenge from Jeremy Mayfield while sailing through Atlanta Motor Speedway's 24-degree banks. Mayfield took the lead for the first time with 77 laps remaining and grabbed it again with 21 to go, but yielded to Earnhardt and finished second, the third consecutive runner-up finish for Evernham Motorsports.

Matt Kenseth's emotions were the polar opposite of Earnhardt's after the UAW-DaimlerChrysler 400 at Las Vegas. The Roush Racing Ford driver had just scored his second consecutive win of the still-new season and moved from second in the NASCAR NEXTEL Cup Series standings into the lead. With 523 points, he was a comfortable 88 in front of Tony Stewart, who finished third in Nevada and moved from sixth to second in the standings. That was quite a morale boost for Stewart, as the sponsor of his No. 20 Joe Gibbs Racing Chevrolet, The Home Depot, is headquartered in Atlanta.

Elliott Sadler, who was ranked No. 8 in points for the first two weeks of the season, stepped up at Las Vegas with a sixth-place finish in the No. 38 M&M's Ford, his best finish at the 1.5-mile oval in five starts there. That moved him up five positions to third in points.

With 405 markers, he was 118 behind Kenseth and just one in front of Jeff Gordon.

Gordon had somewhat of a disappointing day at Vegas in the No. 24 DuPont Chevrolet. He finished 15th – his first time out of the top 10 this season – but the result was good enough to move him up a notch in points from fifth to fourth.

Following a ninth-place run in Nevada, Kurt Busch came into the Atlanta event fifth in points with 400. That put him 123 out of the lead, but he had moved up in the standings two spots and was looking for another good finish in the No. 97 Roush Racing/IRWIN Industrial Tools Ford.

Kevin Harvick's 21st-place showing at Las Vegas was his first outside of the top 15 in three starts, and consequently he dropped three spots in points from third to sixth. Yet, the battle for the title here remained close.

Harvick headed into Atlanta with 399 points, one less than Busch and just one in front of Earnhardt Jr.

As noted, Earnhardt Jr. suffered greatly at the desert oval. A 35th-place finish there saw him plummet from first in points to seventh. It marked the first time the Budweiser Chevrolet driver had been outside of the top five in the chase for the title since he was ranked 10th going into the Atlanta race one year ago.

The NASCAR NEXTEL Cup Series' latest "wunderkind," Kasey Kahne, finished second to Kenseth at Las Vegas, making it his second consecutive runner-up finish to the defending champion in as many races. Instead of dropping like Earnhardt Jr., the Evernham Motorsports Dodge driver shot up to eighth in points from 21st. That put him in the top 10 for the first time in his career and also put him into the lead in Raybestos Rookie of the Year points with 46 versus 34 for Scott Wimmer.

A season-best fourth-place finish at Vegas was good enough to move Chip Ganassi Racing's Texaco/Havoline Dodge driver, Jamie McMurray, into the top 10 in points for the first time since he made his NNCS debut in

(Above) Ryan Newman receives service at the end of pit road with Kasey Kahne pitted right behind. Good work in the pits was at a premium in the race, which was slowed only three times by the yellow flag.

(Left) Jimmie Johnson and his Lowe's crewmates earned every bit of a fourth-place effort at Atlanta after fighting an ill-handling race car all day long. Their reward? A leap in the points from 19th to ninth.

*(Right) Dale Jarrett (88) battles for position with Roush driver Greg Biffle in the National Guard Ford. Biffle eventually completed the pass before the two finished together, with Biffle taking eighth place ahead of Jarrett in ninth.*

*(Below) Tony Stewart (20) chases CAT driver Scott Wimmer with Kasey Kahne on his tale. Stewart's Home Depot Chevrolet proved to be very strong in the race, which allowed him to lead four times for 127 laps and take the lap-leader bonus.*

October 2002. He advanced from 11th to ninth in points, four spots better than his 13th-place finish to the 2003 season.

Team owner Chip Ganassi and his partner, Felix Sabates, had another reason to smile going into the Atlanta 500-miler. McMurray's teammate, Casey Mears, finished seventh in Vegas for his first series career top-10 showing. That vaulted him from 15th in points to 10th, only 156 out of the lead. Yet with 367 markers, he was only seven in front of 11th-place Bobby Labonte and 11 ahead of No. 12-ranked Rusty Wallace.

Remember "Front Row Joe" Nemechek? He got the nickname a while back because he seemed to have found a knack for qualifying faster than anyone else. Nemechek is still running, but as far as the Bud Pole Award is concerned, "First-Run Ryan" Newman has replaced him.

Newman did it again at Atlanta, his third straight pole at the 1.54-mile superspeedway. His speed of 193.575 mph in time trials on March 12, put him on the inside front row for the fifth time in the past eight races, dating back to the end of last season. The Penske Racing Dodge driver was just a tick faster than rookie Brian Vickers, who recorded a lap at 192.634 mph in the Hendrick/GMAC Financial Services Chevrolet.

It was the third time that Newman had "taken" the pole from Vickers, who started next to the ALLTEL Dodge at Phoenix and Rockingham in November 2003.

"You run 200 (mph) here and it feels like it's 400," Newman said. "It's not me; I'm the lucky nut behind the wheel.

"It's a team sport, and qualifying is no different than the race."

"We should have been on the pole," a frustrated Vickers said. "I knew it was a pole lap all the way around until I got to the center of turns three and four. I got on the apron a little bit, and the car shot up the track and I had to get out of it."

Vickers' teammates, Jimmie Johnson and Jeff Gordon, were third and fourth fastest at 192.380 and 192.366 mph, respectively, while Sadler took starting spot No. 5 with a lap at 191.344 mph. Qualifying sixth through 10th fastest were Dale Jarrett, Earnhardt Jr., Harvick, Mears and Bobby Labonte.

While there was little actual wrangling for the lead and just three yellow flags for 17 laps – two for oil on the track surface and one for debris – Earnhardt Jr. had to choose his moves and watch for lapped traffic. He took the lead for the first time later in the event, pacing laps 214-216, and led again from lap 266 through lap 301.

Mayfield grabbed the first position on the 305th circuit, but his Dodge was a tad bit weaker than Earnhardt Jr.'s Chevrolet. When "Junior" made his final move with 16 circuits left, the race was his.

Mayfield's teammate, Kahne, took third (it was his third top-three finish of the season), while Johnson and Newman were fourth and fifth. Kenseth recovered from a pit-road mishap – his car's brakes locked up and he spun out while trying to make a pit stop – to finish sixth, while Stewart, Greg Biffle, Jarrett and J. Gordon completed the top 10.

"I credit the team for making great pit stops and for the adjustments they made," said the winner, who completed the event in 3 hours, 9 minutes and 15 seconds at an average speed of 158.679 mph and left Georgia $180,078 richer.

*The Budweiser Chevrolet streaks down the frontstretch en route to Dale Earnhardt Jr.'s second victory and third top five of the young season. The win also boosted him back to third in points after a dismal showing the previous weekend at Las Vegas.*

## Golden Corral 500 *final race results*

| Fin. Pos. | Start Pos. | Car No. | Driver | Team | Fin. Pos. | Start Pos. | Car No. | Driver | Team |
|---|---|---|---|---|---|---|---|---|---|
| 1 | 7 | 8 | Dale Earnhardt Jr. | Budweiser Chevrolet | 23 | 15 | 15 | Michael Waltrip | NAPA Chevrolet |
| 2 | 16 | 19 | Jeremy Mayfield | Dodge Dealers/UAW Dodge | 24 | 36 | 5 | Terry Labonte | Kellogg's Chevrolet |
| 3 | 12 | 9 | Kasey Kahne | Dodge Dealers/UAW Dodge | 25 | 17 | 10 | Scott Riggs | Valvoline Chevrolet |
| 4 | 3 | 48 | Jimmie Johnson | Lowe's Chevrolet | 26 | 24 | 49 | Ken Schrader | Schwan's Home Service Dodge |
| 5 | 1 | 12 | Ryan Newman | ALLTEL Dodge | 27 | 37 | 22 | Scott Wimmer | Caterpillar Dodge |
| 6 | 30 | 17 | Matt Kenseth | DEWALT Power Tools Ford | 28 | 27 | 45 | Kyle Petty | Georgia-Pacific/Brawny Dodge |
| 7 | 19 | 20 | Tony Stewart | Home Depot Chevrolet | 29 | 5 | 38 | Elliott Sadler | M&M's Ford |
| 8 | 13 | 16 | Greg Biffle | National Guard Ford | 30 | 39 | 30 | Johnny Sauter | America Online Chevrolet |
| 9 | 6 | 88 | Dale Jarrett | UPS/Arnold Palmer Tribute Ford | 31 | 33 | 21 | Ricky Rudd | U.S. Air Force/Motorcraft Ford |
| 10 | 4 | 24 | Jeff Gordon | DuPont Chevrolet | 32 | 8 | 29 | Kevin Harvick | GM Goodwrench Chevrolet |
| 11 | 14 | 23 | Dave Blaney | Bill Davis Racing Dodge | 33 | 25 | 77 | Brendan Gaughan | Kodak Easy Share Dodge |
| 12 | 20 | 97 | Kurt Busch | IRWIN Industrial Tools Ford | 34 | 9 | 41 | Casey Mears | Target Dodge |
| 13 | 21 | 0 | Ward Burton | NetZero Hi-Speed Chevrolet | 35 | 11 | 2 | Rusty Wallace | Miller Lite Dodge |
| 14 | 28 | 6 | Mark Martin | Viagra Ford | 36 | 35 | 4 | Kevin Lepage | Morgan-McClure Chevrolet |
| 15 | 26 | 01 | Joe Nemechek | U.S. Army Chevrolet | 37 | 22 | 42 | Jamie McMurray | Texaco/Havoline Dodge |
| 16 | 31 | 40 | Sterling Marlin | Coors Light Dodge | 38 | 34 | 50 | Derrike Cope | Arnold Development Co. Dodge |
| 17 | 23 | 31 | Robby Gordon | Cingular Wireless Chevrolet | 39 | 41 | 02 | Andy Belmont | Intell Transportation Pontiac |
| 18 | 10 | 18 | Bobby Labonte | Interstate Batteries Chevrolet | 40 | 42 | 72 | Kirk Shelmerdine | Tucson Ford |
| 19 | 18 | 43 | Jeff Green | Cheerios/Betty Crocker Dodge | 41 | 38 | 98 | Todd Bodine | Lucas Oil Ford |
| 20 | 32 | 99 | Jeff Burton | SKF Ford | 42 | 43 | 80 | Andy Hillenburg | Commercial Truck & Trailer Ford |
| 21 | 2 | 25 | Brian Vickers | GMAC Financial Services Chevrolet | 43 | 40 | 09 | Joe Ruttman | Miccosukee Resort Dodge |
| 22 | 29 | 32 | Ricky Craven | Tide Chevrolet | | | | | |

# CAROLINA DODGE DEALERS 400

DARLINGTON RACEWAY
MARCH 21, 2004

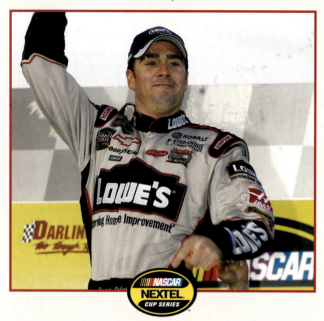

*"I can't believe I won Darlington ... This has always been a goal of mine."*

— *Jimmie Johnson*

One thing seems to be certain as far as Darlington Raceway is concerned: It takes a lot more than modifying the 1.366-mile physical layout to affect it's recent propensity for providing nail-biting finishes.

A year ago, this event came down to a dogfight between Ricky Craven and Kurt Busch that ended when Craven edged his rival by just 0.002-second at the checkered flag. It turned out to be the closest finish in a NASCAR NEXTEL Cup Series event since electronic scoring had been introduced over a decade earlier.

The battle to decide the winner of this year's version of the race was just about as exciting and close, but instead of a fight at the finish line, the event was actually decided in the pits. The crew of Jimmie Johnson's No. 48 Hendrick Motorsports/Lowe's Chevrolet was on its toes (almost literally) all day and reeled off a trio of consecutive lightning-fast 12.6-second pit stops. The last one, brought on by a late-race mishap, did the trick, and Johnson ended up holding off a rapidly closing Bobby Labonte by 0.132-second as they went under the checkered flag.

"These guys got me in the lead early in the race, and they got me out front again when it really counted," said the exuberant victor. "I really wanted a caution to come because I thought with the pit stops we'd been having, we'd have a chance to win the race."

*Jeff Gordon's DuPont Monte Carlo bounces off the fence after colliding with Andy Hillenburg, who had already crashed following contact with Tony Stewart. Neither car could return to action, which dropped Gordon to 41st in the finishing order ahead of Hillenburg in 42nd.*

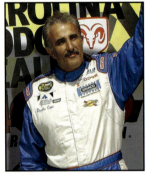

*(Top) Kasey Kahne (9) takes the green flag to begin the Carolina Dodge Dealers 400 with Dale Earnhardt Jr. on his right and Greg Biffle behind in third.*

*(Above) Derrike Cope waves to the fans during driver introductions before starting the race from the fifth position in a Dodge fielded by Arnold Motorsports.*

*(Right) Kasey Kahne capitalizes on his access to veteran Bill Elliott (right), a five-time Darlington victor with 51 career starts on the venerable South Carolina oval.*

*(Below Right) Even with Elliott's advice, Kahne was unable to avoid earning his "Darlington Stripe" after a brush with the wall in practice.*

The win was Johnson's seventh in an 80-race NASCAR NEXTEL Cup Series career and his first of the 2004 season. He also became the 41st different race winner at the track which first opened in 1950, and he left as the eighth different winner there in as many consecutive events. It was, however, his first time in Darlington's victory lane in five visits to the South Carolina super speedway.

Going into the Darlington 400-miler Johnson was ninth in NNCS points following a fourth-place finish in the previous race, the Golden Corral 500 at Atlanta Motor Speedway. With 480 markers, he arrived at Darlington 193 behind Matt Kenseth, the defending series champion.

Kenseth's sixth-place run in the Golden Corral 500 was his fourth top-10 finish of the season, including two victories, and that kept the driver of Roush Racing's DeWalt Tools Ford comfortably in front in the points battle. With 673, he led runner-up Tony Stewart by 82 as the series headed into Darlington.

Stewart, in the No. 20 Joe Gibbs Racing/Home Depot Chevrolet, finished seventh at Atlanta, his third top-10 showing of the year, and with 591 points, he held second by just a few whiskers – eight – over Dale Earnhardt Jr., who came away from Atlanta with his second win of the season and 583 total points.

Kasey Kahne, in the Ray Evernham No. 9 Dodge, continued to belie his rookie status with another strong run. Kahne finished third at Atlanta Motor Speedway – his third top-10 showing of the year – and that put him fourth in points (with 550), 123 behind the leader.

*(Left) Ryan Newman (12) tries to best Robby Gordon (31) on the inside in Darlington's treacherous turns. The two finished together in the race, with Newman picking up a season-best third place ahead of Gordon, who led all drivers by improving 25 positions during the day to finish fourth.*

*(Below) Kevin Harvick tries to stick the nose of his GM Goodwrench Chevrolet inside the Viagra Ford of Mark Martin, while Jeremy Mayfield measures the move from behind. Harvick's challenge proved unsuccessful, and the three finished together with Martin in seventh ahead of Harvick, eighth, and Mayfield in ninth.*

*(Bottom) A double-wide pack uses up the racing groove in Darlington's 23-degree-banked fourth turn, outfitted for the first time with the energy-absorbing SAFER wall barrier.*

It was also the fourth time he'd completed a race as the highest-finishing Raybestos Rookie of the Year candidate.

Jeff Gordon, Johnson's Hendrick Motorsports teammate, finished 10th at Atlanta, his third top-10 run of the year, and with 543 points, he was 130 out of the lead going into the Darlington event but just seven behind Kahne and 16 in front of sixth-place Busch. After finishing 12th in the Golden Corral 500, Busch was hoping to at least equal his finish of a year ago at Darlington.

After a lackluster start in 2004, Jeremy Mayfield gave Earnhardt Jr. a bit of competition at Atlanta and came away with a second-place finish, his first top-10 showing of the year. The run was not only a morale boost for the Evernham Dodge driver, it put him seventh in points, 13 behind Busch.

Elliott Sadler had somewhat of a difficult day at Atlanta. He ended up finishing 29th in the Yates Racing/M&M's Ford, and found himself eighth in points going into Atlanta with 481, just one in front of Johnson, who finished fourth in the Golden Corral 500. Johnson had just 11 more points than 10th-place Bobby Labonte, who was 18th in the

Atlanta event, while Ryan Newman (467 points), Kevin Harvick (466), Joe Nemechek (465), Ward Burton (459) and Dale Jarrett (445) – 11th through 15th in points – were all nipping at Labonte's heels.

With nine caution flags spread evenly throughout the 293-lap event, pit crews had plenty of work in providing fresh rubber for the gritty Darlington asphalt. At right, Elliott Sadler's crew springs into action on the M&M's Ford, helping their driver secure his best finish of the season so far in fifth. Below, Kurt Busch arrives for service from his Sharpie mates. Like Sadler, Busch posted a season-best result, finishing just behind the M&M's driver, in sixth.

Kahne a rookie? The casual bystander might be hard pressed to believe that, considering that the driver who "inherited" the No. 9 Dodge from the semi-retired Bill Elliott attacked the "Track Too Tough to Tame" and, in his first outing at Darlington, captured the Bud Pole for the Dodge Dealers 400 with a time and speed of 28.638 seconds and 171.716 mph. It was his second pole of the year, as he'd qualified fastest two races ago at Las Vegas.

Still feeling the results of his Atlanta victory, Earnhardt Jr. lapped the 1.366-mile track in the No. 8 DEI/Budweiser Chevrolet in 28.732 seconds to take the No. 2 qualifying spot with a speed of 171.154 mph. Greg Biffle, Busch and Derrike Cope (a surprise in an under-funded Dodge) took the next three starting positions, while only one driver, Stanton Barrett, wasn't quick enough to make the field.

"It's definitely a surprise that all this (success) has come so quickly," Kahne admitted. The new SAFER energy absorbing barrier that shaved off about three feet of running room – and in place at Darlington for the first time – didn't seem to have an effect on the first-year driver's style. But he did admit that he took the advice of his crew chief, Tommy Baldwin, who

told him to face the track the same way he did the slightly smaller venue at Rockingham, N.C., earlier in the year. Baldwin gave his driver an egg and told him to pretend it was under the gas pedal and not to crack it.

"The egg is back," Kahne said.

Ryan Newman, his teammate, Rusty Wallace, Stewart, Gordon and Sadler filled in the top 10 qualifying spots. Four drivers, including Michael Waltrip, had to use provisional starts.

Including Kahne, who led the first 11 laps but ended up finishing 13th, 12 drivers swapped the lead 22 times. Busch tried to make up for last year's narrow loss and went to the front five times for 76 laps. Events, though, conspired against him and he was sixth at the conclusion of the race.

The man of the day was Johnson, who led three times for 69 circuits that encompassed laps 166-185, 188-221 and 279-293. Things started turning in his favor when the fifth of nine yellow flags for 58 laps went into effect on lap 162 because of a six-car mishap. The first of those ultra-rapid pit stops put the Lowe's Chevrolet driver into the lead when the race went green on lap 170, a lead he held through the next yellow-flag period (laps 185-190).

The restart after caution flag No. 7 came on lap 239 and saw Busch in the lead and Johnson

running fifth. The restart after the race's eighth interruption came on the 283rd lap, and from there on out (including the last yellow flag) it was Johnson's race.

"We just couldn't get by him," a dejected Labonte said. " We tried our best and just couldn't do it."

"I can't believe I won Darlington. This is unbelievable," Johnson said. "This has always been a goal of mine."

Johnson completed the race in 3 hours, 30 minutes and 39 seconds at an average speed of 114.001 mph and won $151,150.

*Jimmie Johnson (48) grabs the checkered flag a mere 0.132 second ahead of hard-charging Bobby Labonte after a furious four-lap shootout following the day's final caution. Johnson credited his crew for an outstanding final pit stop that gave him the lead by mere inches over Labonte, an advantage he was able to hold over the final 15 laps.*

## Carolina Dodge Dealers 400 *final race results*

| Fin. Pos. | Start Pos. | Car No. | Driver | Team | Fin. Pos. | Start Pos. | Car No. | Driver | Team |
|---|---|---|---|---|---|---|---|---|---|
| 1 | 11 | 48 | Jimmie Johnson | Lowe's Chevrolet | 23 | 28 | 25 | Brian Vickers | GMAC Financial Services Chevrolet |
| 2 | 12 | 18 | Bobby Labonte | Interstate Batteries Chevrolet | 24 | 30 | 43 | Jeff Green | Cheerios/Betty Crocker Dodge |
| 3 | 6 | 12 | Ryan Newman | ALLTEL Dodge | 25 | 5 | 50 | Derrike Cope | Arnold Development Co. Dodge |
| 4 | 29 | 31 | Robby Gordon | Cingular Wireless Chevrolet | 26 | 24 | 30 | Johnny Sauter | America Online Chevrolet |
| 5 | 10 | 38 | Elliott Sadler | M&M's Ford | 27 | 37 | 77 | Brendan Gaughan | Kodak Easy Share Dodge |
| 6 | 4 | 97 | Kurt Busch | Sharpie Ford | 28 | 31 | 4 | Kevin Lepage | Morgan-McClure Chevrolet |
| 7 | 20 | 6 | Mark Martin | Viagra Ford | 29 | 7 | 2 | Rusty Wallace | Miller Lite Dodge |
| 8 | 23 | 29 | Kevin Harvick | GM Goodwrench Chevrolet | 30 | 27 | 10 | Scott Riggs | Valvoline Chevrolet |
| 9 | 18 | 19 | Jeremy Mayfield | Dodge Dealers/UAW Dodge | 31 | 15 | 17 | Matt Kenseth | DeWalt Power Tools Ford |
| 10 | 2 | 8 | Dale Earnhardt Jr. | Budweiser Chevrolet | 32 | 22 | 88 | Dale Jarrett | UPS Ford |
| 11 | 33 | 99 | Jeff Burton | Hot Wheels Ford | 33 | 25 | 21 | Ricky Rudd | Motorcraft Ford |
| 12 | 3 | 16 | Greg Biffle | Travel Lodge/National Guard Ford | 34 | 32 | 45 | Kyle Petty | Georgia-Pacific/Brawny Dodge |
| 13 | 1 | 9 | Kasey Kahne | Dodge Dealers/UAW Dodge | 35 | 39 | 15 | Michael Waltrip | NAPA Chevrolet |
| 14 | 17 | 40 | Sterling Marlin | Coors Light Dodge | 36 | 36 | 32 | Ricky Craven | Tide Chevrolet |
| 15 | 19 | 41 | Casey Mears | Target Dodge | 37 | 42 | 02 | Andy Belmont | Continental Fire & Safety Pontiac |
| 16 | 14 | 22 | Scott Wimmer | Caterpillar Dodge | 38 | 38 | 89 | Morgan Shepherd | Voyles/Carter Royal Dispos-all Dodge |
| 17 | 8 | 20 | Tony Stewart | Home Depot Chevrolet | 39 | 41 | 72 | Kirk Shelmerdine | Tucson Ford |
| 18 | 13 | 0 | Ward Burton | NetZero Hi-Speed Chevrolet | 40 | 35 | 98 | Todd Bodine | Lucas Oil Ford |
| 19 | 26 | 5 | Terry Labonte | Kellogg's Chevrolet | 41 | 9 | 24 | Jeff Gordon | DuPont Chevrolet |
| 20 | 34 | 01 | Joe Nemechek | U.S. Army Chevrolet | 42 | 43 | 80 | Andy Hillenburg | Hover Motorsports Ford |
| 21 | 21 | 42 | Jamie McMurray | Texaco/Havoline Dodge | 43 | 40 | 09 | Joe Ruttman | Miccosukee Resort Dodge |
| 22 | 16 | 49 | Ken Schrader | Schwan's Home Service Dodge | | | | | |

# FOOD CITY 500

*"The way you have to approach Bristol every time is you show up with the frame of mind just to survive."*

— Kurt Busch

Kurt Busch knew he was facing a type of love-hate relationship with Bristol Motor Speedway and many of the fans who regularly pack its grandstands. So approaching the sixth NASCAR NEXTEL Cup Series race of the 2004 season, the first of two annual events at the ultra-steep 0.533-mile oval, he had to make sure he didn't think too hard about the race and suffer from self-imposed pressure that might affect his performance.

First, the driver of Roush Racing's No. 97 Sharpie Ford knew he was going for the so-called "hat trick." He'd won the last two consecutive events at Bristol (as well as three of the last four), thus making it tough for a gambler to wager he'd win again.

Second, although he'd captured the August 2003 race at BMS, it wasn't a popular victory with the crowd of 160,000 fans. He'd gotten into a physical altercation with driver Jimmy Spencer at Michigan Speedway, the event before Bristol, and while Busch was cleared to race in Tennessee, Spencer was barred from participating. Spencer was rightly contrite about the incident in the Michigan garage, but Busch fanned the flames by not letting the matter rest. He said the "wrong things" and was rewarded with a round of catcalls as he celebrated in victory lane at Bristol.

*Jeff Burton (99) gets out of shape after being roughed up from behind by Kevin Harvick just past the 100-lap mark in the Food City 500. Burton's battered car was eventually black-flagged for being unable to maintain the minimum speed, while Harvick drove on to a third-place finish.*

Going into the Food City 500, Busch ranked fourth in the standings with 687, following a sixth-place finish in the Carolina Dodge Dealers 400, the week before in Darlington, S.C.

Kenseth, Busch's Roush teammate had a rough day at Darlington in the No. 17 DeWalt Ford. He finished 31st, four laps down, but still left the track with 743 points. That was 21 more points than runner-up Dale Earnhardt Jr., who finished 10th at Darlington (for his fourth top-10 showing of the season) in the DEI/Budweiser Chevrolet.

Tony Stewart also had a mediocre race at Darlington, finishing 17th in the No. 20 Home Depot Chevrolet. But with three top-10 finishes in five starts, he found himself third in the standings, 35 out of the lead. Rookie sensation Kasey Kahne started on the pole at Darlington but finished 13th in the race and headed into Bristol fifth in points with 679, putting him 64 in arrears of Kenseth.

Jimmie Johnson left the 400-miler at Darlington on a really high note. He'd won the race, giving him his third top-five finish in five starts, and was just 14 points behind Kahne, ranking sixth in the standings and just 78 out of the lead. Jeremy Mayfield recorded a ninth-place finish in the Dodge Dealers 400 and approached Bristol seventh in points, only 13 behind Johnson and a mere eight in front of Bobby Labonte.

With 644 points, Labonte (who ran second at Darlington) was 99 behind the leader and only seven in front of ninth-ranked Ryan Newman, who finished third in South Carolina. Elliott Sadler recorded a fifth-place finish in the Darlington event and that put him just one point behind Newman with 636.

Kevin Harvick headed into Bristol 11th in points with 608. Mark Martin and Jeff Gordon were tied with 583 markers each, as were Joe Nemechek and Ward Burton, who completed the top 15, both with 568 points.

If racing had a title "Chairman of the Pole," it would have to belong to Ryan Newman. The Penske Racing Dodge driver snared his 21st Bud Pole in 86 starts with a time and speed of 14.954 seconds at 128.313 mph. That didn't beat his own track record of 14.908 seconds, set one year ago, but it was a tad better than anyone else. Jeff Gordon was second quickest in time trials with a speed of 128.288 mph, while

Greg Biffle, Rusty Wallace and Kasey Kahne scored starting spots three through five with lap speeds of 128.176, 128.074 and 127.860 mph, respectively.

"We set the bar last spring," said Newman, who now has three poles in six 2004 starts. "We came back (to Bristol) in the fall and didn't qualify as well, but we were more competitive in the race.

"This time, we look forward to being good in both."

Gordon, who had been suffering through somewhat of a recent rough patch, was heartened by his 14.957-second lap in the Hendrick Motorsports/DuPont Chevrolet. It marked the fifth straight time he'd scored a front-row start at the track, a place where he'd been a front-runner in eight of the past nine races.

Rounding out the top 10 in qualifying were Jamie McMurray, Brendan Gaughan, Michael Waltrip, Sadler and Johnny Sauter. The only driver who failed to make the field was Morgan Shepherd.

Although Busch qualified 13th for the race, with three wins in his last four visits to the concrete speedbowl, he must have been doing something right.

(Above) Jamie McMurray (42) slides into his pit stall between Jeff Gordon (24) and Michael Waltrip's NAPA Chevrolet. All three started in the top 10 and finished there as well, with McMurray eighth, Gordon ninth and Waltrip in 10th.

(Above Right) Robby Gordon (31) spins into the path of Jeremy Mayfield (19) while (in order) Ken Schrader, Jeff Green and Johnny Sauter slip past on the outside. Everyone managed to avoid the Cingular car without incident and Gordon went on to complete all 500 laps.

(Below Right) Greg Biffle (16) and Kasey Kahne (9) try to chase down a fleet-running Rusty Wallace (2) in early-race action. Both drivers took turns at the front in chunks over the first half of the race.

"The way you have to approach Bristol every time is you show up with the frame of mind just to survive. The guy who usually has the cleanest looking car at the end of the race usually has the best chance of going to victory lane."

The Las Vegas native obviously took his own advice. Not only did he avoid the slings and arrows that racing at Bristol can toss your way, his reception from the crowd was certainly quite a bit different from that of the previous summer when he pulled his Ford into the track's victory circle for the third time in a row. Busch himself had gambled this time. He'd gone against the advice of his crew chief, Jimmy Fennig, and his call turned out to be just what was needed.

When the sixth of 11 caution flags for 85 of 500 laps was displayed on lap 380, Fennig wanted his driver to join the crowd on pit road for a change of tires. Instead, Busch, who had pitted under green about 20 laps earlier, defied the order and remained on the track where he took the lead for the first time – a lead he would somehow manage to hold for the final 119 circuits.

At the finish, he held off Rusty Wallace's No. 2 Penske/Miller Dodge by just 0.428-second. Wallace, a nine-time winner at Bristol,

was trying to snap a 103-race winless streak but again came up frustratingly short.

"This (Bristol victory), by far, has got to be the sweetest because of what we had to overcome," Busch said. "Our engine had about 1,000 RPM less all day. I just couldn't get the car to handle right. It's just unreal."

Not only was it his ninth career victory, it also propelled Busch into second in points behind leader Matt Kenseth.

Wallace, who led four times for 100 laps, found himself in fifth place after the crucial sixth yellow-flag period ended. He'd advanced to third at the end of yellow No. 8 on lap 437 and was in second when the 10th interruption ended on lap 487.

The 11th and final yellow flag came out on the 494th lap because of a crash, and the race was red-flagged to clear the track of debris. The green came out with two laps left, and Wallace bumped Busch – to no avail – and had to back off when his tactic failed.

"Man, we didn't need those cautions. I was about to pass him that one time," Wallace said. "I wanted that bad. So close."

Busch later apologized – sort of – for going against his crew chief. He said he'd gotten himself into a tough situation and had to "bail myself out" of it. In any case, after completing the event in 3 hours, 13 minutes and 34 seconds at an average speed of 82.607 mph, he left the track $173,965 richer.

*Nine-time Bristol winner Rusty Wallace (2) does his best to chase down Kurt Busch (97), but he simply ran out of laps after a late caution. Busch went on to take his third straight win at the Tennessee half mile.*

## Food City 500 *final race results*

| Fin. Pos. | Start Pos. | Car No. | Driver | Team | Fin. Pos. | Start Pos. | Car No. | Driver | Team |
|---|---|---|---|---|---|---|---|---|---|
| 1 | 13 | 97 | Kurt Busch | Sharpie Ford | 23 | 21 | 6 | Mark Martin | Viagra Ford |
| 2 | 4 | 2 | Rusty Wallace | Miller Lite Dodge | 24 | 12 | 20 | Tony Stewart | Home Depot Chevrolet |
| 3 | 14 | 29 | Kevin Harvick | GM Goodwrench Chevrolet | 25 | 36 | 45 | Kyle Petty | Georgia-Pacific/Brawny Dodge |
| 4 | 17 | 40 | Sterling Marlin | Coors Light Dodge | 26 | 37 | 50 | Derrike Cope | Arnold Development Co. Dodge |
| 5 | 23 | 17 | Matt Kenseth | DeWalt Power Tools Ford | 27 | 26 | 01 | Joe Nemechek | U.S. Army Chevrolet |
| 6 | 19 | 49 | Ken Schrader | Schwan's Home Service Dodge | 28 | 39 | 0 | Ward Burton | NetZero Hi-Speed Chevrolet |
| 7 | 1 | 12 | Ryan Newman | ALLTEL Dodge | 29 | 29 | 43 | Jeff Green | Cheerios/Betty Crocker Dodge |
| 8 | 6 | 42 | Jamie McMurray | Texaco/Havoline Dodge | 30 | 35 | 4 | Kevin Lepage | Food City Chevrolet |
| 9 | 2 | 24 | Jeff Gordon | DuPont Chevrolet | 31 | 42 | 02 | Hermie Sadler | East Tennessee Trailers Pontiac |
| 10 | 8 | 15 | Michael Waltrip | NAPA Chevrolet | 32 | 38 | 94 | Stanton Barrett | AmericInn Chevrolet |
| 11 | 18 | 8 | Dale Earnhardt Jr. | Budweiser Chevrolet | 33 | 27 | 18 | Bobby Labonte | Wellbutrin XL (bupropion HCl) Chevrolet |
| 12 | 3 | 16 | Greg Biffle | National Guard/Jackson Hewitt Ford | 34 | 28 | 10 | Scott Riggs | Valvoline/Harlem Globetrotters Chevrolet |
| 13 | 20 | 22 | Scott Wimmer | Caterpillar Dodge | 35 | 22 | 25 | Brian Vickers | GMAC Chevrolet |
| 14 | 9 | 38 | Elliott Sadler | Pedigree/M&M's Ford | 36 | 24 | 41 | Casey Mears | Target Dodge |
| 15 | 10 | 30 | Johnny Sauter | America Online Chevrolet | 37 | 15 | 21 | Ricky Rudd | Rent-A-Center/Motorcraft Ford |
| 16 | 11 | 48 | Jimmie Johnson | Lowe's Chevrolet | 38 | 31 | 99 | Jeff Burton | Roush Racing Ford |
| 17 | 16 | 19 | Jeremy Mayfield | Dodge Dealers/UAW Dodge | 39 | 34 | 98 | Geoffrey Bodine | Lucas Oil Ford |
| 18 | 33 | 5 | Terry Labonte | Kellogg's Chevrolet | 40 | 5 | 9 | Kasey Kahne | Dodge Dealers/UAW Dodge |
| 19 | 32 | 31 | Robby Gordon | Cingular Wireless Chevrolet | 41 | 41 | 72 | Kirk Shelmerdine | Freddie B's Ford |
| 20 | 7 | 77 | Brendan Gaughan | Kodak/Punisher Dodge | 42 | 40 | 09 | Joe Ruttman | Miccosukee Resort Dodge |
| 21 | 30 | 88 | Dale Jarrett | UPS Ford | 43 | 43 | 80 | Andy Hillenburg | Commercial Truck & Trailer Ford |
| 22 | 25 | 32 | Ricky Craven | Tide Chevrolet | | | | | |

# SAMSUNG/RADIOSHACK 500

## TEXAS MOTOR SPEEDWAY
### APRIL 4, 2004

*"To come back and win at this track is very special. It's a very special weekend for my family and me."*

— *Elliott Sadler*

It had been a long time since Elliott Sadler had steered his car off the track and into victory lane following a NASCAR NEXTEL Cup Series race – 108 events to be exact – but the faith placed in him by Robert Yates Racing finally paid off in the flatlands of the Lone Star State.

Luck – and being in the right place at the right time – finally smiled on the Emporia, Va., native at Texas Motor Speedway, though, and Sadler provided Ford Motor Co., Yates Racing and team sponsor M&M's with a chance to celebrate.

Sadler had finished 14th at Bristol (Tenn.) Motor Speedway, the site of the previous week's race (and where he won for the first time in 2001) and headed to Texas ninth in points, 141 behind Matt Kenseth, the point leader. Kenseth, with 898 points after a fifth-place finish at Bristol, had a narrow 21-point lead over Roush Racing teammate Kurt Busch, who had won the event at Bristol.

Earnhardt Jr. finished 11th in the Bristol event and left the track third in points with 857. A few days later, though, he was fined $10,000 and docked 25 points for admitting he'd intentionally spun his car late in the Food City 500 so he could make a pit stop and have his crew attend to a problem. Yet, with 832 points, he was still third in the standings, 28 in front of Tony Stewart.

*Elliott Sadler's crew services the M&M's Ford at Texas Motor Speedway. Their teamwork kept Sadler up with the leaders all day and put him in position to capture the lead when the opportunity presented itself.*

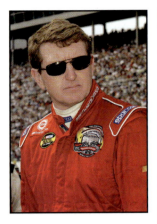

(Above) Bill Elliott, on hand at Texas to make his second start of the season, had an outstanding qualifying run that put him on the front row at the start. It would go for naught, however, when a flat tire late in the race sent him careening into the wall.

(Right) Texas native Bobby Labonte consults with car chief Scott Zipadelli in the TMS garage after taking his first Bud Pole of the year, the 26th of his career.

Stewart had a rough day at Bristol; he finished 24th, two laps down. Going into Texas, he had a 16-point lead on Ryan Newman, who won the Bud Pole at Bristol and finished seventh in the race for his fourth top-10 finish of the season.

With 785 points, Jimmie Johnson was 113 out of the lead but just three in back of Newman with 785. Kevin Harvick ran well at Bristol – he started 14th and finished third – and that put him seventh in the standings with 773 points. He was only 12 markers in back of Johnson, but with 764 points, Jeremy Mayfield was breathing down his neck in eighth place.

Sterling Marlin also had a decent day at his Tennessee "home track," where he started 17th and finished fourth. That gave him his second top-10 finish of 2004 (he also finished

fourth at Rockingham), and with 727 points, he was 30 behind Sadler but just five in front of 11th-place Kasey Kahne, who in turn, headed to Texas a single point in front of 12th-place Jeff Gordon. Also lurking in the wings was Bobby Labonte, in 13th place. With 708 points, he headed to Texas 190 behind Kenseth.

Bobby Labonte (18) drops to the inside in a three-abreast fight with Brian Vickers (25) and Dale Earnhardt Jr. (8). Labonte took the lead at the 200-lap mark, but a battery failure a short time later dropped him from contention.

To call Texas Motor Speedway Bobby Labonte's "home track" is kind of stretching things, but ... aw shucks ... the state is so big that it once was its own country. So even though Corpus Christi, Labonte's hometown, is 7-1/2 hours south of the Fort Worth area, winning the Bud Pole for the Samsung/RadioShack 500 was something of a homecoming for the Joe Gibbs Racing Chevrolet driver. It was also special because Labonte notched the No. 1 starting spot for last year's version of the race and thus became the first two-time pole winner at the track.

"I really do appreciate everybody's support here. It's a fantastic crowd just for qualifying," Labonte said after lapping the track in 27.849 seconds at 193.903 mph. "I did hear the ovation when I came back to the pits, and it's pretty cool to do this in your home state."

The pole belonged to the semi-retired Bill Elliott until Labonte made his run. He clocked in with a lap of 27.874 seconds at 193.729 mph, in an unsponsored Evernham Motorsports Dodge, which was a tad quicker than the speed of 193.673 mph recorded by his teammate, Kahne.

"We don't have anybody on the car, so if you want to throw in a couple of bucks, I'm sure Ray (Evernham) will talk to you," Elliott quipped.

Greg Biffle was fourth quickest in a Ford at 193.195 mph, and Joe Nemechek, in a Chevrolet, took the fifth starting spot with a speed of 193.188 mph. Rounding out the top 10 were Casey Mears (Dodge), Earnhardt Jr. (Chevrolet), Jimmie Johnson (Chevrolet), Jeff Gordon (Chevrolet) and Rusty Wallace (Dodge).

*(Above) Scott Wimmer (22) takes a hard lick from Jeremy Mayfield (19) following a late-race restart. The incident began when Brian Vickers (25) tapped Wimmer from behind, turning him into the path of Mayfield's Dodge.*

*(Left) Kurt Busch sails into the Texas banking with Casey Mears hot on his tail in their battle for position. Busch would fend off Mears' challenge and they finished together, with Busch taking sixth place ahead of Mears in seventh, matching his career best set earlier in the year at Las Vegas.*

Kyle Busch, Morgan Shepherd, Andy Hillenburg and Andy Belmont failed to make the 43-car race.

It was actually the fourth of seven caution-flag periods for 45 of 334 laps that paved the way for Sadler's second career victory while turning events against the dynamic rookie, Kasey Kahne, who again ended up the brides-maid. Kahne, who led six times for 148 laps, had pitted under green just before the crucial yellow flag came out. Sadler hadn't, so he immediately dove into the pits and re-entered the event running second to Jeff Gordon, while Kahne's Evernham Motorsports Dodge got trapped and temporarily was listed as being a lap down.

Although Kahne, the first car a lap in arrears, was the recipient of the "lucky dog" award (he got his lap back), he had to struggle through the final three yellow-flag periods, while things only got better for Sadler. The guy in the catbird's seat was actually Hendrick Motorsports/DuPont Chevrolet driver Gordon. The four-time series champion went into the lead on lap 262, and when the green flag flew for the final time on lap 302 he was handily in front of Sadler.

Five laps later, though, Gordon's car bobbled and slowed with a dying battery, and Sadler went into the lead. Dale Earnhardt Jr. moved his Chevrolet into second place, while Kahne worked his way back up to third. Twenty laps from the finish, Kahne got by Earnhardt's No. 8

Budweiser Monte Carlo and started after Sadler but came up a scant 0.028-second short at the checkered flag.

Gordon flipped a switch that activated a backup battery and got by Earnhardt to finish third, while Rusty Wallace trailed Earnhardt across the line in fifth. Rounding out the top 10 finishers were Kurt Busch, Casey Mears, Tony Stewart, Jimmie Johnson and Jamie McMurray.

"The chips fell in my direction and we were able to pull it off there at the end," Sadler said. "To come back and win at this track is very special. It's a very special weekend for my family and me.

"A lot of things were lifted off my shoulders.

"I was (mentally) coaching Dale Jr. to hold him (Kahne) off as long as he could," Sadler said of the race's final laps. "I knew Kasey would be coming, and once he got around Earnhardt, boy, he started making up time."

"We were dominant all day," noted Kahne, who recorded his fourth top-five finish in seven races. "It's satisfying but a little bit frustrating. I don't know when we'll get another chance to win."

The race lead changed hands 24 times with 12 drivers going to the front. Besides the winner, Kahne and Earnhardt Jr., Gordon, Elliott, Nemechek, Marlin, Wallace, Kyle Petty, Johnny Sauter and Busch took turns pacing the field.

Pole winner Labonte lost the lead on the first lap and led just once for five circuits. He pitted just after the 220-lap mark to have his car's battery replaced and ended up finishing 25th, four laps down. Elliott led twice for 26 laps, but a flat tire sent him into the wall on lap 276 and he finished 36th.

Sadler completed the event in 3 hours, 36 minutes and 30 seconds at an average speed of 138.845 mph and won $507,733.

### Samsung/RadioShack 500 *final race results*

| Fin. Pos. | Start Pos. | Car No. | Driver | Team | Fin. Pos. | Start Pos. | Car No. | Driver | Team |
|---|---|---|---|---|---|---|---|---|---|
| 1 | 19 | 38 | Elliott Sadler | M&M's Ford | 23 | 18 | 31 | Robby Gordon | Cingular Wireless Chevrolet |
| 2 | 3 | 9 | Kasey Kahne | Dodge Dealers/UAW Dodge | 24 | 37 | 30 | Johnny Sauter | America Online Chevrolet |
| 3 | 9 | 24 | Jeff Gordon | DuPont Chevrolet | 25 | 1 | 18 | Bobby Labonte | Interstate Batteries Chevrolet |
| 4 | 7 | 8 | Dale Earnhardt Jr. | Budweiser Chevrolet | 26 | 14 | 40 | Sterling Marlin | Coors Light Dodge |
| 5 | 10 | 2 | Rusty Wallace | Miller Lite Dodge | 27 | 23 | 99 | Jeff Burton | Roush Racing Ford |
| 6 | 12 | 97 | Kurt Busch | IRWIN Industrial Tools Ford | 28 | 40 | 32 | Ricky Craven | Tide Chevrolet |
| 7 | 6 | 41 | Casey Mears | Fuji Film/Target Dodge | 29 | 42 | 4 | Jimmy Spencer | Featherlite Luxury Coaches Chevrolet |
| 8 | 17 | 20 | Tony Stewart | Home Depot Chevrolet | 30 | 35 | 14 | Larry Foyt | Smith ChryslerDodge/FtWorth HD Dodge |
| 9 | 8 | 48 | Jimmie Johnson | Lowe's Chevrolet | 31 | 4 | 16 | Greg Biffle | National Guard Ford |
| 10 | 26 | 42 | Jamie McMurray | Texaco/Havoline Dodge | 32 | 27 | 0 | Ward Burton | NetZero Hi-Speed Chevrolet |
| 11 | 20 | 23 | Dave Blaney | Batesville Speedway/BadBoyMowers Dodge | 33 | 32 | 22 | Scott Wimmer | Caterpillar Dodge |
| 12 | 13 | 25 | Brian Vickers | GMAC Chevrolet | 34 | 21 | 19 | Jeremy Mayfield | Dodge Dealers/UAW Dodge |
| 13 | 22 | 29 | Kevin Harvick | GM Goodwrench/Icebreakers Chevrolet | 35 | 33 | 43 | Jeff Green | Cheerios/Betty Crocker Dodge |
| 14 | 5 | 01 | Joe Nemechek | U.S. Army Chevrolet | 36 | 2 | 91 | Bill Elliott | Evernham Motorsports Dodge |
| 15 | 24 | 10 | Scott Riggs | Valvoline Chevrolet | 37 | 31 | 50 | Derrike Cope | Arnold Development Co. Dodge |
| 16 | 25 | 17 | Matt Kenseth | DeWalt Power Tools Ford | 38 | 16 | 77 | Brendan Gaughan | Kodak Easy Share Dodge |
| 17 | 28 | 6 | Mark Martin | Viagra Ford | 39 | 15 | 12 | Ryan Newman | ALLTEL Dodge |
| 18 | 11 | 88 | Dale Jarrett | UPS Ford | 40 | 34 | 09 | Johnny Benson | Miccosukee Resorts Dodge |
| 19 | 39 | 49 | Ken Schrader | Schwan's Home Service Dodge | 41 | 30 | 5 | Terry Labonte | Kellogg's/Delphi Chevrolet |
| 20 | 41 | 15 | Michael Waltrip | NAPA Chevrolet | 42 | 43 | 72 | Kirk Shelmerdine | Freddie B's Ford |
| 21 | 38 | 45 | Kyle Petty | Georgia-Pacific/Brawny Dodge | 43 | 36 | 98 | Todd Bodine | Lucas Oil Ford |
| 22 | 29 | 21 | Ricky Rudd | Keep It Genuine Ford | | | | | |

*(Top) Elliott Sadler (38) tries to catch Jeff Gordon (24) for the late-race lead. The DuPont Monte Carlo appeared unstoppable as the laps wound down, until an electrical problem caused it to slow. Gordon recovered quickly, but not before Sadler took over the point.*

*(Above Left) Kasey Kahne (9) closes in on Sadler's Ford after the hot-driving rookie fought all the way back from the pit-road setback.*

*(Above) At the finish, Sadler had just enough to hold off Kahne's challenge and take the win by a mere 0.028-second margin of victory. It was Kahne's third runner-up finish in seven events, two of those by less than a car length.*

# ADVANCE AUTO PARTS 500

## MARTINSVILLE SPEEDWAY
### APRIL 18, 2004

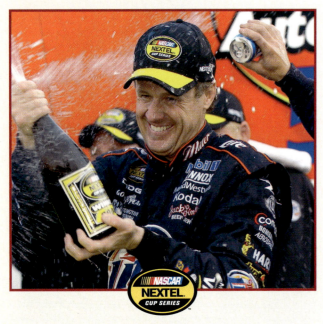

*"I thought if we could get this right or that right we'd get back in victory lane. You know I'm not a quitter."*

— Rusty Wallace

On a clear day in Henry County, Va., Jeff Gordon's winless drought extended itself – in a way, he fell "deeper into a hole" – and Rusty Wallace saw his streak of failing to make it into victory lane finally come to an end after 105 consecutive NASCAR NEXTEL Cup Series events.

Since his last victory on April 29, 2001, at Fontana, Calif., Wallace, a part owner of his team, had tried various arrangements of car setups and team personnel to break the slump. The latest combination, with Larry Carter as crew chief, appeared to do the trick.

"It's been so long and we've been so close," Wallace said of his 55th career victory and seventh at Martinsville. "I thought if we could get this right or that right we'd get back in victory lane. You know I'm not a quitter.

"If anything, I keep moving things around to complement what I have."

Kurt Busch didn't win the race before Martinsville – he finished sixth at Texas Motor Speedway – but the finish was more than good enough to give him the lead in NASCAR NEXTEL Cup Series points. With 1,032 markers, he was 19 in front of Roush Racing teammate Matt Kenseth, who finished a mediocre 16th in the Samsung/RadioShack 500. He had led in the standings since the third race of the season at Las Vegas.

Rusty Wallace (2) charges toward victory at Martinsville while fending off the challenges of Bobby Labonte (18) and Dale Earnhardt Jr. (8), who finished second and third, respectively. Wallace took the lead for the first time in the race with 45 circuits to go and drove to his seventh career win at the Virginia half-mile.

Going into Martinsville, Earnhardt Jr. remained third in points with 997, just 35 behind the leader. The DEI/Bud-weiser Chevrolet driver finished fourth at Texas, which marked his fifth top-10 finish of the season, four of those in the top five.

A solid eighth-place run at Texas enabled Tony Stewart to retain the fourth slot in the points. Texas was the Joe Gibbs Racing/Home Depot Chevrolet driver's fourth top-10 finish of the year, and with 946 points, he was just 86 behind Busch and 51 in back of Earnhardt Jr. Stewart headed into his 11th start at Martinsville, where he had won in October 2000.

A stirring victory in Texas saw Elliott Sadler jump from ninth to fifth in the standings. With 942 points, the driver of Robert Yates Racing's No. 38 M&M's Ford was just 90 out of first place, four behind Stewart and 19 in front of sixth-place Jimmie Johnson. In that spot for the past three consecutive races, Johnson, in the No. 48 Hendrick/Lowe's Chevrolet, finished ninth at Texas and, like Sadler, earned his fourth top-10 run of the year.

A second-place run at Texas Motor Speedway, his third runner-up finish of the year, was good news for rookie Kasey Kahne. He left the track with 902 points and jumped up four spots in the standings, from 11th to seventh. Along with Earnhardt Jr., he headed to Martinsville as the only driver with four top-five finishes in the year's first seven races.

A 13th-place run in the Lone Star State dropped RCR/GM Goodwrench Chevrolet pilot Kevin Harvick down a spot in points, from seventh to eighth. With 897 markers, he was 135 in back of Busch but just five behind Kahne and a scant six in front of Jeff Gordon.

At Texas, Gordon exhibited a bit of the skill that had earned him four series championships. He finished third in the race, his fifth top 10 of the year, and moved from 12th to ninth in points. Statistically, he headed to Virginia 141 points out of the lead and a semi-comfortable 57 ahead of No. 10 Ryan Newman. A mid-race accident in the Samsung/RadioShack 500 saw Newman finish 39th and fall five places in the standings, from fifth to 10th. That put him 198 points behind leader Busch.

Heading to the 0.526-mile Martinsville track the drivers who were 11th-15th in the standings were all within 33 points of cracking the top 10. Both Jeremy Mayfield and Wallace were only nine points in back of Newman, while Jaime McMurray was 16, Sterling Marlin 17 and Bobby Labonte 33.

If ever there was a place, Gordon thought, to post his first win of 2004 this was it. He had won here five times in his career, including a season sweep of the events last year. And although he didn't come anywhere near

*Ryan Newman (12) catches the sliding rear end of his ALLTEL Dodge while Tony Stewart (20) tries to sneak past on the inside. Stewart had a tough weekend – he qualified 30th and salvaged a 14th-place finish – while Newman, who started third, took advantage of a late-race two-tire stop and brought his Penske Intrepid home in fifth.*

Tony Stewart's record-setting Bud Pole run of 95.371 mph, set in September 2000, his time and speed of 20.252 seconds at 93.502 mph was all it took to notch the No. 1 starting spot for the Advance Auto Parts 500. Not only was it his 48th career Bud Pole Award in 373 starts, it was also his third straight at Martinsville.

"I took off, and the car did everything I really wanted it to," Gordon said. "I couldn't ask for much more than I got out of it. We came here with our basic setup ... and we had to make some adjustments.

"We tweaked it, and at the end of practice, I felt we hit on some things."

Jamie McMurray was second quickest in qualifying with a lap of 20.309 seconds at 93.239 mph, while Ryan Newman was third quickest (93.102 mph), Earnhardt Jr. fourth (93.015) and Kevin Harvick fifth (93.001). Rounding out the top 10 fastest qualifiers were Ward

Burton, Busch, Johnson, Sadler and Jeremy Mayfield. Five drivers had to take provisional starts and one, Kirk Shelmerdine, didn't make the cut.

In a way it was fitting for Gordon to put Hendrick Motorsports' No. 24 DuPont Chevrolet on the pole. It added to his team's celebration of its first win, here with Geoffrey Bodine 20 years ago. In tribute, Bodine made a ceremonial pace lap before the start of the race in the same No. 5 Chevrolet in which he won in 1984.

So it was unfortunate events ended up conspiring against Gordon, who, after leading the most times (three) and most laps (180), saw his day go sour through no fault of his own. He was running in the top five when the day's seventh yellow flag was waved on lap 284 because of a crash. During the caution, the race was halted because of a large hole that appeared in the concrete surface in turn three.

*(Below Left) Track workers repair the turn-three pothole that brought the race to a temporary halt on lap 290.*

*(Below Right) The DuPont crew affects repairs to the right front of Gordon's Monte Carlo, damaged by the chunk of concrete that broke loose in the third turn. Although their bid for victory ended, great teamwork combined with Gordon's driving prowess salvaged a sixth-place result and moved Gordon from ninth to seventh in points.*

*(Bottom) Eleven cautions during the day helped keep 19 cars on the lead lap, which made the pits a very busy place as teams and drivers fought for track position both on the speedway and along pit road.*

Unfortunately, Gordon's car had hit the chunk of debris that came out of the hole and damaged his Chevrolet's right front. Gordon asked officials that his crew be allowed to repair the damage during the red-flag period – it took track workers over 77 minutes to fill in the chasm – but his plea was denied. After the race resumed on lap 302, Gordon made a pit stop to make his car raceable again, and he salvaged a top-10 finish.

"It's unfortunate the race track came apart. I hear they're going to repave it," Gordon said. "I guess we were just one race early.

"It definitely took away any chance we had of winning, but I guess that is just part of it. The car wasn't quite the same."

When the ninth of 11 yellow flags for 106 laps came out on lap 415, Johnson, who had taken over first place four laps earlier, and crew chief Chad Knaus opted not to pit. Wallace, however, stopped for four tires, while his teammate, Ryan Newman, took on two. Johnson kept the lead through the 10th caution period (laps 430-439) with Newman, Wallace, Labonte and Dale Earnhardt Jr. right behind him. Then, one lap before the final yellow flag

was displayed on lap 457, Wallace, who had already dispatched Earnhardt Jr. and Newman, grabbed the lead and kept it until the end.

Bobby Labonte made a valiant effort to catch Wallace but ended up second in front of Earnhardt Jr., Johnson and Newman. Gordon, Jamie McMurray, Matt Kenseth, Sterling Marlin and Dale Jarrett completed the top 10 finishers.

In leading the final 45 of 500 laps, Wallace gave Dodge its first win of the year and first at the track since the retired Dave Marcis won at Martinsville in 1975. It was also Wallace's first victory in a Dodge.

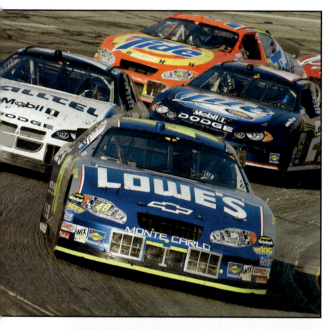

Part of it for Wallace, though, was staying calm and collected and concentrating on his job once he realized Johnson had given him an opening. He did just that and was 0.538-second in front of the runner-up at the final flag. He completed the race in 3 hours, 51 minutes and 29 seconds at an average speed of 68.169 mph and left the tight little race track with an extra $164,998 in his pocket.

*(Above) The Miller Lite crew falls to work to give their driver a set of fresh Goodyears. Wallace's call for four new tires on a late-race caution ultimately proved to be the difference that allowed Rusty to overtake the leaders and notch the victory.*

*(Left) Jimmie Johnson (48) holds the point ahead of Ryan Newman (12) and Rusty Wallace (2) after the lap 440 restart following the 10th caution of the race. Within 15 laps, Wallace had passed Newman, who earlier opted for two tires, and Johnson, who took none, taking the lead he would carry to the checkered flag.*

## Advance Auto Parts 500 *final race results*

| Fin. Pos. | Start Pos. | Car No. | Driver | Team | Fin. Pos. | Start Pos. | Car No. | Driver | Team |
|---|---|---|---|---|---|---|---|---|---|
| 1 | 17 | 2 | Rusty Wallace | Miller Lite Dodge | 23 | 28 | 5 | Terry Labonte | Kellogg's Chevrolet |
| 2 | 23 | 18 | Bobby Labonte | Interstate Batteries Chevrolet | 24 | 33 | 43 | Jeff Green | Cheerios/Betty Crocker Dodge |
| 3 | 4 | 8 | Dale Earnhardt Jr. | Budweiser Chevrolet | 25 | 27 | 99 | Jeff Burton | Team Caliber Racing Ford |
| 4 | 8 | 48 | Jimmie Johnson | Lowe's Chevrolet | 26 | 37 | 02 | Hermie Sadler | TheFanZcar Chevrolet |
| 5 | 3 | 12 | Ryan Newman | ALLTEL Dodge | 27 | 20 | 01 | Joe Nemechek | U.S. Army Chevrolet |
| 6 | 1 | 24 | Jeff Gordon | DuPont Chevrolet | 28 | 13 | 10 | Scott Riggs | Valvoline Chevrolet |
| 7 | 2 | 42 | Jamie McMurray | Texaco/Havoline Dodge | 29 | 16 | 22 | Scott Wimmer | Caterpillar Dodge |
| 8 | 29 | 17 | Matt Kenseth | DeWalt Power Tools Ford | 30 | 21 | 31 | Robby Gordon | Cingular Wireless Chevrolet |
| 9 | 18 | 40 | Sterling Marlin | Coors Light Dodge | 31 | 22 | 30 | Johnny Sauter | America Online Chevrolet |
| 10 | 25 | 88 | Dale Jarrett | UPS Ford | 32 | 42 | 89 | Morgan Shepherd | Voyles/Carter Dispos-all Dodge |
| 11 | 7 | 97 | Kurt Busch | IRWIN Industrial Tools Ford | 33 | 40 | 50 | Derrike Cope | Arnold Development Co. Dodge |
| 12 | 9 | 38 | Elliott Sadler | M&M's Ford | 34 | 19 | 6 | Mark Martin | Viagra Ford |
| 13 | 35 | 25 | Brian Vickers | GMAC Chevrolet | 35 | 24 | 16 | Greg Biffle | National Guard Ford |
| 14 | 30 | 20 | Tony Stewart | Home Depot Chevrolet | 36 | 10 | 19 | Jeremy Mayfield | Dodge Dealers/UAW Dodge |
| 15 | 39 | 15 | Michael Waltrip | NAPA Chevrolet | 37 | 12 | 41 | Casey Mears | Target Dodge |
| 16 | 32 | 32 | Ricky Craven | Tide Chevrolet | 38 | 34 | 4 | Jimmy Spencer | Featherlite Custom Trailers Chevrolet |
| 17 | 11 | 77 | Brendan Gaughan | Kodak Easy Share Dodge | 39 | 43 | 98 | Todd Bodine | Lucas Oil Ford |
| 18 | 31 | 45 | Kyle Petty | Georgia-Pacific/Brawny Dodge | 40 | 26 | 49 | Ken Schrader | Schwan's Home Service Dodge |
| 19 | 5 | 29 | Kevin Harvick | GM Goodwrench Chevrolet | 41 | 36 | 94 | Stanton Barrett | W.W. Motorsports Chevrolet |
| 20 | 14 | 21 | Ricky Rudd | Motorcraft Ford | 42 | 41 | 80 | Andy Hillenburg | Commercial Truck & Trailer Ford |
| 21 | 15 | 9 | Kasey Kahne | Dodge Dealers/UAW Dodge | 43 | 38 | 09 | Joe Ruttman | Miccosukee Resorts Dodge |
| 22 | 6 | 0 | Ward Burton | NetZero Hi-Speed Chevrolet | | | | | |

# AARON'S 499

## TALLADEGA SUPERSPEEDWAY
### APRIL 25, 2004

*"I thought that we were ahead, (but) neither of us really knew ...
I had no idea what was going to happen."*

— *Jeff Gordon*

Jeff Gordon wasn't concerned that the reception he got from some of the fans was less than generous after he narrowly edged Dale Earnhardt Jr. just before the final yellow flag of the day came out late in an action-packed 500-miler. For in winning under caution, he broke an 11-race winless streak dating back to Atlanta last fall.

In a NASCAR NEXTEL Cup Series race that featured 54 lead changes among 23 drivers and 11 yellow-flag periods – the most ever at the 2.66-mile Alabama oval – Gordon's Hendrick/DuPont Chevrolet and the Dale Earnhardt Inc./Budweiser Chevrolet of Earnhardt Jr. were going at it side by side in the fourth corner with less than five of the event's 188 laps remaining. Then on the 184th circuit, Gordon's teammate, rookie Brian Vickers, looped his Chevrolet in the fourth turn.

The caution period went into effect immediately after the spin and the race up front was so close it was tough to tell just who was leading – but the replays told the story. Gordon was in front by a hair and because the race wasn't restarted, he went to victory lane and broke a lock DEI drivers seemed to have in restrictor-plate events at Talladega and Daytona.

*Ricky Rudd (21), Jeff Gordon (24) and Sterling Marlin (40) stack it up three wide on the high banks at Talladega Superspeedway. Rudd, with a fresh paint job reminiscent of the 1970s when David Pearson wheeled the Wood Brothers' cars to great success, set the pace in qualifying and grabbed his first Bud Pole in nearly two years.*

*(Above) Kevin Harvick (29) tries to hold position in the middle groove with Michael Waltrip (15) charging on the inside and Joe Nemechek (01) using the high side. Waltrip and Nemechek qualified well in second and fourth, respectively, but it was Harvick who stayed out of trouble and took a top-five finish in third.*

*(Right) Jimmie Johnson (48), Tony Stewart (20), Jamie McMurray (42) and Jeff Gordon (24) make themselves a Schwan's sandwich with Ken Schrader's Dodge (49). Johnson and McMurray hung with the lead pack for the most part and picked up finishes in the top 10 behind Gordon.*

NASCAR officials said they didn't restart the event for reasons of safety. There had been enough bumping and banging in the race, including a 10-car wreck just before the halfway point. A vocal minority of fans disagreed, though, and pelted the track with debris.

"When they told me there was a wreck behind us, I thought that we were ahead, (but) neither of us really knew," Gordon said of his 65th career victory. "That was pretty exciting. I had no idea what was going to happen."

"I was a car length by him when I went by a caution light that was not on," Earnhardt said. "I thought I was miles ahead of him. I didn't even think it was close."

After he looked at video replays, though, Richie Gilmore, director of motorsports operations for Earnhardt's team, concurred that Gordon was the winner.

"They definitely had some good video showing it," Gilmore said. "The '24' (Gordon) was probably about two inches ahead of us when the '25' (Vickers) started to spin."

Going into the season's ninth event, things were already heating up in the point standings. Earnhardt Jr. parlayed a third-place finish in the Advance Auto Parts 500 at Martinsville, Va., the week before into first place in series points. It was a series-leading fifth top-five performance, and with 1,167 points he headed to Alabama five in front of Kurt Busch, the former leader.

Busch wound up 11th at Martinsville, thus surrendering his one-race lead in the standings. His Martinsville run ended a string of consecutive top-10 finishes at three.

With 1,155 points, Busch's teammate, Matt Kenseth, found himself third in the running for the title, dropping him down one spot from the previous week. Kenseth, however, finished eighth at Martinsville for his sixth top-10 finish of the season, which put him just 12 points in arrears of Earnhardt.

Jimmie Johnson came home fourth at Martinsville in the No. 48 Lowe's Chevrolet,

and that moved him up two spots in points from sixth to fourth. He had been ranked sixth for the past three races but was now just 67 points behind Kenseth and 79 behind Earnhardt.

Elliott Sadler's 12th-place effort at the Virginia half mile neither helped nor harmed his place in the standings. With 1,069 he remained fifth in points for the second straight race and was still one of just four drivers to be ranked in the top 10 all season. He left Martinsville 19 points behind Johnson but just

*The biggest accident of the day occurred between turns three and four near the 82-lap mark. The incident was triggered when Tony Stewart turned Kurt Busch (97), who spun in front of a pack containing Kenny Wallace (00), Rusty Wallace (2), Terry Labonte (5), Derrike Cope (50), Kasey Kahne (9), Scott Riggs (10) and Dave Blaney (23). Ricky Rudd (21) was able to scoot by the mess on the infield grass.*

*(Above) Scott Riggs (10), Sterling Marlin (40) and Jeff Burton (99) fan out on Talladega's spacious racing surface. Riggs had a career-best qualifying run to start fifth in the Aaron's 499, and Burton, who started 25th, posted a season-best seventh place at the end of the event.*

*(Right) Dale Earnhardt Jr. (8) and Jeff Gordon (24) idle around the track together after the race was slowed for the final time with a handful of laps remaining. Replays confirmed the call from the tower that Gordon had edged past the Budweiser Chevrolet when the caution light came on, and the results stood to give Gordon his first win of the season.*

race track. The run was also beneficial in that he advanced from ninth in points to seventh, 116 behind leader Earnhardt. The Martinsville showing was also his third top-10 finish in a row, and with 1,051 points he was just 16 points in back of Stewart and 41 in front of Rusty Wallace.

Ranked eighth in points after the Advance Auto Parts 500 – where he snapped a lengthy winless streak with a victory – Wallace also moved up three spots and into the top 10 for the first time in 2004. The win was his seventh at Martinsville and 55th overall.

Kasey Kahne's finish of 21st at Martinsville – just the third time in the season he'd finished out of the top 15 in a race – dropped him two spots in points from seventh to ninth. Heading to Talladega, he found himself 160 points out of the lead with 1,007 and just four in front of 10th-ranked Kevin Harvick. On an up note, he exited Martinsville leading in Raybestos Rookie of the Year points by 34 over Scott Wimmer.

Harvick ended up with a 19th-place showing at Martinsville, which knocked him down to 10th in points from eighth. Yet, it marked his third consecutive week in the top 10. Harvick, however, had four drivers outside the top 10 within 48 points of his position.

It's hard to say if "going retro" had anything to do with it, but Ricky Rudd was the fastest of 45 drivers who took a shot at the Bud Pole for the Aaron's 499. His Wood Brothers Ford was painted to look like the cars that David Pearson

two in front of sixth-ranked Tony Stewart.

Stewart had another rough go of it at Martinsville – for him anyway – finishing 14th. That dropped him down two spots in points, from fourth to sixth, marking just the second time in 2004 he had fallen out of the top five. With 1,067 points, he was an even 100 behind the leader and 21 behind Johnson.

Jeff Gordon had continued his show of recent strength with a sixth-place finish at Martinsville, even though his car was damaged by a chunk of concrete that put a hole in the

found so much success with in the 1970s, and his lap of 50.089 seconds at 191.180 mph gave the Wood's team its first pole since March 1984.

"When the car used to look like this it ran fast, and today it ran fast again," Rudd said. "We'll probably have to keep this thing like this all year long; it looks great."

It was Rudd's first pole at Talladega and first since 2002 at Watkins Glen, N.Y., 59 races ago. He was also the only driver to eclipse the 191 mph mark in qualifying for this race.

Chevrolet drivers set the next four quickest speeds. Michael Waltrip (190.974 mph) took the outside front row spot, Earnhardt Jr. (190.336) was third fastest, Joe Nemechek (190.109) was fourth and Scott Riggs (190.019) was fifth. Rounding out the top 10 in time trails were Mark Martin, Dale Jarrett, Johnson, Sterling Marlin and Ward Burton.

Larry Foyt and Todd Bodine weren't quick enough to make the field, and Kirk Shelmerdine chose not to make a qualifying lap.

Jeff Gordon started the race in 11th place, took the lead for the first time on lap 31 and ran in front for five laps. He also led laps 37-39 and lap 78. After surviving an extremely physical race, he went to the front for the final time six laps from the finish and ended up with the lowest average finishing speed ever set at Talladega, 129.396 mph.

Kevin Harvick came home third, Jimmie Johnson was fourth and Robby Gordon fifth. All were in Chevrolets, while Roush Racing

teammates Mark Martin and Jeff Burton drove Fords to sixth and seventh place, respectively. Casey Mears (eighth) and Jamie McMurray (ninth) were in Dodges, while 10th-place finisher Bobby Labonte was in a Chevrolet.

Earnhardt Jr. led the most times (11) and laps (57), but fate was on Gordon's side this time around. He left the track with the winner's purse of $320,258 and renewed optimism for the still long season.

"Anytime Junior doesn't win here and he's got a shot, it's going to be controversial, because he's got so many people pulling for him," Gordon noted. "I don't mind a little controversy ... but I wanted to enjoy the moment."

*Jimmy Spencer pits the Morgan McClure Motorsports Chevrolet, which spouts water from the engine cooling overflow. Despite the water temperature, Spencer, who was making his third start of the season in the No. 4, remained on the lead lap and gave the team its best finish of the year so far, in 20th.*

## Aaron's 499 *final race results*

| Fin. Pos. | Start Pos. | Car No. | Driver | Team | Fin. Pos. | Start Pos. | Car No. | Driver | Team |
|---|---|---|---|---|---|---|---|---|---|
| 1 | 11 | 24 | Jeff Gordon | DuPont/Pepsi Chevrolet | 23 | 40 | 49 | Ken Schrader | Schwan's Home Service Dodge |
| 2 | 3 | 8 | Dale Earnhardt Jr. | Budweiser Chevrolet | 24 | 28 | 45 | Kyle Petty | Georgia-Pacific/Brawny Dodge |
| 3 | 14 | 29 | Kevin Harvick | GM Goodwrench Chevrolet | 25 | 13 | 5 | Terry Labonte | Kellogg's Chevrolet |
| 4 | 8 | 48 | Jimmie Johnson | Lowe's Chevrolet | 26 | 35 | 04 | Eric McClure | 77 Sports.com/I Can Learn Chevrolet |
| 5 | 21 | 31 | Robby Gordon | Cingular Wireless Chevrolet | 27 | 39 | 25 | Brian Vickers | GMAC Chevrolet |
| 6 | 6 | 6 | Mark Martin | Viagra Ford | 28 | 12 | 38 | Elliott Sadler | M&M's Ford |
| 7 | 25 | 99 | Jeff Burton | Round Up Ford | 29 | 34 | 09 | Johnny Benson | Miccosukee Resorts Dodge |
| 8 | 16 | 41 | Casey Mears | Target Dodge | 30 | 26 | 9 | Kasey Kahne | Dodge Dealers/UAW Dodge |
| 9 | 33 | 42 | Jamie McMurray | Texaco/Havoline Dodge | 31 | 9 | 40 | Sterling Marlin | Coors Light Dodge |
| 10 | 19 | 18 | Bobby Labonte | Wellbutrin XL Chevrolet | 32 | 4 | 01 | Joe Nemechek | U.S. Army Chevrolet |
| 11 | 17 | 12 | Ryan Newman | ALLTEL Dodge | 33 | 32 | 2 | Rusty Wallace | Miller Lite Dodge |
| 12 | 2 | 15 | Michael Waltrip | NAPA Chevrolet | 34 | 5 | 10 | Scott Riggs | Valvoline Chevrolet |
| 13 | 20 | 77 | Brendan Gaughan | Kodak Easy Share Dodge | 35 | 36 | 33 | Kerry Earnhardt | Bass Pro Shops Chevrolet |
| 14 | 29 | 30 | Johnny Sauter | America Online Chevrolet | 36 | 22 | 97 | Kurt Busch | Sharpie Ford |
| 15 | 18 | 16 | Greg Biffle | National Guard/Subway Ford | 37 | 27 | 00 | Kenny Wallace | Aaron's Sales & Lease Chevrolet |
| 16 | 7 | 88 | Dale Jarrett | UPS Ford | 38 | 41 | 50 | Derrike Cope | Arnold Development Co. Dodge |
| 17 | 1 | 21 | Ricky Rudd | Keep It Genuine Ford | 39 | 42 | 23 | Dave Blaney | Bill Davis Racing Dodge |
| 18 | 30 | 22 | Scott Wimmer | Caterpillar Dodge | 40 | 10 | 0 | Ward Burton | NetZero Hi-Speed Chevrolet |
| 19 | 15 | 43 | Jeff Green | Cheerios/Betty Crocker Dodge | 41 | 43 | 89 | Morgan Shepherd | Carter Dispos-all Dodge |
| 20 | 23 | 4 | Jimmy Spencer | Morgan McClure Motorsports Chevrolet | 42 | 31 | 17 | Matt Kenseth | DeWalt Power Tools Ford |
| 21 | 38 | 19 | Jeremy Mayfield | Dodge Dealers/UAW Dodge | 43 | 24 | 32 | Ricky Craven | Tide Chevrolet |
| 22 | 37 | 20 | Tony Stewart | Home Depot Chevrolet | | | | | |

# AUTO CLUB 500

*"I think when you've got a team like this and a car like this ... well, we've got momentum right now."*

— *Jeff Gordon*

Jeff Gordon and Bobby Labonte had at least one thing in common at the conclusion of a 250-lap test of stamina on an unusually hot spring day at Fontana, Calif.'s 2.5-mile California Speedway: Both drivers' Chevrolets were out of fuel.

There was this difference, though: While Labonte's No. 18 Interstate Batteries machine ran out of gasoline on the final lap, dropping him to fifth at the finish, Gordon's No. 24 DuPont Monte Carlo had enough of Sunoco's premium blend left for him to do a victory-lap burnout before his crew pushed it into the winner's circle at his home-state track.

Not only was the triumph Gordon's second straight of the 2004 season, it was also his third at Fontana in eight starts, securing his position as the track's only multiple NASCAR NEXTEL Cup Series winner. He won the inaugural event at Fontana in 1997 and went to victory lane again two years later.

Going into the California event Dale Earnhardt Jr. had his eye on Gordon. The week before he'd finished second in the Aaron's 499 at Talladega, Ala., in a narrow loss. Yet he was heading west still leading in NASCAR NEXTEL Cup Series points with 1,347. That extended his advantage over second-place pointsman Jimmie Johnson to 94. It was also his fourth week overall as the leader, tying him in that category with Matt Kenseth.

Crew members perform some makeshift body work on Kurt Busch's Irwin Ford after it hit the wall on lap 57 and then spun into the path of Rusty Wallace's Miller Lite Dodge. Busch, the defending race champion, made it back into the race and was only one lap down at the finish, while Wallace got the worst of it and was listed 35th, 57 laps off the winning pace.

*Jeff Green (below) and Scott Riggs (bottom) had outstanding qualifying runs at California and secured the second row on the grid, with Green in third and Riggs fourth. For Riggs, it was his second straight top-five start after taking the fifth spot the week before at Talladega.*

*(Opposite Page, Bottom) Casey Mears (41) and Ward Burton (0) race each other while putting together strong runs on the two-mile California oval. Mears captured eighth place, his fourth top 10 of the season, while Burton ended up 10th in his best result since a ninth place at Rockingham in February.*

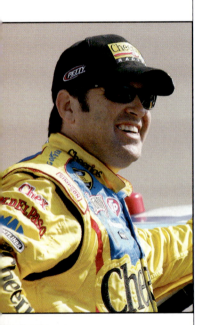

Johnson had a good run at Talladega, finishing fourth for his second consecutive top-five result and fourth in the last six races. The effort moved him up two spots in points from fourth to second. He had high hopes for a good finish, as Fontana was the site of his first series victory in April 2001.

Gordon's win at Talladega, his first of the year and 65th overall, saw him leap from seventh in the standings to third. With 1,236 points, he was 111 out of the lead and only 17 behind Johnson. The move upward was the biggest within the top 10 for the week.

Unlike Gordon, the news for Ford driver Kurt Busch coming out of Talladega was not as good. He finished 36th there because of an accident and dropped from second in points to fourth. It was his first finish in nine starts out of the top 16, and he headed west with 1,222 points, 125 out of the lead but just 14 behind Gordon. On an upscale note, though, he was the defending champion of the Auto Club 500 and planned to return to his winning ways at California.

Busch's Roush Racing teammate, Kenseth, also took a bit of a hit in points. The defending series champion finished a season-worst 42nd at Talladega because of engine problems, falling

The San Bernardino Mountains provide a scenic back-drop for the crowd estimated at 120,000 on an unusually warm, but beautifully clear day in Southern California for the eighth running of the Auto Club 500.

from third to fifth in points. That gave him a total of 1,192, putting him 155 behind Earnhardt and 30 in arrears of Busch.

Richard Childress Racing driver Kevin Harvick matched his season best with a third-place run at Talladega and moved up four spots in points from 10th to sixth. The jump in ranking matched him with Gordon for the largest gain of the week. With 1,173 points, he was just 19 behind Kenseth and 174 out of the lead. The run in Alabama was his third top-five showing of the year and second in his last four starts.

Tony Stewart, Bobby Labonte's Joe Gibbs Racing teammate, could do no better than 22nd

*(Right) Bobby Labonte gets tires and fuel from his Interstate crew during an early-race caution. Labonte mounted a challenge against Jeff Gordon late in the event before his fuel cell ran dry less than a lap from the finish.*

*(Below) Penske driver Brendan Gaughan (77) hugs the inside line while teammate Ryan Newman (12) and Terry Labonte (5) take the long way around. A native of nearby Las Vegas, Nev., Gaughan must have felt at home in California; he posted career bests in qualifying (fifth) and in the race with a strong sixth-place finish.*

at Talladega and fell a spot in the standings from sixth to seventh. It became his lowest ranking in points for the year, but the good news for him was that he was only four points behind Harvick and 23 in arrears of Kenseth. In other words, he was far from out of the hunt for the championship.

Robert Yates Racing's Elliott Sadler ended a two-week stay as number five on the points ladder with a 28th-place effort in the Aaron's 499 and left the track in the eighth position with 1,153. It marked the first time in the last five events he'd finished outside of the top 15, but he remained as just one of four drivers to be ranked in the top 10 for the entire season to date. He was also just 16 points behind Stewart and 194 out of the lead.

Penske Racing Dodge pilot Ryan Newman found himself 218 points in back of leader Earnhardt Jr. heading to California, but with an 11th-place run at Talladega, he moved back into the top 10 in points, from 11th to ninth, after an absence of one week. He was only 24 markers in back of Sadler and 19 in front of

10th-place Bobby Labonte, who was previously ranked 12th. A 10th-place run at Talladega put Labonte within shouting distance of the title, as he went into the California 500-miler 237 points out of the lead.

Kasey Kahne didn't come close to setting a Bud Pole qualifying record at California Speedway on April 30. But his time and speed of 38.515 seconds at 186.940 mph was more than enough to put the Evernham Motorsports driver of the No. 9 Dodge squarely on the pole for the Auto Club 500. It was the Raybestos Rookie of the Year candidate's third Bud Pole of the year, and the accomplishment came in his first outing on the 2.5-mile track.

It was also the sixth pole spot of the year for Dodge, in 10 events, leaving Chevrolet and Ford with two each.

"I love qualifying ... and I know I'm learning new things (at) every race," Kahne said. "We were good in practice, but to run three-tenths (of a second) quicker in qualifying says a lot for the team."

Joe Nemechek, in a Chevrolet, was close on Kahne's heels. His speed of 186.737 put him next to the rookie on the front row, while Jeff Green, in the No. 43 Petty Enterprises Dodge, was third quickest at 186.316 mph. Scott Riggs (186.148 mph), Brendan Gaughan (185.845) and Brian Vickers (185.806), also all rookie contenders, completed the top six fastest qualifiers, while Ryan Newman, Sterling Marlin, Rusty Wallace and Earnhardt Jr. rounded out the top 10.

Gordon led the Auto Club 500 on five occasions for 81 laps and went to the front for the final time on lap 204. Bobby Labonte moved into second place on the 222nd lap and was gaining on Gordon when, midway through the final circuit, disaster struck.

"Nobody told me we were going to be short and I didn't ask," noted a disappointed Labonte. "I'm sure we didn't miscalculate; we just came up a little bit short after that last run."

The victory firmly put to rest the notion that Jeff Gordon was in some kind of "slump."

"I think when you've got a team like this and a car like this ... well, we've got momentum right now," Gordon said. "It's been amazing the last few weeks.

"I went around to do my burnout, spun around and ran out of gas."

Gordon beat teammate and fellow Californian Jimmie Johnson by a "comfortable" 12.871 seconds. Had it not been for Labonte's misfortune, things might have been different. Johnson ran up front all day, but by the end of the event he thought he'd have to settle for a fifth-place finish. Then, with the final lap in sight, the three drivers in front of him, Bobby Labonte, Jeremy Mayfield and pole winner Kahne all ran out of gas.

"I was excited. We'll take it any way we can get it," Johnson said.

Ryan Newman and Matt Kenseth finished third and fourth, while Brendan Gaughan was sixth. Terry Labonte sweetened the pot for Hendrick Motorsports with a seventh-place showing, while Casey Mears, Kevin Harvick and Ward Burton were eighth through 10th.

Labonte, as noted, was disappointed, but like a veteran shrugged off his bad luck. Teammates Kahne, who finished 13th, and Mayfield, in 14th (the first driver a lap down), however, were stunned.

"I had no idea we were running out of gas," Mayfield noted. "I didn't know we were that close. I thought we were just barely going to make it."

"I'm fine, just a little burned out," Kahne added. "I'm not sure what happened out there."

*Jeff Gordon (24) sets sail through the smooth, 14-degree banking with Jimmie Johnson (48) and Jeff Green (43) in pursuit. Gordon led five times for 81 laps, including the final 47, on the way to his third victory in eight starts at Fontana, Calif.*

## Auto Club 500 *final race results*

| Fin. Pos. | Start Pos. | Car No. | Driver | Team | Fin. Pos. | Start Pos. | Car No. | Driver | Team |
|---|---|---|---|---|---|---|---|---|---|
| 1 | 16 | 24 | Jeff Gordon | DuPont Chevrolet | 23 | 21 | 97 | Kurt Busch | IRWIN Industrial Tools Ford |
| 2 | 19 | 48 | Jimmie Johnson | Lowe's Chevrolet | 24 | 31 | 88 | Dale Jarrett | UPS Ford |
| 3 | 7 | 12 | Ryan Newman | Mobil 1/ALLTEL Dodge | 25 | 4 | 10 | Scott Riggs | Valvoline Chevrolet |
| 4 | 25 | 17 | Matt Kenseth | DeWalt Power Tools Ford | 26 | 30 | 99 | Jeff Burton | Roundup Ford |
| 5 | 27 | 18 | Bobby Labonte | Interstate Batteries Chevrolet | 27 | 8 | 40 | Sterling Marlin | Coors Light Dodge |
| 6 | 5 | 77 | Brendan Gaughan | Kodak Easy Share Dodge | 28 | 2 | 01 | Joe Nemechek | U.S. Army Chevrolet |
| 7 | 29 | 5 | Terry Labonte | Kellogg's Chevrolet | 29 | 6 | 25 | Brian Vickers | GMAC Chevrolet |
| 8 | 13 | 41 | Casey Mears | Target Dodge | 30 | 39 | 22 | Scott Wimmer | Caterpillar Dodge |
| 9 | 24 | 29 | Kevin Harvick | GM Goodwrench Chevrolet | 31 | 36 | 50 | Derrike Cope | Bennet Lane Winery Dodge |
| 10 | 15 | 0 | Ward Burton | NetZero Hi-Speed Chevrolet | 32 | 17 | 15 | Michael Waltrip | NAPA Chevrolet |
| 11 | 26 | 6 | Mark Martin | Viagra Ford | 33 | 18 | 16 | Greg Biffle | National Guard/Subway Ford |
| 12 | 23 | 31 | Robby Gordon | Cingular Wireless Chevrolet | 34 | 41 | 98 | Todd Bodine | Lucas Oil Ford |
| 13 | 1 | 9 | Kasey Kahne | Dodge Dealers/UAW Dodge | 35 | 9 | 2 | Rusty Wallace | Miller Lite Dodge |
| 14 | 20 | 19 | Jeremy Mayfield | Dodge Dealers/UAW Dodge | 36 | 38 | 89 | Morgan Shepherd | Voyles Equip./Carter Dispos-all Dodge |
| 15 | 12 | 42 | Jamie McMurray | Texaco/Havoline Dodge | 37 | 3 | 43 | Jeff Green | Cheerios/Betty Crocker Dodge |
| 16 | 11 | 20 | Tony Stewart | Home Depot Chevrolet | 38 | 22 | 4 | Jimmy Spencer | Morgan-McClure Motorsports Chevrolet |
| 17 | 35 | 21 | Ricky Rudd | "Keep It Genuine" Ford | 39 | 28 | 45 | Kyle Petty | Georgia-Pacific/Brawny Dodge |
| 18 | 34 | 32 | Ricky Craven | Tide Chevrolet | 40 | 43 | 94 | Stanton Barrett | AmericInn Chevrolet |
| 19 | 10 | 8 | Dale Earnhardt Jr. | Budweiser Chevrolet | 41 | 40 | 02 | Hermie Sadler | The FanZCar Chevrolet |
| 20 | 32 | 49 | Ken Schrader | Schwan's Home Service Dodge | 42 | 42 | 72 | Kirk Shelmerdine | 2nd Chance Race Parts Ford |
| 21 | 37 | 30 | Johnny Sauter | AOL/IMAX NASCAR 3D Chevrolet | 43 | 33 | 09 | Joe Ruttman | Miccosukee Resort Dodge |
| 22 | 14 | 38 | Elliott Sadler | Pedigree Ford | | | | | |

# CHEVY AMERICAN REVOLUTION 400

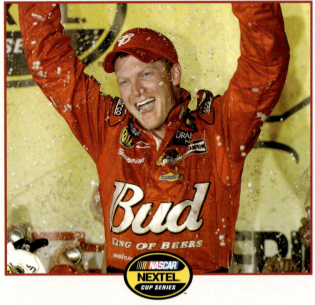

*"It was about as good as it was going to get ... I had 40 laps and plenty of race car left."*

— *Dale Earnhardt Jr.*

A moment of temporary deafness paid off handsomely for Dale Earnhardt Jr. Saturday night in Richmond, Va.

The driver of the No. 8 DEI/Budweiser Chevrolet said he failed to hear a call from Tony Eury Jr., the team's car chief, to come in for tires and fuel when what turned out to be the event's ninth – and final – yellow-flag period began on lap 344. While other front-runners did make stops, Earnhardt Jr. remained on the track, then took the lead with 55 circuits to go and bested fellow Chevrolet driver Jimmie Johnson by 1.481 seconds at the finish.

Going into the Chevy American Revolution 400, Earnhardt Jr. was first in points for the third consecutive event. Overall, he was one of four drivers to be ranked among the top 10 for the entire season to date. Actually, he exited the 500-mile race at Fontana, Calif., in the top 10 for the 43rd consecutive event dating back to March 2003 at Atlanta.

"Junior," though, had a close challenger in Johnson. With 1,428 points going into Richmond, the Hendrick Motorsports/Lowe's Chevrolet driver was just 25 behind the leader. Thanks to three consecutive top-five finishes, including a second-place run at Fontana, Johnson was within whispering distance of the points lead. Also, he was tied with Earnhardt in top-five finishes for the year with six.

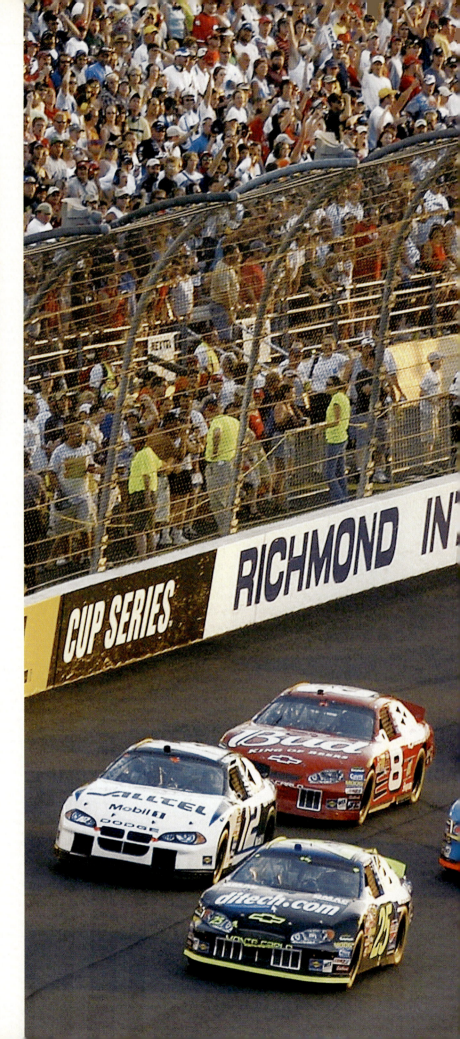

*The starting field takes the green flag for the Chevy American Revolution 400 led by Brian Vickers (25) and Ryan Newman (12) on the front row followed by Jeff Green (43) and Dale Earnhardt Jr. (8). For Green, this was his second consecutive start from the inside second row, having started third at California as well.*

*After six qualifying efforts of sixth or better in his first 15 career starts, Brian Vickers finally collects his first Anheuser-Busch Pole Award after setting a track record speed of 129.983 mph on the freshly repaved Richmond oval.*

With two consecutive race wins under his belt (California and Talladega, Ala.), Gordon remained third in the standings with 1,426 points, which separated him from teammate Johnson by just two markers. Gordon's record for the year also included finishes in the top 10 in his last five starts overall.

The defending series champion, Matt Kenseth, following the Fontana event, swapped points positions with his Roush Racing teammate, Kurt Busch, moving up from fifth place to fourth. Kenseth had been ranked among the top 10 for the entire season to date and headed to Virginia with 1,357 points, 96 behind Earnhardt. Also, he now had remained among the top 10 for 45 consecutive races, dating back to February 2003, and led all drivers in that category.

Busch, with 1,316 points, wasn't that far behind Kenseth and was tied in markers with Kevin Harvick. Busch had stayed within the top five for the sixth consecutive week and in the top 10 for the past nine races. He was ranked ahead of Harvick because of the tiebreaker rule – the best finish to date.

Harvick remained sixth in the standings for the second week in a row and nearly cracked the top five for the first time since the February event at Rockingham, N.C., when he was ranked third. Harvick, however, had been in the top 10 for the last five weeks and eight weeks overall.

Ryan Newman's consistency paid off a bit between the California and Richmond events, as he jumped two positions in points from ninth to seventh. The Penske Racing/ALLTEL Dodge

(Above) Racing at Richmond doesn't get much tighter than this! Robby Gordon (31), Sterling Marlin (40) and Tony Stewart (20) roar off the fourth turn three wide while bearing down on the rear bumper of Jeff Burton's RoundUp Ford. After starting 28th, Stewart, a three-time Richmond winner, picked up 24 positions before posting his third top-five finish of the season.

(Left) Jamie McMurray (42) and Joe Nemechek (01) slide in tandem after making contact in the second turn. Neither driver was able to finish the race, spoiling a strong eighth-place start for the U.S. Army Chevrolet driver, his fourth top-10 qualifying effort in the last five events.

(Top) Jeff Burton (99) tries the upper line around RIR's 14-degree-banked corners above Scott Riggs (10), Matt Kenseth (17) and Dave Blaney in the No. 7 Ultra Motorsports Dodge. Kenseth came out on top in this pack with a fifth place at the end of the night, his fifth top five of the season.

(Above) Veterans Bobby Labonte (18) and Mark Martin (6) go at it side by side in their battle for position. Both drivers did well on the Virginia short track with Labonte posting his fourth consecutive top 10 in third, and Martin taking his fourth top 10 of the year in seventh.

driver left Fontana with 1,299 points and had registered top-five finishes in two of his last three starts. He was just 17 points out of fifth place, heading to a track where he'd won once (last September) and finished second twice in just four career starts.

Tony Stewart, driver of the No. 20 Joe Gibbs Racing/Home Depot Chevrolet fell from seventh to eighth in the standings and had dropped a spot in the top 10 for the third straight week. Yet, with 1,284 points, he was just 169 out of the lead and remained only one of four drivers to be ranked 10th or better for the entire year.

Stewart's teammate, Bobby Labonte, began to heat up a bit as he'd posted top-10 finishes in his last three starts. One result was that the No. 18 Interstate Batteries Chevrolet driver moved up a notch in points from 10th to ninth. With 1,265 points to his credit following

Fontana, he was 188 in arrears of the leader, just 19 behind Stewart and 15 in front of 10th-ranked Elliott Sadler.

Sadler needed to finish better than he did in California and dropped from eighth in points to 10th. Although the M&M's Ford driver stayed with that group of four who'd been ranked 10th or better in points all year, 11th-place Kasey Kahne was within 41 points of the top 10, while 12th place Jamie McMurray was within 50.

Due, no doubt, to a fresh coat of asphalt, Bud Pole qualifying at Richmond International Raceway was fast and a bit tricky. Yet, 29 drivers eclipsed the former track time-trial record speed of 21.195 seconds (127.389 mph) set by Ward Burton in May 2002. At the top of the heap this time was rookie Brian Vickers, who, in the No. 25 Hendrick Motorsports Chevrolet, rounded the 0.75-mile track in 20.772 seconds at 129.983 mph.

It was Vickers' first pole in 16 starts and came in his first race at the capital city speedway. The accomplishment was a bit sweeter for the young driver, as he edged pole-run "specialist" Ryan Newman out of the No. 1 slot by a mere 0.002 second.

"Our No. 1 priority wasn't to sit on the pole," Vickers said. "It was to get a good, smooth lap in. I think that's what helped us sit on the pole. It was awesome.

"It was nice to turn the tables on him (Newman). Everybody kept telling me to be patient ... it was just a matter of time before we had our pole. But we were getting anxious."

Jeff Green, Earnhardt Jr. and Johnson took

the third through fifth starting spots, while Robby Gordon, Rusty Wallace, Joe Nemechek, Casey Mears and Greg Biffle rounded out the top 10 in qualifying.

Earnhardt Jr. quickly adapted to the 0.75-mile speedway's new surface; he took the lead for the first time on lap 33 and dominated the event by leading a total of five times for 115 of 400 laps.

"My car was really, really loose on brand-new tires. It was about as good as it was going to get," the winner said when asked about not pitting with the others on the final yellow. "I had 40 laps and plenty of race car left.

"A lot of times in these races you get a lot of cautions at the end when guys get racy. I thought staying out front was a good choice."

Although the event would see no more yellow flags, the Budweiser driver's decision not to come in for fresh rubber still paid off. It was his third victory of the year, 12th of his career and second at Richmond, where he won in 2000, his rookie season. He strengthened his lead in the point standings and continued to set himself up for the final 10-race "Chase for the NASCAR NEXTEL Cup" in the fall.

The race was aptly named as Chevrolet drivers took seven of the top 10 finishing positions. Behind Johnson came Joe Gibbs Racing teammates Bobby Labonte and Stewart, in Chevys, while Kenseth was fifth, in a Ford. Jeff Gordon, Martin, pole winner Vickers, Newman and Michael Waltrip were sixth through 10th, respectively.

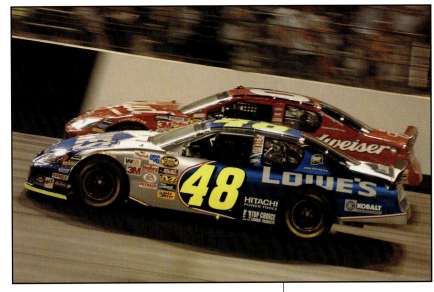

Earnhardt Jr., who said he believes his style of racing is more akin to that of his grandfather, Ralph Earnhardt, instead of his famous dad's, still showed a bit of his "intimidating" side during the 300-mile race. For instance, after a restart on the 130th lap, he jumped up along side Johnson and ran him hard until the next caution flag came out on lap 139.

"I am normally not that aggressive with the car, (but) just for a second I felt like my daddy," he said. "It was kind of neat. I don't know if it had really come over me before."

In any event, this time "neat" spelled victory. The winner completed the event in 3 hours, 3 minutes and 12 seconds at an average speed of 98.253 mph and won $285,053.

*Jimmie Johnson (48) and Dale Earnhardt Jr. take their battle for the top of the point standings to the Richmond asphalt. At the end, Earnhardt padded his slim lead by 15 points over Johnson by picking up not only the win, but the lap-leader bonus as well. Johnson's runner-up finish was his second straight and his fourth consecutive top-five run.*

## Chevy American Revolution 400 *final race results*

| Fin. Pos. | Start Pos. | Car No. | Driver | Team |
|---|---|---|---|---|
| 1 | 4 | 8 | Dale Earnhardt Jr. | Budweiser Chevrolet |
| 2 | 5 | 48 | Jimmie Johnson | Lowe's Chevrolet |
| 3 | 27 | 18 | Bobby Labonte | Interstate Batteries Chevrolet |
| 4 | 28 | 20 | Tony Stewart | Home Depot Chevrolet |
| 5 | 29 | 17 | Matt Kenseth | DeWalt Power Tools Ford |
| 6 | 13 | 24 | Jeff Gordon | DuPont Chevrolet |
| 7 | 12 | 6 | Mark Martin | Viagra Ford |
| 8 | 1 | 25 | Brian Vickers | GMAC Chevrolet |
| 9 | 2 | 12 | Ryan Newman | ALLTEL Dodge |
| 10 | 18 | 15 | Michael Waltrip | NAPA Chevrolet |
| 11 | 30 | 21 | Ricky Rudd | Rent-a-Center/Motorcraft Ford |
| 12 | 14 | 38 | Elliott Sadler | Pedigree Ford |
| 13 | 31 | 88 | Dale Jarrett | UPS Ford |
| 14 | 17 | 99 | Jeff Burton | RoundUp Ford |
| 15 | 32 | 40 | Sterling Marlin | Coors Light Dodge |
| 16 | 7 | 2 | Rusty Wallace | Miller Lite Dodge |
| 17 | 26 | 09 | Bobby Hamilton Jr. | Miccosukee Resort Dodge |
| 18 | 19 | 5 | Terry Labonte | Kellogg's Chevrolet |
| 19 | 35 | 30 | Johnny Sauter | America Online Chevrolet |
| 20 | 15 | 0 | Ward Burton | NetZero Hi-Speed Chevrolet |
| 21 | 10 | 16 | Greg Biffle | National Guard Ford |
| 22 | 11 | 19 | Jeremy Mayfield | Dodge Dealers/UAW Dodge |
| 23 | 34 | 49 | Ken Schrader | Schwan's Home Service Dodge |
| 24 | 6 | 31 | Robby Gordon | Cingular Wireless Chevrolet |
| 25 | 20 | 29 | Kevin Harvick | GM Goodwrench Chevrolet |
| 26 | 21 | 32 | Ricky Craven | Tide Chevrolet |
| 27 | 22 | 45 | Kyle Petty | Georgia-Pacific/Brawny Dodge |
| 28 | 39 | 9 | Kasey Kahne | Dodge Dealers/UAW Dodge |
| 29 | 41 | 50 | Derrike Cope | Chesapeake Mobile Home Sales Dodge |
| 30 | 25 | 22 | Scott Wimmer | Caterpillar Dodge |
| 31 | 23 | 97 | Kurt Busch | IRWIN Industrial Tools Ford |
| 32 | 9 | 41 | Casey Mears | Target Dodge |
| 33 | 36 | 98 | Todd Bodine | Lucas Oil Ford |
| 34 | 40 | 77 | Brendan Gaughan | Jasper Engines & Trans./Kodak Dodge |
| 35 | 16 | 10 | Scott Riggs | Valvoline Chevrolet |
| 36 | 8 | 01 | Joe Nemechek | U.S. Army Chevrolet |
| 37 | 3 | 43 | Jeff Green | Cheerios/Betty Crocker Dodge |
| 38 | 37 | 42 | Jamie McMurray | Texaco/Havoline Dodge |
| 39 | 42 | 89 | Morgan Shepherd | Voyles/Carter Royal Dispos-all Dodge |
| 40 | 24 | 7 | Dave Blaney | Ultra Motorsports Dodge |
| 41 | 38 | 4 | Jimmy Spencer | Morgan-McClure Motorsports Chevrolet |
| 42 | 33 | 02 | Hermie Sadler | Jenkins & Jenkins Chevrolet |
| 43 | 43 | 80 | Randy LaJoie | Commercial Truck & Trailers Ford |

# NASCAR NEXTEL ALL-STAR CHALLENGE

## LOWE'S MOTOR SPEEDWAY
### MAY 22, 2004

*"It took everything I had there, and he finally slipped a little bit coming out of (turn) four and I was able to get by."*

— *Matt Kenseth*

Matt Kenseth streaks toward the start/finish line at Lowe's Motor Speedway 0.571 second ahead of Ryan Newman on his way to collecting the $1 million check for winning the NASCAR NEXTEL All-Star Challenge.

Eleven laps into the first segment of the 20th version of the non-points NASCAR NEXTEL Cup Series "fans'" race – newly named the NASCAR NEXTEL All-Star Challenge – team owner Jack Roush was probably wondering if the annual event designed for maximum spectator entertainment value was really worth the effort.

One of his five drivers in the series, Kurt Busch, had plowed into the rear end of teammate Greg Biffle and taken them both out of the race. They joined Roush driver Jeff Burton in the garage, who had crashed out of the companion NEXTEL Open earlier in the evening.

At the end of the Challenge's third segment, though, the incidents were at least temporarily forgotten. Another of Roush Racing's "all-star" quintet was heading toward victory lane and a paycheck of $1,044,000.

Matt Kenseth, the defending Series champion, had slipped past Penske Racing Dodge driver Ryan Newman with four laps left and gone on to win the NASCAR NEXTEL All-Star Challenge for the first time in four attempts.

"A million bucks, boys," Kenseth yelled over the radio, as he took the final checkered flag.

*(Above Left) Rusty Wallace answers questions posed by reporters shortly after accepting his award for winning the pole for the NASCAR NEXTEL All-Star Challenge. Wallace completed the three-lap qualifying run that included a stop on pit road for four tires in just over two minutes.*

*(Above Middle) Tony Stewart chats with Dick Berggren following the main event. Although he didn't win, his showing of first, second and third in the three segments, respectively, made for a satisfying evening of racing.*

*(Above Right) Kerry Earnhardt had lots to smile about when he learned that he had been chosen by the fans to advance into the feature event. Unfortunately, an accident in the NEXTEL Open eliminated him seven laps short of the finish.*

While, as it was last year, the event was divided into three "legs" of 40, 30 and 20 laps, respectively, the rules were again tweaked to keep the competitors on their toes. First, everyone had to make a pit stop between laps 10 and 35. There was a 10-minute intermission between the first and second segments, where teams could make adjustments to their cars, and there was a voluntary pit stop included between segments two and three.

A random drawing to determine how many cars would be inverted in the second segment was again included. This time, however, instead of being determined by the fans, a number was

"pulled" by a FOX TV broadcaster. And this time around, drivers weren't eliminated via the rules at the end of the first and second legs.

Although the winner of the NEXTEL Open was again automatically included in what was to be a 24-car Challenge field, there was a new twist. Fans were asked to vote for a "favorite" to be added to the main event. Kerry Earnhardt got the nod. But because he wasn't around at the end of his race, the honor went to Ken Schrader, who made it into the feature for the first time since 1995.

It all added up to a somewhat strange but fun-filled race format with a dandy ending.

Starting on the pole, Rusty Wallace, right next to teammate Newman, got the jump off the start and led the first nine circuits, staying in front, even though the race was interrupted on the fourth lap because of an accident. Newman took over on lap 10, but the next time around a melee brought about by Busch crashing into Biffle ended in a 12-car accident and a red-flag period to clean up the debris.

While Biffle was less than pleased about getting the boot so early in the race, Busch (who apologized to everyone involved) said he was merely trying to "bump-draft" his teammate and help him move up in the field.

"My car just lifted him instead of pushing him," Busch explained. "I have to get myself in check, I guess."

The red flag was withdrawn after a 15-minute delay. And Newman and Tony Stewart were at the point on the lap-16 restart with 15 drivers behind them. Stewart pitted on lap 19, giving the lead to Newman, who in turn pitted on the 25th circuit, passing the No. 1 spot to Dale Earnhardt Jr.

"Junior" made his stop on lap 28. Stewart then retook the front spot, beat Kenseth to the checkered flag by 0.387 second and won $75,000.

*(Below) Greg Biffle's National Guard Ford shows the effects of a lap-11 crash triggered by his teammate, Kurt Busch. A total of six cars, including Biffle's and Busch's, were eliminated in the incident.*

*(Bottom) Sterling Marlin limps the Coors Light Dodge toward the garage after being involved in the multi-car accident on lap 11 of the All-Star Challenge. Marlin made the field by winning the NEXTEL Open preliminary event for the fourth time.*

(Above) Defending All-Star champion Jimmie Johnson comes off the fourth turn in the midst of a spin during the event's second segment. Johnson was able to keep his already-damaged car off the wall, but decided to park the ill-handling Chevrolet and call it a night.

(Below) Ryan Newman (12) and Tony Stewart (20) pace the field for the evening's first restart after the original field of 24 had been reduced by seven in the early going. Stewart went on to win the first segment while Newman won the second.

The top eight finishers were inverted for the second segment, which put Michael Waltrip on the pole for the lap-41 restart, Terry Labonte in second and Newman in third, while Kenseth started seventh and Stewart in eighth. Labonte led the first lap, but a spinning car slowed the pace on the second. On the restart, Newman and Earnhardt moved around Labonte for first and second place, while Stewart moved up to fourth.

Jimmie Johnson, the race's defending champion, brought out the fourth (and last) caution flag on the 54th lap when he spun out. As his Chevrolet was "pretty beat up" from being collected in the Biffle-Busch incident, he took it to the garage for good.

Everyone but Newman and Stewart pitted, and that paved the way for them finishing first and second in segment No. 2., while Kenseth,

Earnhardt Jr. and Waltrip rounded out the top five.

The event's finale was set up when everyone but Newman decided to pit for fresh rubber at the end of the second segment. The Penske Dodge driver and his crew chief, Matt Borland, opted for track position, hoping their car's tires would be good enough to last for 20 more laps. It was a risky gamble that almost paid off.

Starting first, Newman led laps 71-73 before falling victim to Kenseth's Ford. By now a two-car race for the win, Newman bounced back to lead laps 75-86, but his tires weren't good enough to earn him the win. Coming off the fourth corner on the 87th lap, Newman lost the lead – and the big paycheck – and finished 0.571-second behind Kenseth. Stewart was hoping something would happen to the dueling duo, but nothing did and he had to be content with third place. Waltrip and Earnhardt Jr. completed the top five.

"With the new tires, I was actually a little loose for the start of the last 20 laps," Kenseth noted. "So it was probably good I was running behind Ryan.

"It took everything I had there, and he finally slipped a little bit coming out of (turn) four and I was able to get by."

"We had an awesome car all night. This Dodge was fast," Newman said. "The guys did an awesome job in the pits (and) we just ran

out of tires there at the end. We were about three or four laps short of being too confident. That's about it."

"In a situation like that, no matter what you do, someone is going to do the opposite. Our best bet was to stay out and gamble that way. But finishing second in this race is almost the same as 25th," noted Borland, who saw his driver pick up the second-place check for $306,400.

It took Kenseth just 1 hour, 28 minutes and 9 seconds to become a million-dollar winner.

Sterling Marlin is well on his way to becoming "king of the prelim." He handily stayed out of the way in a first-lap multicar crash in the 30-lap NEXTEL Open and powered by Ganassi Racing teammate Jamie McMurray on the last of 30 laps and won the race for a fourth time.

The event was split into segments of 20 and 10 laps, and McMurray easily came home first in the initial segment. In the 10-lap conclusion, though, he succumbed not only to Marlin, but also to Jeremy Mayfield, who finished second. Jeff Green and Scott Wimmer rounded out the top five in a race that took less than 37 minutes to complete.

Qualifying the night before for the NASCRAR NEXTEL All-Star Challenge was a show in itself, as drivers had to complete three laps and come in on a mandatory pit stop for a change of four tires. Rusty Wallace and his Penske Dodge crew did everything right, came away with no penalties and took the pole with an overall time of 2 minutes and 3.998 seconds at an average speed of 130.647 mph. Newman, Kenseth, Mark Martin and Tony Stewart completed the five fastest qualifiers.

The pole would have gone to Kurt Busch, who ran through the paces in a little more than two minutes. He, however, was docked 20 seconds for exceeding the 45 mph entry speed into the pits and ended up 14th on the next night's starting grid.

Matt Kenseth (17) races hard with Ryan Newman (12) over the final laps, giving the crowd yet another thrilling NASCAR NEXTEL All-Star finish. Newman elected not to pit for tires and started the final segment from the pole with Kenseth right behind shod with fresh rubber.

## NASCAR NEXTEL All-Star Challenge *final race results*

### Segment 1 (40 laps)

| Fin. Pos. | Start Pos. | Car No. | Driver |
|---|---|---|---|
| 1 | 5 | 20 | Tony Stewart |
| 2 | 3 | 17 | Matt Kenseth |
| 3 | 4 | 6 | Mark Martin |
| 4 | 15 | 8 | Dale Earnhardt Jr. |
| 5 | 1 | 2 | Rusty Wallace |
| 6 | 2 | 12 | Ryan Newman |
| 7 | 13 | 5 | Terry Labonte |
| 8 | 8 | 15 | Michael Waltrip |
| 9 | 18 | 88 | Dale Jarrett |
| 10 | 7 | 38 | Elliott Sadler |
| 11 | 11 | 48 | Jimmie Johnson |
| 12 | 12 | 25 | Brian Vickers |
| 13 | 17 | 24 | Jeff Gordon |
| 14 | 9 | 18 | Bobby Labonte |
| 15 | 16 | 9 | Kasey Kahne |
| 16 | 24 | 49 | Ken Schrader |
| 17 | 22 | 98 | Geoffrey Bodine |
| 18 | 23 | 40 | Sterling Marlin |
| 19 | 10 | 16 | Greg Biffle |
| 20 | 14 | 97 | Kurt Busch |
| 21 | 21 | 31 | Robby Gordon |
| 22 | 6 | 29 | Kevin Harvick |
| 23 | 19 | 01 | Joe Nemechek |
| 24 | 20 | 32 | Ricky Craven |

### Segment 2 (30 laps)

| Fin. Pos. | Start Pos. | Driver |
|---|---|---|
| 1 | 3 | Ryan Newman |
| 2 | 8 | Tony Stewart |
| 3 | 7 | Matt Kenseth |
| 4 | 5 | Dale Earnhardt Jr. |
| 5 | 1 | Michael Waltrip |
| 6 | 9 | Dale Jarrett |
| 7 | 6 | Mark Martin |
| 8 | 4 | Rusty Wallace |
| 9 | 13 | Jeff Gordon |
| 10 | 14 | Bobby Labonte |
| 11 | 12 | Brian Vickers |
| 12 | 15 | Kasey Kahne |
| 13 | 10 | Elliott Sadler |
| 14 | 2 | Terry Labonte |
| 15 | 16 | Ken Schrader |
| 16 | 17 | Geoffrey Bodine |
| 17 | 11 | Jimmie Johnson |

### Segment 3 (30 laps)

| Fin. Pos. | Start Pos. | Driver |
|---|---|---|
| 1 | 3 | Matt Kenseth |
| 2 | 1 | Ryan Newman |
| 3 | 5 | Tony Stewart |
| 4 | 7 | Michael Waltrip |
| 5 | 4 | Dale Earnhardt Jr. |
| 6 | 9 | Jeff Gordon |
| 7 | 11 | Kasey Kahne |
| 8 | 2 | Elliott Sadler |
| 9 | 6 | Rusty Wallace |
| 10 | 8 | Mark Martin |
| 11 | 10 | Dale Jarrett |
| 12 | 14 | Brian Vickers |
| 13 | 15 | Ken Schrader |
| 14 | 13 | Terry Labonte |
| 15 | 12 | Bobby Labonte |
| 16 | 16 | Geoffrey Bodine |

# COCA-COLA 600

## LOWE'S MOTOR SPEEDWAY
### MAY 30, 2004

*"It really was a lot of fun ... Luckily, we were able to not make any mistakes in the pits or on the car."*

— *Jimmie Johnson*

If this event had been the fall 500-mile NASCAR NEXTEL Cup Series race at Lowe's Motor Speedway, Jimmie Johnson, driver of Hendrick Motorsports' No. 48 Lowe's Chevrolet, might have led every lap.

Although it was the Memorial Day weekend Coca-Cola 600, the longest contest on the tour, Johnson made it look like an autumn evening hayride. Johnson was awesome in winning the 600-mile day-into-night event on the 1.5-mile super speedway for the second time in a row. Starting on the pole, he led eight times for 334 of 400 laps or 501 of the 600 miles. Only Jim Paschal did better at LMS, leading 335 laps when he was victorious in this event in May 1967.

Nothing, it seemed could stop Johnson from trouncing the field. While there were seven yellow-flag periods for 37 laps, the first didn't go into effect until lap 161 when Johnny Sauter clipped the wall in the second corner. The event also ended under the yellow after Kasey Kahne tagged Bobby Labonte, also in turn two, on the final lap. But by then Johnson was safely heading toward victory lane for the second time in 2004.

"It really was a lot of fun," Johnson said. "But in some cases it's almost better to be in second (place) or third trying to move up. When you're up front, you have the bulls-eye on you. All the other teams are trying to outdo your times.

*Tony Stewart (20), Rusty Wallace (2) and Casey Mears (41) blast down the frontstretch three abreast at Lowe's Motor Speedway during the Coca-Cola 600. All three drivers had respectable evenings by finishing in the top 10 with Mears in seventh, tying his season best, ahead of Stewart in ninth and Wallace in 10th.*

*(Top Left) John Andretti discusses the handling of his car with crew chief Tony Gibson. Andretti was making his third start of the season, all for DEI, and his first since Rockingham in February.*

*(Top Right) Michael Waltrip is all business as he prepares for the grueling, 600-mile event. He took a much-needed second place at the finish, his first top five of the season.*

*(Above Left) There's no doubt who this little guy's rootin' for! The No. 8 came away with sixth place and remained on top of the point standings.*

*(Above Right) Bobby Hamilton Jr. is focused on his task before making his second start of the year for Phoenix Racing. Unfortunately, the NASCAR Busch Series standout had to wrestle an ill-handing Dodge and retired after 73 laps.*

"Luckily, we were able to not make any mistakes in the pits or on the car."

Michael Waltrip, who made a late-race stop for two fresh tires, finished second in a DEI Chevrolet, Matt Kenseth was third in a Roush Racing Ford, Jamie McMurray was fourth in a Dodge and Elliott Sadler took fifth in a Ford. In all, just 13 of the 43 starters went the entire distance.

Heading into the Coca-Cola 600, Dale Earnhardt Jr. still led in NASCAR NEXTEL Cup Series points, but that lead was shrinking. Coming off his third victory of the season in the Chevy American Revolution 400 at Richmond,

Va., the driver of the No. 8 DEI Chevrolet had amassed 1,643 points. He went to the top of the standings four races ago and had led for a series-leading six events.

Beginning to breathe down "Junior's" neck, however, was Johnson, who exited Richmond tied in top-five finishes with Earnhardt, as each had seven. On a roll in the past four races (he was fourth or better in each), Johnson left the Virginia short track with 1,603 points, just 40 behind Earnhardt Jr.

Johnson's record included back-to-back runner-up finishes at Richmond and Fontana, Calif., and he'd been ranked a season-high No. 2 in points for the previous three events. He finished 39th at LMS in his series debut three years ago, and he had continually gotten better there ever since. Included was winning the Bud Pole for the Coca-Cola 600 in 2002.

Jeff Gordon, Johnson's teammate and mentor, left Richmond in the same spot in points he was going in: third. With 1,581 markers he was 62 out of the lead. It was his third week in the No. 3 spot, and six consecutive top-10 finishes had moved him from 13th place to within sight of the lead. Headed into the Coca-Cola 600, he led in top-10 finishes with nine in 11 starts.

Defending champion Matt Kenseth remained fourth in points and had been positioned among the top five in the title chase for 10 of 11 weeks and had been in the top 10 since February 2003. He exited Richmond with 1,517 points, which was 64 behind Gordon and 126 in arrears of the leader.

Kenseth won the Coca-Cola 600 four years ago and had just one finish worse than second in four events with an 18th-place showing in 2001. The driver of the Roush Racing/No 17 DeWalt Tools Ford also carried momentum with him, as he'd won the NASCAR NEXTEL All-Star Challenge at LMS the week before.

Tony Stewart left the 400-miler at Richmond with a smile on his face – and for good reason. His fourth-place showing there was his best effort of the season since finishing third and Las Vegas. Better yet, it launched him from eighth in points to fifth.

The driver of the No. 20 Joe Gibbs Racing/Home Depot Chevrolet headed toward Charlotte with 1,449 points, just 68 behind Kenseth and 194 in back of Earnhardt Jr. It also ranked him among the top five in points for the seventh time this season, and he remained just one of four drivers to be ranked in the top 10 for the entire season to date.

Penske Racing South Dodge pilot Ryan Newman had posted three top-10 finishes in his last four starts, and a ninth-place showing at Richmond was good enough to move him up a notch in points from seventh to sixth. That put him one spot shy of his season-best ranking of fifth following the event at Bristol, Tenn.

Although Newman left Richmond 201 points out of the lead, with 1,442 to his credit, he was only seven behind Stewart. Also, he'd finished

*(Below) Kevin Harvick (29) and John Andretti (1) come off the turn together with Kyle Busch measuring them from behind in the CarQuest Chevrolet. Busch, winner of the previous night's NASCAR Busch Series event, was driving his second big-league race in a Monte Carlo fielded by Hendrick Motorsports.*

*Jeff Gordon bears down on his Hendrick teammate, Jimmie Johnson (48), with (in order) Hendrick-driving Brian Vickers (25), Ryan Newman, Tony Stewart and Elliott Sadler all trying to keep pace. Sadler had the best shot of all, leading four times for 41 laps, but no one really had a challenge for the Lowe's Chevrolet this night.*

*(Above) Fans take in the action under the lights from their own personal ringside seats atop their vehicles in the Lowe's Motor Speedway infield.*

*(Lower Right) Jimmie Johnson's Lowe's crew provides swift service for their driver during a late-race caution. Their efforts contributed heavily toward the team's success, as Johnson held the lead on four of the event's six restarts, helping him take full command of the 400-lapper.*

fifth in the 600 a year ago, second in the fall race at LMS and second in the NASCAR NEXTEL All-Star Challenge a week ago.

Stewart's JGR teammate, Bobby Labonte, ran third at Richmond and benefited by jumping from ninth to a season-best seventh in points. In his last four starts the No. 18 Interstate Batteries Chevrolet driver had finished 10th or better. He headed into the Coca-Cola 600 with 1,430 points, putting him just 12 behind Newman and 19 in back of Stewart.

Kevin Harvick had a troublesome night at Richmond, finishing 25th, three laps down in the RCR Enterprises/GM Goodwrench Chevrolet. That set him back two spots in points from sixth to eighth. The good news was that he remained in the top 10 in the standings for the sixth straight race and ninth week overall.

Harvick entered the 600-miler at LMS with 1,404 points, which put him 26 behind Labonte and 239 out of the lead.

Kurt Busch also managed to take the checkered flag at Richmond, but in a troublesome evening finished 14 laps down in the 31st position. That experience saw the driver of Roush Racing's No. 97 Irwin Ford dive from fifth to

ninth in the standings. Although he was 252 points out of the lead, with 1,391 markers, he was still 14 in front of 10th-ranked Elliott Sadler.

Fifty-two drivers attempted to qualify for the Bud Pole in the Coca-Cola 600, nine more than needed for a 43-car field. It turned out that Johnson combined skill, a powerful car and the luck of the draw to come up with a track qualifying record time and speed of 28.869 seconds at 187.052 mph. The effort knocked Ryan Newman, who time-trialed at 186.948 mph, off the pole and broke the existing record of 186.657 mph set by Newman last fall.

"It's amazing what a roller coaster you can take in terms of confidence," said Johnson, who

was the last driver to take a lap. "When I saw our draw for qualifying, my confidence skyrocketed. Then when Ryan went out and busted that lap, it kind of plateaued."

Qualifying had begun under the afternoon sun, and by the time Johnson made his attempt the track surface temperature had gone down about 20 degrees. The result: Advantage Johnson.

It was an advantage that he kept all weekend. After he took the lead away from McMurray on lap 384, he stayed in command through one more caution flag and a short red-flag period and motored away to finish up in 4 hours, 12 minutes and 10 seconds at an average speed of 142.763 mph and win $426,350.

*(Above Right) The post-race celebration begins with a championship-style burnout for the fans after Jimmie Johnson scored his second straight Coca-Cola 600 victory.*

*(Above Left) Team owner Rick Hendrick (middle) and crew chief Chad Knaus (right) join the winner in victory lane. For Rick Hendrick, this trophy would join six others won by his drivers in this event, two by Darrell Waltrip (1988-89), three by Jeff Gordon (1994, 1997-98) and now two by Johnson.*

## Coca-Cola 600 *final race results*

| Fin. Pos. | Start Pos. | Car No. | Driver | Team | Fin. Pos. | Start Pos. | Car No. | Driver | Team |
|---|---|---|---|---|---|---|---|---|---|
| 1 | 1 | 48 | Jimmie Johnson | Lowe's Chevrolet | 23 | 23 | 29 | Kevin Harvick | GM Goodwrench Chevrolet |
| 2 | 12 | 15 | Michael Waltrip | NAPA Chevrolet | 24 | 26 | 32 | Ricky Craven | Tide Chevrolet |
| 3 | 37 | 17 | Matt Kenseth | Smirnoff Ice/DEWALT Ford | 25 | 28 | 10 | Scott Riggs | Valvoline Chevrolet |
| 4 | 21 | 42 | Jamie McMurray | Texaco/Havoline Dodge | 26 | 40 | 21 | Ricky Rudd | U.S. Air Force/Motorcraft Ford |
| 5 | 4 | 38 | Elliott Sadler | Pedigree Ford | 27 | 8 | 43 | Jeff Green | Cheerios/Great American Bake Sale Dodge |
| 6 | 10 | 8 | Dale Earnhardt Jr. | Budweiser Chevrolet | 28 | 29 | 22 | Scott Wimmer | Caterpillar Dodge |
| 7 | 14 | 41 | Casey Mears | Target Dodge | 29 | 24 | 4 | Jimmy Spencer | Morgan-McClure Motorsports Chevrolet |
| 8 | 15 | 19 | Jeremy Mayfield | Dodge Dealers/UAW Dodge | 30 | 3 | 24 | Jeff Gordon | DuPont Chevrolet |
| 9 | 6 | 20 | Tony Stewart | Home Depot Chevrolet | 31 | 41 | 49 | Ken Schrader | Schwan's Home Service Dodge |
| 10 | 16 | 2 | Rusty Wallace | Miller Lite Dodge | 32 | 27 | 84 | Kyle Busch | CarQuest Chevrolet |
| 11 | 32 | 97 | Kurt Busch | IRWIN Industrial Tools Ford | 33 | 7 | 77 | Brendan Gaughan | Kodak Easy Share/Jasper Dodge |
| 12 | 19 | 9 | Kasey Kahne | Dodge Dealers/UAW Dodge | 34 | 38 | 50 | Derrike Cope | Bennett Lane Winery Dodge |
| 13 | 9 | 18 | Bobby Labonte | Interstate Batteries/Shrek 2 Chevrolet | 35 | 2 | 12 | Ryan Newman | ALLTEL Dodge |
| 14 | 13 | 01 | Joe Nemechek | U.S. Army Chevrolet | 36 | 18 | 6 | Mark Martin | Viagra Ford |
| 15 | 5 | 25 | Brian Vickers | GMAC Chevrolet | 37 | 35 | 5 | Terry Labonte | Kellogg's Chevrolet |
| 16 | 17 | 0 | Ward Burton | NetZero Hi-Speed Chevrolet | 38 | 42 | 45 | Kyle Petty | Krazy Kritters/GP/Brawny Dodge |
| 17 | 11 | 23 | Dave Blaney | Whelen Dodge | 39 | 36 | 40 | Sterling Marlin | U.S. Marine Corp./Coors Light Dodge |
| 18 | 33 | 88 | Dale Jarrett | UPS Ford | 40 | 39 | 30 | Johnny Sauter | America Online Chevrolet |
| 19 | 25 | 1 | John Andretti | Snap-On Chevrolet | 41 | 43 | 02 | Hermie Sadler | Zapf Creations Chevrolet |
| 20 | 20 | 31 | Robby Gordon | Cingular Wireless Chevrolet | 42 | 31 | 09 | Bobby Hamilton Jr. | Miccosukee Resorts Dodge |
| 21 | 30 | 16 | Greg Biffle | National Guard/Subway Ford | 43 | 22 | 51 | Kevin Lepage | negotiationsseminar.com Chevrolet |
| 22 | 34 | 99 | Jeff Burton | RoundUp Ford | | | | | |

# MBNA 400
# "A SALUTE TO HEROES"

*"I had forgotten what this feels like ... Everything went our way today. The car got stronger and stronger ..."*

— *Mark Martin*

The 13th race of the 2004 NASCAR NEXTEL Cup Series season happened to fall on the 60th anniversary of D-Day, the historic Allied invasion of Europe that was a turning point in the eventual outcome of World War II.

The 400-mile race on the one-mile speedway was named to honor the day's participants, and it provided a fitting drama. Including a record run for the Bud Pole by Dodge-driving Jeremy Mayfield, the four-hour-plus marathon featured 11 interruptions for 90 laps, two red-flag periods, a huge pileup that changed the course of the race and a surprise winner, Mark Martin.

Going into Dover, the 13th of 26 races that determine who will be eligible for the final "Chase for the NASCAR NEXTEL Cup," things had tightened up a bit in the point standings. Earnhardt Jr., who had finished sixth in the previous week's Coca-Cola 600 at Lowe's Motor Speedway, was still leading in points, but not by much!

His 40-point advantage going into the 600 had shrunk considerably. With 1,798 markers, he was a scant five in front of Jimmie Johnson, who had won the series' longest race. Yet, Earnhardt was able to maintain his No. 1 ranking for the fifth consecutive race and seventh overall. He also was one of four drivers ranked among the top 10 all season, and for 45 consecutive events dating back to 2003.

Mark Martin gets a set of fresh tires and a load of fuel under caution at Dover. The veteran driver drove a smart race, stayed out of trouble and was in position to take over the lead with 19 laps remaining to end a 72-race winless streak with his 34th career victory.

(Above) Members of a military honor guard stand at attention along pit road during pre-race ceremonies for the MBNA 400 "A Salute to Heroes," aptly named as the race was held on the 60th anniversary of D-Day.

(Right) In honor of the occasion, Bobby Labonte's Chevrolet carried a commemorative paint scheme and was officially listed as the "MBNA D-Day 60th Anniversary Chevrolet."

Hendrick Motorsports Chevrolet driver Johnson was dominant at LMS and kept his second-place berth in points for the fourth week in a row. His second win of the year (the other came at Darlington, S.C.) saw him shave 35 points off "Junior's" advantage and come away with his fifth consecutive top-five performance.

Defending series champion Matt Kenseth had a strong run in the Coca-Cola 600, and a third-place finish bumped him up a notch in points from fourth to third. He headed to Dover with 1,687 points, which put him 111 out of the lead and 106 in back of Johnson. Yet the Roush Racing Ford driver's showing at LMS was his third straight top-five finish and sixth of the season. He also extended his streak of being listed among the top 10 in the standings to 47 events, starting in February 2003 at Rockingham, N.C.

The news coming out of the 600-mile race wasn't as good for Jeff Gordon. He went into the event third in points and left in fourth. The reason was a 30th-place finish that snapped a run of six straight in the top 10. After spending the past three weeks in third place, he left Charlotte with just his second finish of the year out of the top 15. But with 1,654 points he was still within shouting distance of Kenseth.

Tony Stewart, pilot of Joe Gibbs Racing's No. 20 Home Depot Chevrolet, finished ninth in the 600-mile race and stayed fifth in points for the second straight week. The finish was also his

second consecutive in the top 10 and sixth of the year. Just 67 points behind Gordon, he headed to the Delaware one-miler with a record of nine top-10 finishes in 10 starts on the concrete oval.

Bobby Labonte's 13th-place finish in the Coca-Cola 600 was a mixture of bad and good news: it broke a four-race string of top-10 finishes, but the run was good enough to move him up a notch in points from seventh to sixth. That ranking was a season high for the No. 18 Interstate Batteries Chevrolet driver, and he approached Dover with 1,554 points, 244 out of the lead.

The Coca-Cola 600 was also a good experience for Robert Yates Racing's Elliott Sadler. After finishing fifth, he left the track seventh in points, up three spots from 10th. It was Sadler's highest ranking since he was fifth following the mid-April event at Martinsville, Va. He approached Dover just 17 points behind Labonte and 261 behind the leader.

Kurt Busch ended a three-race skid outside the top 20 by running 11th at LMS. That also

moved him up a position in the standings from ninth to eighth place and marked his best finish since also running 11th at Martinsville four races ago. He exited the 600-miler 16 points behind Sadler, 33 in back of Labonte and 277 out of the lead.

Engine problems at Charlotte got the better of Penske South Dodge driver Ryan Newman and also hurt him in points. He ended up finishing 35th in the race and nosedived three places in the standings from sixth to ninth. The poor finish in the 600 was just his third outside the top 10 in the last nine events and put him 21 points behind Busch, 37 in back of Sadler and 298 in arrears of Earnhardt Jr.

RCR Racing/GM Goodwrench Chevrolet pilot Kevin Harvick also had less than a stellar time at Lowe's Motor Speedway. He finished 23rd and slid two positions in points from eighth to 10th. Although his total of 1,498 put him 300 behind the leader, he remained in the top 10 for the seventh consecutive week and 10th overall.

Although Mayfield's chances of winning Sunday's race were dashed when he was caught up in one of the many mishaps, he was all

*(Left) Front tire changer Shane Church works in a cloud of brake dust from the Texaco/Havoline Dodge after Jamie McMurray brought it to a sudden stop on pit road.*

*(Left, Below) Jeremy Mayfield waits patiently with lead mechanic Mike Shiplett (left) and team director Kenny Francis (middle) after posting a fast lap at 161.522 mph in qualifying. No one was able to beat the track-record speed, which gave Mayfield his eighth career Bud Pole.*

*(Below) Mayfield's crew hurries to complete their service at the end of pit road while Tony Stewart (20) and Kasey Kahne (9) bolt away from their stops. Stewart got out first three times under caution, which helped him lead an event-high 234 laps.*

*(Top Left) The yellow flag made 11 appearances during the 400-lap race on the concrete oval know as the "Monster Mile."*

*(Top Right) Elliott Sadler (38) and Brendan Gaughan (77) get tangled up in the first turn following a restart on lap 38, bringing out the third caution flag of the day. The two drivers started the race together from the third row with Gaughan in the fifth spot next to Sadler in sixth.*

*(Right) Greg Biffle's crew pushes the battered National Guard Ford down pit road following the day's biggest accident that involved 18 cars. The race was red-flagged to clean up the mess, causing the drivers to park along the frontstretch.*

*(Below Right) Jeff Burton (99) and Kevin Harvick (29) lead the field side by side after an early-race restart. In a strong showing, Burton drove his Roush Ford to the front for 15 laps and brought home a season-best fourth place at the end of the day.*

smiles on "pole day." He took his eighth career Bud Pole Award with a time and speed of 22.288 seconds and 161.522 mph. He handily bested second-fastest qualifier Ryan Newman's effort of 22.410 seconds (160.643 mph) and set aside the old track record of 159.964 mph set by Rusty Wallace in September 1999.

"This is probably the sweetest pole I've ever gotten," Mayfield said. "We went into it with an open mind and said we've got to get what we can get, and the car stuck."

"I wasn't surprised by Jeremy," Newman added. "He was a tenth (of a second) quicker than us in practice. Jeremy had run close to a perfect lap."

The "Monster Mile" truly lived up to its name this time around. In a race that saw almost everyone a lap down at one point, only the first five drivers finished on the lead lap. It was also something of a disaster for Evernham Motorsports drivers Mayfield and Kasey Kahne, and while Tony Stewart and Dale Earnhardt Jr. finished second and third, respectively, it was no picnic for them either.

As the event was winding to its conclusion, it appeared Raybestos Rookie of the Year challenger Kahne was finally en route to his first

*Tony Stewart (20) puts the heat on Mark Martin (6) as the laps wind down. Even with older tires, Martin was able to fend of Stewart's challenge and stretch his lead to a final margin of 1.702 seconds on the way to his fourth Dover win.*

career NNCS victory. While leading on the 381st lap, he ran through a patch of oil from another car's blown engine. His Dodge lost traction, spun into the third-turn wall and was damaged beyond repair.

"I went down into the turn and there was no grip," said Kahne, who finished 21st. "I came to a stop ... and then I was in the (infield medical) care center for a check-up."

From there, Martin, in the No. 6 Roush Racing/Viagra Ford, took the lead and finished the race 1.702 seconds in front of Stewart. Martin's teammate, Jeff Burton, was fourth, rookie Scott Riggs finished fifth and Michael Waltrip was sixth, a lap down.

"I had forgotten what this feels like," said Martin of his 34th career victory but first since

May 2002. "Everything went our way today. The car got stronger and stronger (but) it was just a stroke of luck."

Included in the race were the accidents, a pitting mistake by Stewart, 17 drivers that didn't take the checkered flag and a race-average speed of 97.042 mph, the slowest ever at Dover. Stewart, who led the most laps (234) had to scramble to catch back up, and he and Earnhardt Jr. staged a dogfight for the runner-up spot.

"Tony outran me the first half of the race, and he had new tires on at the end and I didn't," Martin said. "I thought I was going to get my heart broken."

Instead, the 45-year-old driver walked away with the winner's paycheck of $271,900.

## MBNA 400 "A Salute To Heroes" *final race results*

| Fin. Pos. | Start Pos. | Car No. | Driver | Team | Fin. Pos. | Start Pos. | Car No. | Driver | Team |
|---|---|---|---|---|---|---|---|---|---|
| 1 | 7 | 6 | Mark Martin | Viagra Ford | 23 | 3 | 25 | Brian Vickers | GMAC Chevrolet |
| 2 | 10 | 20 | Tony Stewart | Home Depot Chevrolet | 24 | 2 | 12 | Ryan Newman | ALLTEL Dodge |
| 3 | 26 | 8 | Dale Earnhardt Jr. | Budweiser Chevrolet | 25 | 18 | 18 | Bobby Labonte | MBNA D-Day 60th Anniversary Chevrolet |
| 4 | 22 | 99 | Jeff Burton | Roush Racing Ford | 26 | 40 | 16 | Greg Biffle | National Guard Ford |
| 5 | 23 | 10 | Scott Riggs | Valvoline Chevrolet | 27 | 5 | 77 | Brendan Gaughan | Jasper Engines & Transmissions Dodge |
| 6 | 8 | 15 | Michael Waltrip | NAPA Chevrolet | 28 | 17 | 41 | Casey Mears | Target Dodge |
| 7 | 34 | 5 | Terry Labonte | Kellogg's Chevrolet | 29 | 16 | 40 | Sterling Marlin | Coors Light Dodge |
| 8 | 1 | 19 | Jeremy Mayfield | Dodge Dealers/UAW Dodge | 30 | 28 | 21 | Ricky Rudd | "Keep It Genuine" Ford |
| 9 | 21 | 22 | Scott Wimmer | Caterpillar Dodge | 31 | 19 | 43 | Jeff Green | Cheerios/Betty Crocker Dodge |
| 10 | 33 | 29 | Kevin Harvick | GM Goodwrench Chevrolet | 32 | 14 | 48 | Jimmie Johnson | Lowe's Chevrolet |
| 11 | 29 | 88 | Dale Jarrett | UPS Ford | 33 | 27 | 23 | Dave Blaney | Ollie's Bargain Outlet Dodge |
| 12 | 11 | 97 | Kurt Busch | Sharpie/IRWIN Ford | 34 | 15 | 49 | Ken Schrader | Schwan's Home Service Dodge |
| 13 | 4 | 2 | Rusty Wallace | Miller Lite Dodge | 35 | 36 | 50 | Mike Wallace | GEICO Dodge |
| 14 | 24 | 31 | Robby Gordon | Cingular Wireless Chevrolet | 36 | 13 | 24 | Jeff Gordon | DuPont Chevrolet |
| 15 | 9 | 42 | Jamie McMurray | Texaco/Havoline Dodge | 37 | 30 | 45 | Kyle Petty | Georgia-Pacific/Brawny Dodge |
| 16 | 31 | 32 | Ricky Craven | Tide Chevrolet | 38 | 32 | 01 | Joe Nemechek | U.S. Army Chevrolet |
| 17 | 41 | 4 | Jimmy Spencer | Morgan-McClure Motorsports Chevrolet | 39 | 43 | 72 | Kirk Shelmerdine | Freddie B's Ford |
| 18 | 6 | 38 | Elliott Sadler | M&M's Ford | 40 | 35 | 09 | Tony Raines | Miccosukee Resort Dodge |
| 19 | 25 | 0 | Ward Burton | NetZero Hi-Speed Chevrolet | 41 | 38 | 51 | Kevin Lepage | negotiationssolution.com Chevrolet |
| 20 | 37 | 30 | Johnny Sauter | America Online Chevrolet | 42 | 42 | 89 | Morgan Shepherd | Red Line Oil Dodge |
| 21 | 12 | 9 | Kasey Kahne | Dodge Dealers/UAW Dodge | 43 | 20 | 94 | Stanton Barrett | Husqvarna Chevrolet |
| 22 | 39 | 17 | Matt Kenseth | DeWalt Power Tools Ford | | | | | |

# POCONO 500

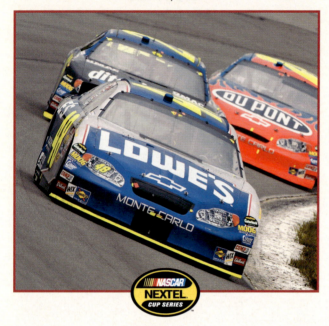

*"The pit stops were fast, the race car was fast (and) the driver was fast."*

*— Jimmie Johnson*

Jimmy Johnson's "magic act" – and yes, that's a cliché comparable to "snatching victory from the jaws of defeat" or "pulling the rabbit out of the hat" – continued on a pleasant afternoon in the Pocono Mountains as he put the Hendrick Motorsports/Lowe's Chevrolet into victory lane for the third time in 2004, second time in two weeks and the ninth time in his career.

Johnson earned every bit of this one, however, and with the win he tied Dale Earnhardt Jr. for the most number of NASCAR NEXTEL Cup Series victories this season with three and, more important, narrowed the gap in points at the top of the standings between him and the driver of the Budweiser Chevrolet.

Earnhardt Jr. had finished third the week before in the MBNA 400 at Dover (Del.) International Speedway, which helped him rebuild his points lead over Johnson from five markers to 98, the largest margin of 2004. The Dover finish also meant "Junior" was able to maintain his No. 1 ranking for the sixth consecutive race and series-leading eighth week overall.

Johnson was happy to leave Dover after getting caught up in a massive pileup there and finishing 32nd. Yet, with 1,865 points, he was not out of the hunt and still had his sights set on the season's final 10-race "Chase for the NASCAR NEXTEL Cup." The Dover accident was just his second DNF (did not finish) of the year, and he remained No. 2 in points for the fifth consecutive event.

*Kasey Kahne prepares to pull his Dodge out of the Pocono garage for a round of practice. The rookie driver continued his impressive qualifying performances by winning his fourth Bud Pole at a track-record speed of 172.533 mph.*

(Top Left) Dale Earnhardt Jr. sits quietly while team members prepare his Budweiser Chevrolet for competition. In the Pocono 500, Earnhardt salvaged a sixth-place finish from a mid-pack start, but still dropped 40 points to Jimmie Johnson in the standings.

(Top Right) Brian Vickers (left) takes some pointers from three-time Pocono winner Jeff Gordon. With the second-fastest qualifying run, Vickers completed an all-rookie front row with pole-winner Kahne.

(Above) Bobby Labonte (18) keeps his Monte Carlo just ahead of Kevin Harvick through Pocono's sweeping third turn. Labonte arrested a two-race skid with a third-place run.

Matt Kenseth also had a less-than-stellar day in Delaware. He crashed and finished 22nd, which ended a string of three consecutive top-five finishes. Still, the driver of the No. 17 DeWalt Tools Ford kept his third-place spot in points and, with 1,784, was just 81 behind Johnson and 179 out of the lead. He also kept another string intact: He'd been in the top 10 in points since February 2003 at Rockingham, N.C.

Tony Stewart brought the No. 20 Home Depot Chevrolet home second at Dover, and that helped him move up a notch in series points from fifth to fourth. The runner-up finish was his third top 10 in a row and seventh of the year, and he remained one of four drivers to be ranked in the top 10 all year long. With 1,767 points, he trailed Kenseth by 17 and Earnhardt Jr. by 196, and he headed to Pocono with anticipation as the race's defending champion.

For the second consecutive week Jeff Gordon endured a finish of 30th or worse with a 36th-place showing at Dover. That dropped the Hendrick Motorsports/DuPont Chevrolet driver from fourth to fifth in points, while a week earlier he'd gone from third to fourth. Gordon was naturally hoping to use his past Pocono record (15 top-10 finishes, including three wins) to improve his luck. With 1,709 points, he was 254 out of the lead and 58 behind Stewart.

Kurt Busch, driver of Roush Racing's No. 97 IRWIN Ford, made the biggest jump in the top 10 between Dover and Pocono. After finishing 12th in the MBNA 400, he shot from eighth place to sixth with 1,648 points. That put him 61 markers behind Gordon and with a fight on his hands to keep from going any lower.

The reason was Elliott Sadler, who, although remaining seventh in the standings for the second straight week, took full advantage of his 18th place at Dover and walked away with 1,646 points, just two less than Busch.

Bobby Labonte, Stewart's teammate, had 11 top-five finishes at Dover in the late 1990s but just one top-10 finish there in the past three events. His sour luck on the "Monster Mile" continued as he finished 25th in the MBNA 400 because of mechanical problems, causing him to slip from sixth to eighth in points. He headed away from Delaware and toward Pennsylvania with 1,642 points, which was only four in back of Sadler but 321 behind Earnhardt Jr.

Coming away from Dover, Kevin Harvick and Ryan Newman had swapped places in the top 10. Harvick had been 10th but edged into ninth, while Newman slid from ninth to 10th.

Among the top 10 in points for the past eight races, Harvick entered Pocono with 1,632 points, just 16 behind sixth-place Busch.

Newman's bid to win his third straight Dover race failed after he was involved in a pit-road mishap and, later, in a multicar accident. It was his first finish outside the top 10 at Dover in five starts and left him with 1,596 points, a healthy 367 in back of Earnhardt Jr.

Raybestos Rookie of the Year challenger Kasey Kahne got his weekend in the Pocono Mountains off to a speedy start by winning the Bud Pole for the Pocono 500. His time and speed of 52.164 seconds at 172.533 mph broke the old record of 52.207 at 172.391 mph, set in July 2000 by Stewart. It was the fourth time in a row and fifth overall that old qualifying records had been eclipsed in 2004. It was also

the fourth pole in just 14 starts for the Evernham Motorsports Dodge pilot.

"The car was perfect; I couldn't believe it," said Kahne. "We were a little bit off in practice ... but I drove a little bit better (in qualifying). (Pocono) is a difficult track. It takes some time to learn."

Fellow rookie Brian Vickers was fast enough to start next to Kahne with a speed of 172.308 mph in his first race at Pocono. Veteran Joe Nemechek was third quickest and Mark Martin, who won at Dover the week before, posted the fourth-fastest time in qualifying.

Jimmie Johnson started the Pocono 500 in fifth place, led eight times for 126 of 200 laps around the massive three-cornered track and had things well in hand when the 500-mile affair ended under caution.

*(Above) Casey Mears patiently observes preparations to his Target Dodge. Mears put together a superb run on the triangular super speedway, hanging with the front-runners for most of the day and finishing with his fifth top 10 in his last eight starts.*

*(Below) Dave Blaney (30) tries to sneak to the inside of Kurt Busch (97) and Ken Schrader (49). Busch picked up 22 positions during the 500-mile affair to end a six-race absence from the top 10. Blaney was making his first start in the AOL Chevrolet for Richard Childress after Johnny Sauter's release from the team.*

(Above) Jimmie Johnson (48) follows the pace car ahead of teammate Brian Vickers, with P.J. Jones (50), making his first start of the season, fronting the lap-down cars on Johnson's left. In spite of problems that dropped him back in the field, Johnson still managed to lead eight times for 126 laps.

(Right) Crew chief Chad Knaus pleads his case with a NASCAR official after his driver lost track position on a caution. The ruling stood, but no matter – Johnson drove back to the point within 10 laps after taking the green flag.

Sounds like an almost-perfect day for the 28-year-old Californian ... right? Well, because of a miscalculation by the pit-road flagman, it almost wasn't. Johnson took the lead on the 11th lap, gave it up briefly on lap 36, and then paced laps 37-50, 55, 57-71, 86-89, 100-113 and went to the front again on lap 132.

He held that lead until lap 156 when the day's sixth of 11 yellow-flag periods for 57 laps was displayed because of a blown engine.

Johnson, following the latest rule, passed the pit-road entrance and prepared to pit on the second time around. What happened, though, was after he and the pace car passed the entrance, an official flagged everyone else into the pits prematurely. While Johnson's rivals were getting serviced, he had to make another 2.5-mile trip around the track before coming in.

NASCAR realized the error, but it was too late for Johnson, who restarted the event on lap 163 in the 20th position. Mad, but undeterred, Johnson quickly made up for lost time. The event's dominant driver survived five more yellow flags, shot past Jeremy Mayfield on the 173rd lap and took off. When the yellow banner was displayed for another blown engine with only four laps left, he had the contest in his pocket. Mayfield finished second, Bobby Labonte was third, Jeff Gordon took fourth and Kurt Busch was fifth.

Earnhardt Jr. didn't lead a lap but finished sixth and salvaged his position at the top of the point standings. Terry Labonte, Robby Gordon, Jamie McMurray and Casey Mears rounded out the top 10, and 21 of the 43 starters completed every lap.

"We were fast all the way through," Johnson said. "The pit stops were fast, the race car was fast (and) the driver was fast.

"Fortunately, we didn't lose the race over (the error). But I was very upset at the time that things weren't corrected to give us the track position back."

Johnson completed the marathon event in 4 hours, 27 minutes and 33 seconds at an average speed of 112.129 mph. In victory lane, he held the winner's check for $186,950.

Jimmie Johnson crosses the finish line under caution with Jeremy Mayfield (19) alongside in second. The win, his third of the season, gave Johnson six top fives in his last seven starts and decreased his deficit in the points to 58 behind Dale Earnhardt Jr.

## Pocono 500 *final race results*

| Fin. Pos. | Start Pos. | Car No. | Driver | Team | Fin. Pos. | Start Pos. | Car No. | Driver | Team |
|---|---|---|---|---|---|---|---|---|---|
| 1 | 5 | 48 | Jimmie Johnson | Lowe's Chevrolet | 23 | 33 | 4 | Jimmy Spencer | Morgan-McClure Motorsports Chevrolet |
| 2 | 7 | 19 | Jeremy Mayfield | Dodge Dealers/UAW Dodge | 24 | 39 | 99 | Jeff Burton | Duke Children's Hospital Ford |
| 3 | 17 | 18 | Bobby Labonte | Interstate Batteries Chevrolet | 25 | 18 | 49 | Ken Schrader | Schwan's Home Service Dodge |
| 4 | 6 | 24 | Jeff Gordon | DuPont Chevrolet | 26 | 10 | 88 | Dale Jarrett | UPS Ford |
| 5 | 27 | 97 | Kurt Busch | IRWIN Industrial Tools Ford | 27 | 8 | 20 | Tony Stewart | Home Depot Chevrolet |
| 6 | 16 | 8 | Dale Earnhardt Jr. | Budweiser Chevrolet | 28 | 43 | 98 | Geoffrey Bodine | Lucas Oil Ford |
| 7 | 19 | 5 | Terry Labonte | Kellogg's Chevrolet | 29 | 29 | 30 | Dave Blaney | America Online Chevrolet |
| 8 | 13 | 31 | Robby Gordon | Cingular Wireless Chevrolet | 30 | 11 | 12 | Ryan Newman | ALLTEL Dodge |
| 9 | 14 | 42 | Jamie McMurray | Texaco/Havoline Dodge | 31 | 20 | 40 | Sterling Marlin | Coors Light Dodge |
| 10 | 21 | 41 | Casey Mears | Target Dodge | 32 | 30 | 2 | Rusty Wallace | Miller Lite Dodge |
| 11 | 9 | 16 | Greg Biffle | Pennzoil/National Guard Ford | 33 | 22 | 15 | Michael Waltrip | NAPA Chevrolet |
| 12 | 12 | 38 | Elliott Sadler | M&M's Ford | 34 | 34 | 32 | Ricky Craven | Tide Chevrolet |
| 13 | 2 | 25 | Brian Vickers | GMAC Chevrolet | 35 | 24 | 22 | Scott Wimmer | Caterpillar Dodge |
| 14 | 1 | 9 | Kasey Kahne | Dodge Dealers/UAW Dodge | 36 | 4 | 6 | Mark Martin | Viagra Ford |
| 15 | 32 | 43 | Jeff Green | Cheerios/Betty Crocker Dodge | 37 | 25 | 45 | Kyle Petty | Georgia-Pacific/Brawny Dodge |
| 16 | 40 | 10 | Scott Riggs | Valvoline Chevrolet | 38 | 41 | 89 | Morgan Shepherd | Racing for Jesus/Arnold Dev. Co. Dodge |
| 17 | 26 | 0 | Ward Burton | NetZero Hi-Speed Chevrolet | 39 | 31 | 77 | Brendan Gaughan | Kodak/Jasper Dodge |
| 18 | 3 | 01 | Joe Nemechek | U.S. Army Chevrolet | 40 | 42 | 72 | Kirk Shelmerdine | L.R. Lyons & Sons Transportation Ford |
| 19 | 35 | 21 | Ricky Rudd | Keep It Genuine Ford | 41 | 38 | 00 | Carl Long | Buyer's Choice Auto Warranty Dodge |
| 20 | 23 | 29 | Kevin Harvick | GM Goodwrench Chevrolet | 42 | 28 | 37 | Todd Bodine | Carter's-Royal Dispos-all Dodge |
| 21 | 15 | 17 | Matt Kenseth | DeWalt Power Tools Ford | 43 | 36 | 51 | Kevin Lepage | negotiationssolution.com Chevrolet |
| 22 | 37 | 50 | P.J. Jones | Arnold Development Co. Dodge | | | | | |

# DHL 400

*"They said there was smoke on the backstretch, but there was no caution .... when I got into turn three, that's when they said the caution is out. I knew at that point (the win) was locked in."*

— Ryan Newman

Although the DHL 400 continued a recent trend in NASCAR NEXTEL Cup Series competition by ending under the yellow flag, it really didn't matter to race winner Ryan Newman.

For the soft-spoken Midwesterner, the feat ended a 21-race no-win streak and came in his 95th series career start. It also ended a string of nine different MIS winners in as many races, as Newman had won on the Brooklyn, Mich., oval in August 2003.

Although Newman had crashed out of the previous week's event at Pocono, Pa., he had run well enough during the year to head to Michigan 10th in NASCAR NEXTEL Cup Series points. With 1,674 markers he was 439 behind point leader Dale Earnhardt Jr.

Earnhardt Jr. finished sixth in the Pocono 500 and held onto his points lead for the seventh consecutive event and ninth overall. He remained just one of four drivers to be ranked in the top 10 in points for the entire season and had been 10th or better for 47 consecutive race weeks. That was the second-longest active streak, second only to Matt Kenseth's run of 49 weeks in a row.

*The starting field for the DHL 400 rumbles down Michigan International Speedway's sweeping frontstretch, led by Jeff Gordon (24) and Brian Vickers (25), on the way to taking the green flag for the 15th event of the 2004 season.*

(Above) Jeff Gordon takes time to accommodate some of the many autograph seekers on hand at Michigan, including one smart fan who brought along his copy of The Official NASCAR Preview and Press Guide 2004.

(Right, Above) Brian Vickers (left), Jimmie Johnson (middle) and Jeff Gordon pose together after writing their names in the NASCAR history book by sweeping the top three starting positions for Hendrick Motorsports.

(Right, Below) Brothers Todd (left) and Geoffrey Bodine get a chance to relax together in the Michigan garage area. Todd was preparing to make his eighth start of the season in a Dodge fielded by Carter Racing, while Geoffrey, currently a regular campaigner in the NASCAR Craftsman Truck Series, was starting his third event of the year driving the Mach 1 Inc. Ford.

Earnhardt, however, was beginning to feel some real heat generated by second-place points runner Jimmie Johnson, who had put his No. 48 Lowe's Chevrolet into victory lane at Pocono for his third win of the year (tying Earnhardt Jr.). Johnson headed to Michigan with 2,055 points, just 58 behind Earnhardt. The victory was Johnson's sixth top-five finish in his last seven starts and allowed him to shave 40 points off Earnhardt's lead.

Although Kenseth ended up 21st at Pocono – it was his second straight race finish outside the top 20 – he maintained third place in points for the third consecutive week. Those two finishes, however, allowed Earnhardt Jr. to more than double his lead over Kenseth, who had a 111-point deficit heading into Dover, Del., but now trailed by 224.

Four-time series champion Jeff Gordon exhibited a bit of the "right stuff" by breaking out of a two-race slump where he'd finished 30th or worse with a fourth-place effort at Pocono. The top-five performance, his fourth of the season and first since his win at California in early May, moved him up one spot in points from fifth to fourth. It marked his sixth consecutive week among the top five. He closed to within 15 points of Kenseth, but with 1,874 to his credit he was still 239 points behind the leader.

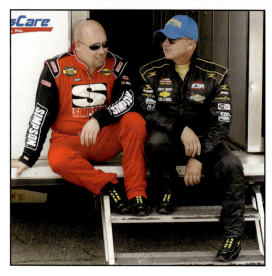

Kyle Petty (45), Scott Wimmer (22) and Kasey Kahne (9) race down the frontstretch in three-wide formation. Kahne started the race all the way back in 34th place but picked up 32 positions to take second after 400 miles, his fourth runner-up finish of the year.

A 27th-place finish in the Pocono 500 knocked Tony Stewart down a spot in the standings from fourth to fifth. It was a season-worst outing for the driver of the Home Depot Chevrolet and ended a run of consecutive top-10 finishes at three. It also marked just the second time in the last eight races Stewart had finished outside the top 16. With 1,854 points he was 20 behind Gordon and 259 out of the lead.

Bobby Labonte fared a bit better than team-mate Stewart at Pocono, and it showed in the standings. As a result of a third-place finish, he moved up two spots in points from eighth to sixth. The Pocono run was the No. 18 Interstate Batteries driver's third top-five fin-ish in the last five races, which helped him advance upward from 10th place over that span of events. He left Pocono 301 points behind Earnhardt, with 1,812, but just nine in front of Kurt Busch.

Although Busch finished fifth at Pocono, he still lost a spot in the standings, falling from sixth to seventh. The Pocono run was his first top-five finish since his victory at Bristol, Tenn., in late March. Still, he kept his hold on being within the top 10 in points for the 13th consec-utive week and headed into the Michigan event as its defending champion.

As did Busch, Elliott Sadler slipped one posi-tion in points following a 12th-place finish at

(Left) As the DHL 400 was held on Father's Day, many drivers took the opportunity to convey good wishes to their dads, including Kyle Petty on the back of his Dodge.

(Below) Matt Kenseth (17) and Elliott Sadler (38) play dueling Fords in their fight for position on the track. Sadler had a strong run, finished in the top five and moved up to seventh in the points, while Kenseth stopped a two-race skid outside the top 20 with a seventh-place effort.

*(Top) Jamie McMurray coasts down pit road after the engine in his Dodge expired near the mid-point of the race. He was one of five drivers unable to finish the event due to engine failure.*

*(Above) Ryan Newman (12) and Brian Vickers (25) match up in early-race action. Both drivers had been on a tear in qualifying, with Vickers making his fifth consecutive start inside the top five, while Newman posted his fourth top-four effort in the last five events.*

*(Right) Jeff Gordon offers his thoughts to members of the media after the engine in his DuPont Chevrolet let go. Although he completed just 88 of 200 laps, he led 81 of those and took the lap-leader bonus for the race.*

Mayfield was just two points behind Newman in 11th place, while Jamie McMurray had two less points than Mayfield. Kasey Kahne, listed in 13th place, was only 23 points from breaking into the top 10.

Gordon didn't set any qualifying records but his time and speed of 37.723 seconds at 190.865 mph were enough to claim his 49th career Bud Pole in 380 races. It was his second pole win of the season and fourth at Michigan. He would be joined on the front row by teammate and pro-tégé Brian Vickers, who turned in a lap of 37.861 seconds at 190.169 mph, while Jimmie Johnson was third quickest at 190.164 mph. The Hendrick Motorsports sweep marked the first time in the sport's history that a single organization had won the top three starting positions for an event.

"We're just trying to make up for (poor fin-ishes) at Charlotte and Dover. Those were kind of ugly for us," Gordon noted. "The car has just been phenomenal since we unloaded it."

Unfortunately for Gordon, he went from tri-umph to adversity in the DHL 400. Gordon led the event's first 78 laps and went on to lead twice for 81 laps (more than anyone else), but then came a telltale puff of smoke as engine failure got the better of his No 24 DuPont Chevrolet. He completed just 88 laps and fin-ished 39th.

"We blew up, which is a rare case for Hendrick Motorsports," he said. "You never

Pocono in the No. 38 M&M's Ford. He dropped from seventh place to eighth, exiting the Pennsylvania event with 1,773 points, 30 in back of Busch and 340 out of the lead. The Pocono showing, though, was his third top-15 finish in the last four races, and he remained one of just four drivers to be ranked in the top 10 for the entire season to date.

Kevin Harvick brought the No. 29 GM Goodwrench Chevrolet home 20th at Pocono and remained ninth in points for the second straight week. Pocono marked the third time in the last four races that Harvick had finished no better than 20th. Despite his troubles, he headed to Michigan with 1,735 points, just 38 behind Sadler and 77 in back of Labonte.

Newman crashed his No. 12 ALLTEL Dodge at Pocono and ended up with a 30th-place finish, but he held onto the 10th spot in points for a second straight week. He headed toward Michigan with 1,674 points (439 behind the leader) and some competition for a spot in the final "Chase for the NASCAR NEXTEL Cup" hot on his heels. Jeremy

blow up when you're running 30th ... it's always when you're leading or running up front when you have a shot for the lead."

Newman led twice for 22 laps, including the last 17. He took the lead away from Dale Jarrett following the end of the race's seventh caution on lap 178, gave way to Jarrett's Ford on lap 183 but regained the lead on the next circuit and held on for the win.

The last of nine caution flags for 33 of 200 laps was displayed on the final circuit around the two-mile super speedway because of an accident in the second corner. By then, though, it became a moot point. Newman's No. 12 Penske Racing South/ALLTEL Dodge was just far enough ahead of the hard-charging Kasey Kahne to collect the victory.

Jarrett faded in the closing laps and had to settle for third place behind Kahne. Jimmie Johnson finished fourth, while Jarrett's teammate, Elliott Sadler, came home fifth.

"I was on the back straightaway and I saw somebody turn sideways before we got the white-flag lap," Newman said of the final incident. "I said, 'That's it right there.' They said there was smoke on the backstretch, but there was no caution.

"Then we went around again and ... when I got into turn three, that's when they said the caution is out. I knew at that point (the win) was locked in."

Newman went to victory circle to collect a check for $176,367 after working for 2 hours, 52 minutes and 18 seconds.

*Four-time Michigan winner Dale Jarrett (88) tries to catch Ryan Newman (12) from behind in a late-race battle for victory. The two drivers swapped the lead three times over a six-lap stretch before the ALLTEL driver took control for good with 17 circuits remaining.*

## DHL 400 *final race results*

| Fin. Pos. | Start Pos. | Car No. | Driver | Team | Fin. Pos. | Start Pos. | Car No. | Driver | Team |
|---|---|---|---|---|---|---|---|---|---|
| 1 | 4 | 12 | Ryan Newman | ALLTEL Dodge | 23 | 13 | 16 | Greg Biffle | National Guard/Subway Ford |
| 2 | 34 | 9 | Kasey Kahne | Dodge Dealers/UAW Dodge | 24 | 27 | 20 | Tony Stewart | Home Depot Chevrolet |
| 3 | 37 | 88 | Dale Jarrett | UPS Ford | 25 | 35 | 50 | P.J. Jones | Arnold Development Companies Dodge |
| 4 | 3 | 48 | Jimmie Johnson | Lowe's Chevrolet | 26 | 31 | 5 | Terry Labonte | Kellogg's Chevrolet |
| 5 | 22 | 38 | Elliott Sadler | M&M's Ford | 27 | 23 | 43 | Jeff Green | Cheerios/Betty Crocker Dodge |
| 6 | 24 | 40 | Sterling Marlin | Coors Light Dodge | 28 | 36 | 4 | Jimmy Spencer | Morgan-McClure Motorsports Chevrolet |
| 7 | 18 | 17 | Matt Kenseth | Carhartt/DEWALT Power Tools Ford | 29 | 26 | 32 | Ricky Craven | Tide Chevrolet |
| 8 | 12 | 18 | Bobby Labonte | Interstate Batteries Chevrolet | 30 | 14 | 0 | Ward Burton | NetZero Hi-Speed Chevrolet |
| 9 | 2 | 25 | Brian Vickers | GMAC Chevrolet | 31 | 9 | 41 | Casey Mears | Target Dodge |
| 10 | 19 | 15 | Michael Waltrip | NAPA Chevrolet | 32 | 42 | 98 | Geoffrey Bodine | Lucas Oil Ford |
| 11 | 7 | 97 | Kurt Busch | Sharpie Ford | 33 | 5 | 31 | Robby Gordon | Cingular Wireless Chevrolet |
| 12 | 25 | 21 | Ricky Rudd | "Keep It Genuine" Ford | 34 | 15 | 6 | Mark Martin | Viagra Ford |
| 13 | 17 | 99 | Jeff Burton | Roush Racing Ford | 35 | 16 | 01 | Joe Nemechek | U.S. Army Chevrolet |
| 14 | 29 | 22 | Scott Wimmer | Caterpillar Dodge | 36 | 38 | 37 | Todd Bodine | Carter's-Royal Dispos-all Dodge |
| 15 | 39 | 30 | Dave Blaney | America Online Chevrolet | 37 | 30 | 42 | Jamie McMurray | Texaco/Havoline Dodge |
| 16 | 6 | 77 | Brendan Gaughan | Jasper Engines/Kodak Dodge | 38 | 1 | 24 | Jeff Gordon | DuPont Chevrolet |
| 17 | 21 | 29 | Kevin Harvick | GM Goodwrench Chevrolet | 39 | 28 | 49 | Ken Schrader | Schwan's Home Service Dodge |
| 18 | 33 | 45 | Kyle Petty | Georgia-Pacific/Brawny Dodge | 40 | 40 | 89 | Morgan Shepherd | Red Line Oil/Racing with Jesus Dodge |
| 19 | 8 | 19 | Jeremy Mayfield | Dodge Dealers/UAW Dodge | 41 | 32 | 51 | Kevin Lepage | negotiationssolution.com Chevrolet |
| 20 | 20 | 10 | Scott Riggs | Valvoline Chevrolet | 42 | 43 | 02 | Derrike Cope | The FanZcar/ETT Chevrolet |
| 21 | 11 | 8 | Dale Earnhardt Jr. | Budweiser Chevrolet | 43 | 41 | 72 | Kirk Shelmerdine | Freddie B's Ford |
| 22 | 10 | 2 | Rusty Wallace | Miller Lite Dodge | | | | | |

# DODGE/SAVE MART 350

## INFINEON RACEWAY
### JUNE 27, 2004

*"Today, I was challenged by my physical fitness ... I'm so beat right now, it's hard for (the win) to sink in."*

— *Jeff Gordon*

For Jeff Gordon, a four-time NASCAR NEXTEL Cup Series champion, dropping from fourth to sixth in series points after finishing 38th in the DHL 400 at Michigan because of engine failure was about the last straw.

That, combined with previous runs of 36th at Dover, Del., and 30th in the Coca-Cola 600 at Concord, N.C., put him into a fighting mood as he headed west to the road course at Sonoma, Calif. He said his battle plan for the road race at the 1.99-mile, 10-turn Infineon Raceway was simple: "Attack, attack, attack."

Gordon followed up his feisty promise not just by "attacking" his foes. He simply overwhelmed everyone from beginning to end. Starting on the Bud Pole (the 50th of his career), the driver of the No 24 DuPont Chevrolet dominated the event by leading 92 of 110 laps and beating runner-up Jamie McMurray in Chip Ganassi's Dodge to the checkered flag by 1.032 seconds. It was his third victory of the season, fourth at Sonoma and the third win there after starting on the pole.

Going into the season's first of two road races, Jimmie Johnson, who finished fourth at Michigan in the No. 48 Lowe's Chevrolet, was the new points leader. His showing was a series-leading 10th top-five performance, and it allowed him to knock Dale Earnhardt Jr. out of the lead after a reign of seven weeks. With 2,220 markers, though, he was just seven in front of Earnhardt Jr. It took Johnson six straight weeks at No. 2 to finally dislodge the driver of the Budweiser Chevrolet.

Jamie McMurray attacks the course on his way to a season-best runner-up finish in the Dodge/Save Mart 350. McMurray led a strong trio of drivers from Chip Ganassi's stable, all of who benefited from a test at the Sonoma, Calif., track held earlier in the year.

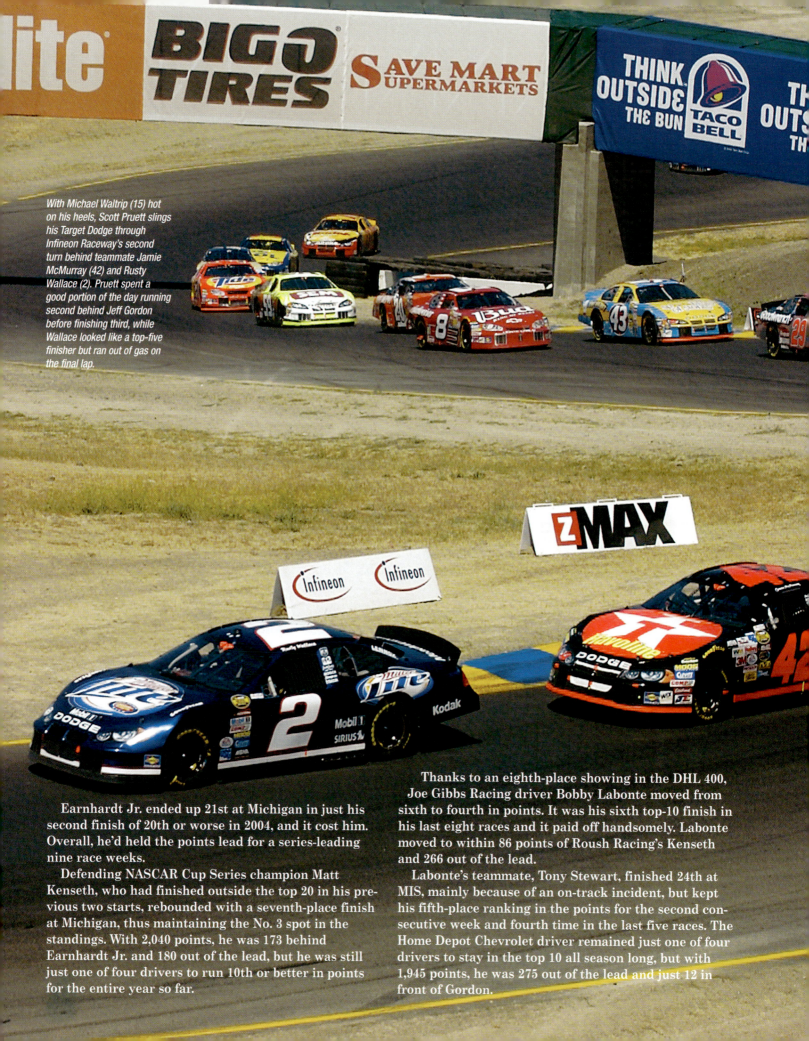

*With Michael Waltrip (15) hot on his heels, Scott Pruett slings his Target Dodge through Infineon Raceway's second turn behind teammate Jamie McMurray (42) and Rusty Wallace (2). Pruett spent a good portion of the day running second behind Jeff Gordon before finishing third, while Wallace looked like a top-five finisher but ran out of gas on the final lap.*

Earnhardt Jr. ended up 21st at Michigan in just his second finish of 20th or worse in 2004, and it cost him. Overall, he'd held the points lead for a series-leading nine race weeks.

Defending NASCAR Cup Series champion Matt Kenseth, who had finished outside the top 20 in his previous two starts, rebounded with a seventh-place finish at Michigan, thus maintaining the No. 3 spot in the standings. With 2,040 points, he was 173 behind Earnhardt Jr. and 180 out of the lead, but he was still just one of four drivers to run 10th or better in points for the entire year so far.

Thanks to an eighth-place showing in the DHL 400, Joe Gibbs Racing driver Bobby Labonte moved from sixth to fourth in points. It was his sixth top-10 finish in his last eight races and it paid off handsomely. Labonte moved to within 86 points of Roush Racing's Kenseth and 266 out of the lead.

Labonte's teammate, Tony Stewart, finished 24th at MIS, mainly because of an on-track incident, but kept his fifth-place ranking in the points for the second consecutive week and fourth time in the last five races. The Home Depot Chevrolet driver remained just one of four drivers to stay in the top 10 all season long, but with 1,945 points, he was 275 out of the lead and just 12 in front of Gordon.

Oddly enough, Gordon, Elliott Sadler and Kurt Busch all headed to California with 1,933 points but, according to the NASCAR system, were ranked sixth, seventh and eighth in the standings, respectively, 287 behind leader Johnson.

Sadler, by finishing fifth at Michigan to earn his second top-five finish in the last four races, moved up a notch in the standings, while Busch, who finished 11th in the DHL 400, fell from seventh to eighth but stayed in the top 10 for the 14th consecutive week.

Penske Racing South Dodge driver Ryan Newman notched his first win of the year at Michigan and jumped up one spot in points from 10th to ninth. The victory was his second at MIS and 10th of his career. It also ended a brief slump in which he'd finished 24th or worse in the last three races. Newman also became the ninth different winner in 15 races run to date and went into the event at Sonoma with 1,859 points, 361 in back of the leader.

Kevin Harvick had a "middling" finish at Michigan in 17th, which knocked him down a spot in points from

ninth to 10th. He did, however, extend his running-at-the-finish streak to 54 consecutive races, dating back to Rockingham, N.C., in February 2002. Going into the Dodge/Save Mart 350, he was 373 points out of the lead, 12 behind Newman and just 26 in front of 11th-place Kasey Kahne.

Gordon is acknowledged by some to be a master road racer, but in Bud Pole qualifying, Infineon Raceway's new track surface almost mastered him. Gordon's car bounced around the twisting track, almost tagged the wall at one point and actually went airborne for a moment and landed in the dirt.

Yet Gordon still ended up going quicker in less time than anyone else. He whipped around the course in 75.968 seconds at 94.303 mph, breaking the old record of 93.620 mph set by Boris Said a year ago. Rusty Wallace, in a Dodge, was second fastest at 94.174 mph, and teammates Busch and Mark Martin were third and fourth, respectively, at 93.852 and 93.701 mph, also eclipsing the old record.

(Above and Right) Road-racing champion Scott Pruett was on hand at Sonoma to pilot the No. 39 Target Dodge for team owner Chip Ganassi. In a stellar performance, Pruett overcame the disadvantage of driving only two races a year (both on road courses) and probably had the best shot at chasing down Jeff Gordon, but he lost valuable track position when he was blocked in his pit stall on his final stop of the day.

(Below) A very determined Jeff Gordon and his powerful DuPont Chevrolet were simply an unbeatable combination on the Infineon road course. Gordon trounced the field by leading 92 of 110 laps, 82 more than his closest challenger, on the way to his third win of the season.

"We're on a mission," Gordon said after his run. We're not happy with the way things have been going lately.

"The track has a lot of grip. I was really disappointed when I made the run because I felt like I left the door wide open for other guys to knock us down the list."

Kenseth, Pruett, Greg Biffle, Harvick, Joe Nemechek and Bobby Labonte completed the top 10 in qualifying. The only driver not to make the 43-car field was Morgan Shepherd, and German road racer Klaus Graf took the 38th starting spot in a BAM Racing Dodge. He was the first German driver to make it into a NASCAR NEXTEL Cup Series event since Rolf Stommelon in 1971 at Talladega, Ala.

Busch got the jump on Gordon at the start of the event and led the first lap, but Gordon regained the No. 1 spot the next time around

and led through lap 34. Martin, Stewart and Earnhardt Jr. swapped the lead through lap 45, but Gordon again took over and paced the next 22 circuits plus the final 37. In fact, Gordon was the leader following the restarts of four of the event's six caution-flag periods for 13 laps.

Finishing behind runner-up McMurray was road-racing ace Scott Pruett, also in a Ganassi Racing Dodge, Michael Waltrip, in a DEI Chevrolet, was fourth, and fifth went to Gordon's teammate, Johnson. Neither they nor anyone else, however, could do anything with Gordon, whose biggest foe turned out to be 90-degree weather that made the cockpit of his car almost unbearable.

"Today, I was challenged by my physical fitness," Gordon said. "It wasn't easy. We had to fight for it. It wasn't a gimme.

"I'm so beat right now, it's hard for (the win) to sink in."

Two of the most disappointed drivers were Busch and Robby Gordon, the event's defending champion. The distributor wires in Busch's Ford shorted out and burned a hole in an oil line, and the result was a 36th-place finish. Gordon caused two of the caution flags and was a victim of three flat tires, primarily because the lug nuts on all four wheels of his Chevrolet were loose before the race started. He ended up finishing 34th.

Graf, however, finished on the lead lap and was running 17th when the winner took the checkered flag. The event took 2 hours, 49 minutes and 34 seconds to complete at an average speed of 77.456 mph, and Gordon's take for the day was $388,103.

(Top Left) Klaus Graff rolls through the esses in his SEM Dodge fielded by BAM Racing. In his NASCAR NEXTEL Cup Series debut, the German-born driver nailed down a lead-lap, 17th-place finish.

(Top) Former track record holder Boris Said, driving a Monte Carlo for MB2/MBV Motorsports, started 19th and drove into the top 10 for a solid sixth-place finish.

(Above) Michael Waltrip (15) faced a tough task after dropping to the rear of the field before the event due to an engine change, but deliberately picked his way through traffic and wound up fourth, gaining 36 positions on the day to lead all drivers.

## Dodge/Save Mart 350 *final race results*

| Fin. Pos. | Start Pos. | Car No. | Driver | Team | Fin. Pos. | Start Pos. | Car No. | Driver | Team |
|---|---|---|---|---|---|---|---|---|---|
| 1 | 1 | 24 | Jeff Gordon | DuPont Chevrolet | 23 | 18 | 49 | Ken Schrader | Schwan's Home Service Dodge |
| 2 | 11 | 42 | Jamie McMurray | Texaco/Havoline Dodge | 24 | 14 | 0 | Ward Burton | NetZero Hi-Speed Chevrolet |
| 3 | 6 | 39 | Scott Pruett | Target Dodge | 25 | 25 | 22 | Scott Wimmer | Caterpillar Dodge |
| 4 | 40 | 15 | Michael Waltrip | NAPA Chevrolet | 26 | 33 | 77 | Brendan Gaughan | Kodak/Jasper Dodge |
| 5 | 34 | 48 | Jimmie Johnson | Lowe's Chevrolet | 27 | 36 | 43 | Jeff Green | Cheerios/Spoonfuls of Stories Dodge |
| 6 | 19 | 36 | Boris Said | Centrix Chevrolet | 28 | 2 | 2 | Rusty Wallace | Miller Lite Dodge |
| 7 | 29 | 41 | Casey Mears | Target Dodge | 29 | 9 | 01 | Joe Nemechek | U.S. Army Chevrolet |
| 8 | 4 | 6 | Mark Martin | Viagra Ford | 30 | 21 | 19 | Jeremy Mayfield | Dodge Dealers/UAW Dodge |
| 9 | 13 | 99 | Jeff Burton | Roush Racing Ford | 31 | 30 | 9 | Kasey Kahne | Dodge Dealers/UAW Dodge |
| 10 | 16 | 38 | Elliott Sadler | M&M's Ford | 32 | 27 | 45 | Kyle Petty | Georgia-Pacific/Brawny Dodge |
| 11 | 20 | 8 | Dale Earnhardt Jr. | Budweiser Chevrolet | 33 | 10 | 18 | Bobby Labonte | Interstate Batteries Chevrolet |
| 12 | 8 | 29 | Kevin Harvick | GM Goodwrench Chevrolet | 34 | 24 | 31 | Robby Gordon | Cingular Wireless Chevrolet |
| 13 | 7 | 16 | Greg Biffle | National Guard/TraveLodge Ford | 35 | 12 | 21 | Ricky Rudd | Motorcraft Ford |
| 14 | 22 | 12 | Ryan Newman | ALLTEL Dodge | 36 | 3 | 97 | Kurt Busch | IRWIN Industrial Tools Ford |
| 15 | 17 | 20 | Tony Stewart | Home Depot Chevrolet | 37 | 43 | 98 | Larry Gunselman | Lucas Oil/Gibson Products Dodge |
| 16 | 42 | 32 | Ricky Craven | Tide Chevrolet | 38 | 32 | 61 | Austin Cameron | McMillin Homes/NAPA Auto Care Chev. |
| 17 | 38 | 59 | Klaus Graf | SEM/Color Horizons Dodge | 39 | 31 | 50 | P.J. Jones | Bennett Lane Winery Dodge |
| 18 | 23 | 88 | Dale Jarrett | UPS Ford | 40 | 15 | 5 | Terry Labonte | Kellogg's Chevrolet |
| 19 | 28 | 30 | Jim Inglebright | America Online Chevrolet | 41 | 37 | 02 | Brandon Ash | Fuerza-Ash Mtspts/Health Ed. Coun. Ford |
| 20 | 5 | 17 | Matt Kenseth | DeWalt Power Tools Ford | 42 | 41 | 10 | Scott Riggs | Valvoline Chevrolet |
| 21 | 26 | 40 | Sterling Marlin | Coors Light Dodge | 43 | 35 | 72 | Tom Hubert | Freddie B's Ford |
| 22 | 39 | 25 | Brian Vickers | GMAC Chevrolet | | | | | |

# PEPSI 400

**DAYTONA INTERNATIONAL SPEEDWAY**
JULY 3, 2004

*"I don't think there's any doubt in anybody's mind here which team performed the best all weekend."*

— *Jeff Gordon*

Going into the 400-miler at Daytona International Speedway, the event that traditionally marks the unofficial halfway point of the season, Jimmy Johnson was on a roll. With a fifth-place finish the week before at Sonoma, Calif., he maintained his lock on the points lead and had his eye on the final 10-race Chase for the NASCAR NEXTEL Cup. The run in California was his third consecutive top-five finish and his eighth in the previous nine events, which resulted in a 27-point advantage (2,375-2,348) over second-place Dale Earnhardt Jr. Overall, Johnson now had a series-leading 11 finishes of fifth or better for the year.

Earnhardt Jr. brought the No. 8 Budweiser Chevrolet home 11th at Infineon Raceway, thus keeping Johnson well within his sights. Although he'd lost 20 points to Johnson, it was his second consecutive week at No. 2 in the standings, following seven weeks in a row at No. 1. Overall, he had been the point leader for a season-high nine weeks and had been ranked among the top three for all but one.

Although Ford driver and defending NASCAR Cup Series champion Matt Kenseth had a less than great day in California with a 20th-place finish, he remained third in points and headed to Daytona with 2,143. It was his fifth straight week at No. 3, and he was just one of four drivers to be ranked in the top 10 all year long and for 51 consecutive events. The streak was still the longest in the series overall.

*Brian Vickers (25) and Kurt Busch (97) blast through the tri-oval at Daytona International Speedway side by side, with Casey Mears (41) trying to close in on the outside. With a fourth-place finish, Busch picked up his second top five in the last four events, while Vickers posted his second ninth-place effort in his last three starts.*

(Above) Crew chief Todd Parrott takes refuge under an umbrella while waiting for track drying to be completed. Although delayed by rain, the race eventually got the green flag and ran the entire 400-mile distance.

(Above Right) Brendan Gaughan (77) and Mike Wallace (50) get together against the fourth-turn wall in an incident that brought out the fifth and final caution of the night on lap 78. The damage to Wallace's Dodge did not allow him to continue, while Gaughan returned and was running at the finish.

(Right) Ryan Newman's ALLTEL crew members finish their work on pit road with Casey Mears blasting away from behind. The two drivers not only pitted together, they finished together with Mears in 11th ahead of Newman in 12th.

Gordon's domination of the Dodge/Save Mart 350 at Sonoma paid off in more ways than one. His third win of the year tied him with Johnson and Earnhardt in season victories and let him jump up two spots in points from sixth to fourth. With 2,123 markers he was 252 behind the leader and just 20 in back of Kenseth. The victory also pulled Gordon out of a slump in which he'd finished 30th or worse in three of the previous four events.

Tony Stewart, again ranked fifth in points, made somewhat of a performance improvement at Sonoma. He'd finished outside of the top 20 in the previous two races, but at California he came away with a 15th-place showing and left with 2,068 points, which was 307 out of the

lead, 55 behind Gordon but just one in front of a persistent Elliott Sadler.

Sadler moved up one spot in points, from seventh to sixth, on the strength of a 10th-place finish at Sonoma. It was the Robert Yates Racing Ford driver's second top-10 finish in a row and third in the previous five races. Sadler was still just one of four drivers to be ranked among the top 10 from the start of the year to the present and was heading to a track where he'd scored three top-10 finishes in 11 starts.

Stewart's Joe Gibbs Racing teammate, Bobby Labonte, took a nosedive in points after a disappointing 33rd-place finish at Sonoma. He went into that race fourth in points and left

it in seventh. The three-position slide was the largest of the week among the top 10, and with 2,018 points, he fell 357 behind the leader, 49 in back of Sadler and just 25 in front of eighth-place Kurt Busch.

Busch, in the No.97 Roush Racing Ford, had a day similar to Labonte's in California. There, he tied his season-worst finish of 36th but still managed to hold on to the eighth spot in the standings for the second consecutive week.

Ryan Newman followed up his win at Michigan two races back by finishing 14th in California. Although that was nothing to brag about, the driver of the ALLTEL Dodge remained ninth in points for the second straight week. With 1,980 markers, he was 395 out of the lead going to Daytona but trailed Busch by just 13.

A 12th-place effort in California meant that Richard Childress Racing Chevrolet pilot Kevin Harvick was still in the hunt as the 26-race lead-up to the final 10-race chase ground on.

(Left) Matt Kenseth's team works in an effort to get their driver back into action. Kenseth, who started near the back of the field, took a hit on the track in an early accident, and in the points by falling to fifth after managing only a 39th-place finish in the race.

Outside pole winner Michael Waltrip (15) jumps to an early lead over Jeff Gordon (24), Tony Stewart (20) and Dale Earnhardt Jr. (8). Waltrip, a three-time victor at Daytona and the track's all-time leading money winner, led the Pepsi 400 five times for 57 laps but faded to 13th at the finish.

*(Above) The Fords of Mark Martin (6) and Ricky Rudd hold the inside lane next to the Chevrolets of Terry Labonte (5) and Robby Gordon (31) in their high-speed battle for position. Martin took sixth and gained his second straight top 10, ahead of eighth-place Labonte with his third top 10 in the last five events.*

*(Right) Dale Earnhardt Jr. motors through the wet infield grass after having to dodge another car while leaving pit road on the fourth caution of the race. The incident cost Earnhardt valuable track position, although he was able to recover to finish third.*

He left the road course with 1,974 points, 401 behind the leader. But it was just his second run of 15th or better in the past six races. Also, he had to keep his eye on Jamie McMurray, who was just 82 points behind him in 11th place.

It had been a long time — 23 years — since a driver had won the Pepsi 400 from the pole, but Gordon duplicated Cale Yarborough's accomplishment this time around by first setting a time and speed of 47.705 seconds at 188.659 mph. It was his 51st career Bud Pole Award in 382 races, as well as his third in as many events. The last driver to go three-for-three was Newman, last year, and the man who did it before Newman was Gordon himself in 1996.

"This weekend is really working out awesome for us, so far," said Gordon, who also ran the fastest lap in practice. "For the first time, I felt like the car was really good from the

minute we unloaded it. The Hendrick (horsepower) has been strong."

Michael Waltrip, in the No. 15 NAPA Chevrolet was second quickest in time trials with an effort of 47.715 seconds at 186.620 mph, while Ricky Rudd, Dale Jarrett and Earnhardt Jr. rounded out the top five.

Gordon had to cool his heels for about two hours before he began the journey that would lead to his fourth NASCAR NEXTEL Cup Series victory of the year, second in a row, and second straight in a restrictor-plate race. Heavy rain had soaked the 2.5-mile track, but the event got the go-ahead at about 10 p.m.

Gordon, in the No. 24 DuPont Chevrolet, used a combination of skill, determination and teamwork to grab the win and upstage the teams of Dale Earnhardt, Inc. — up to now the "kings" of restrictor-plate racing — and lead Hendrick Motorsports to a dominating evening at Daytona.

Gordon led the first nine laps under a competition caution to facilitate track drying and make sure it was safe for racing. While Gordon lost the lead to Waltrip on the 10th circuit — the race's first green-flag lap — he went on to pace the field five times for 61 laps, including the final seven.

The five yellow-flag periods for 25 laps all came between laps 1 and 77, and the most dramatic incident of the event was a four-car accident on the 18th circuit. Earnhardt Jr.'s chances of winning were diminished during the fourth caution (laps 72-76). While leading, he pitted and, as he was leaving his pit, got shoved aside by Brian Vickers (who was trying to avoid Gordon) and ended up in the soggy grass. Earnhardt Jr. re-entered the event running 13th and worked his way back toward the front, but he couldn't catch Gordon.

When the checkered flag fell, Gordon's teammate, Johnson, was 0.143 second behind him, while fellow Hendrick drivers Terry Labonte and Vickers were eighth and ninth, respectively.

Of the DEI contingent, Earnhardt Jr. finished third, Waltrip was 13th and John

Andretti finished last due to an accident on the 45th of 160 laps.

"We definitely put on a heck of an effort all the way around as a team this entire weekend," Gordon said. "I don't think there's any doubt in anybody's mind here which team performed the best all weekend.

"We've made gains for sure, and think that was evident."

"Those guys, the Hendricks, they've done their homework," Earnhardt Jr. added. "I have to give credit. They outran us."

Gordon completed the race in 2 hours, 45 minutes and 23 seconds at an average speed of 145.117 mph and won $346,703.

Jeff Gordon (24) and Jimmie Johnson (48) team up on the inside against Tony Stewart (20), as the three drivers fight for the lead. Johnson stayed hooked-up with his Hendrick teammate and helped Gordon to his second straight victory celebration (top), while Stewart brought the Home Depot Chevrolet home in fifth.

## Pepsi 400 *final race results*

| Fin. Pos. | Start Pos. | Car No. | Driver | Team | Fin. Pos. | Start Pos. | Car No. | Driver | Team |
|---|---|---|---|---|---|---|---|---|---|
| 1 | 1 | 24 | Jeff Gordon | DuPont/Pepsi Chevrolet | 23 | 26 | 99 | Jeff Burton | Coca-Cola C2 Ford |
| 2 | 19 | 48 | Jimmie Johnson | Lowe's Chevrolet | 24 | 33 | 45 | Kyle Petty | Georgia-Pacific/Brawny Dodge |
| 3 | 5 | 8 | Dale Earnhardt Jr. | Budweiser Chevrolet | 25 | 31 | 9 | Kasey Kahne | Dodge Dealers/UAW Dodge |
| 4 | 35 | 97 | Kurt Busch | Coca-Cola C2/Sharpie Ford | 26 | 39 | 38 | Elliott Sadler | M&M's Ford |
| 5 | 17 | 20 | Tony Stewart | Home Depot/Coca-Cola C2 Chevrolet | 27 | 27 | 2 | Rusty Wallace | Miller Lite Dodge |
| 6 | 21 | 6 | Mark Martin | Viagra Ford | 28 | 20 | 33 | Kerry Earnhardt | Bass Pro Shops/TRACKER Chevrolet |
| 7 | 15 | 18 | Bobby Labonte | Wellbutrin XL(tm) Chevrolet | 29 | 40 | 4 | Jimmy Spencer | Morgan-McClure Motorsports Chevrolet |
| 8 | 10 | 5 | Terry Labonte | Cheez-It/Spider-Man 2 Chevrolet | 30 | 30 | 43 | Jeff Green | Cheerios/Betty Crocker Dodge |
| 9 | 14 | 25 | Brian Vickers | GMAC Chevrolet | 31 | 9 | 16 | Greg Biffle | Coca-Cola C2/National Guard Ford |
| 10 | 6 | 01 | Joe Nemechek | U.S. Army Chevrolet | 32 | 37 | 22 | Scott Wimmer | Caterpillar Dodge |
| 11 | 24 | 41 | Casey Mears | Target Dodge | 33 | 43 | 89 | Morgan Shepherd | Racing with Jesus/Red Line Oil Dodge |
| 12 | 13 | 12 | Ryan Newman | ALLTEL Dodge | 34 | 42 | 98 | Larry Gunselman | Lucas Oil Ford |
| 13 | 2 | 15 | Michael Waltrip | NAPA Chevrolet | 35 | 29 | 49 | Ken Schrader | Schwan's Home Service Dodge |
| 14 | 11 | 29 | Kevin Harvick | Coca-Cola C2/GM Goodwrench Chevrolet | 36 | 12 | 77 | Brendan Gaughan | Kodak/Jasper Eng. & Trans. Dodge |
| 15 | 23 | 30 | Dave Blaney | AOL Broadband Chevrolet | 37 | 32 | 42 | Jamie McMurray | Texaco/Havoline Dodge |
| 16 | 4 | 88 | Dale Jarrett | UPS Ford | 38 | 38 | 32 | Ricky Craven | Tide Chevrolet |
| 17 | 3 | 21 | Ricky Rudd | Coca-Cola C2/Motorcraft Ford | 39 | 36 | 17 | Matt Kenseth | Smirnoff Ice/DeWalt Ford |
| 18 | 34 | 98 | Bill Elliott | Coca-Cola C2 Dodge | 40 | 8 | 0 | Ward Burton | NetZero Hi-Speed Chevrolet |
| 19 | 25 | 31 | Robby Gordon | Cingular Wireless Chevrolet | 41 | 41 | 50 | Mike Wallace | SportClips Dodge |
| 20 | 22 | 40 | Sterling Marlin | Coors Light Dodge | 42 | 28 | 09 | Bobby Hamilton Jr. | Miccosukee Resorts Dodge |
| 21 | 7 | 10 | Scott Riggs | Valvoline Chevrolet | 43 | 18 | 1 | John Andretti | Coca-Cola C2 Chevrolet |
| 22 | 16 | 19 | Jeremy Mayfield | Dodge Dealers/UAW Dodge | | | | | |

# TROPICANA 400
## Presented by Meijer

### CHICAGOLAND SPEEDWAY
#### JULY 11, 2004

*"We didn't need the accident with (Kahne) to win the race. ...
We had the strongest car."*

— *Tony Stewart*

Tony Stewart gets the "go" signal from his crew after a stop under caution in the Tropicana 400. The Home Depot team did an outstanding job on pit road, returning Stewart to No. 1 position for seven of the day's nine restarts.

Tony Stewart got his meeting with Chicagoland Speedway's wall out of the way two days prior to the Tropicana 400 during a practice session, and then settled down to business, while Jimmie Johnson again clearly showed why he was the leader in NASCAR NEXTEL Cup Series points.

Going into Chicagoland, Johnson was fresh off his fourth consecutive top-five race finish, a second place in the previous week's Pepsi 400 at Daytona Beach, Fla. It was also his ninth finish of fifth or better in the last 10 races, 12th in 17 starts, and with 2,545 points, he was 27 in front of second-place Dale Earnhardt Jr.

The driver of the No. 8 Budweiser Chevrolet wasn't making it easy for Johnson by any means. Earnhardt Jr. finished one spot behind Johnson at Daytona, maintaining his deficit in the points at 27. It was his third consecutive week in second place and his 50th in the top 10, an active streak ranking second only to Matt Kenseth's 52 in a row.

Jeff Gordon, who claimed both the Bud Pole and the race win at Daytona, moved up a spot in the standings from fourth to third and headed into Chicago with 2,313 points, putting him 232 out of first place. The win was his fourth of the year and second straight, and he capitalized on that by gaining three spots in just two weeks. Also, Gordon had been ranked among the top 10 for 15 weeks, including the last 11.

(Above) Dale Jarrett takes advantage of the UPS Ford's ability to hug the bottom of the track to race past Robby Gordon's Chevrolet. Jarrett cited his car's setup as the reason he was able to stay away from trouble on the track and capture a strong finish.

(Right) Crew chief Mike Ford (left) plots strategy with driver Dale Jarrett before getting underway at Chicago. The team's third-place performance matched its season best, that coming three races prior at Michigan.

(Below Right) Ken Schrader (left) shares a laugh with Bobby and Judy Allison in the Chicagoland garage area.

After finishing outside of the top 10 in his last three starts, Stewart rallied at Daytona by finishing fifth and advanced a place in points from fifth to fourth. He hadn't been ranked outside the top five for the past seven weeks, and while he was 342 points out of the lead going into Chicago, he was, with 2,203 markers, just 110 behind Gordon, but a mere 14 in front of fifth-ranked Kenseth.

Defending series champion Kenseth was involved in an accident in the Pepsi 400, finished 39th and fell from third in points to fifth. It was his fourth finish of 20th or worse in the past five events for the usually consistent up-front driver. With 2,189 points, he was well within reach of Stewart but just 25 in front of Bobby Labonte.

Labonte finished a solid seventh in the Pepsi 400 and jumped up a spot in the standings from seventh to sixth place. His ninth top-10 finish of the year helped him rebound from a disappointing 33rd-place showing in Sonoma, Calif., and he headed toward the superspeedway near Chicago with 2,164 points, 381 out of the lead.

Kurt Busch made a positive move of his own after finishing fourth at Daytona, which allowed him to advance a place in the standings from eighth to seventh. Heading out of Florida with 2,153 points, he was just 11 behind Labonte and 36 away from cracking the top five.

Daytona got the better of M&M's Ford pilot Elliott Sadler. He finished 26th and fell from sixth to eighth place in points. It was his worst finish since a 28th at Talladega, Ala., (another restrictor-plate track), but the good news for Sadler was that he left Florida just one point behind Busch and only 12 in arrears of Labonte.

Penske Racing Dodge pilot Ryan Newman remained ninth in points following Daytona, his third consecutive week in that position, and extended his stay in the top 10 to nine straight race weeks. At this point in 2003, he was 16th in the standings, and now he was returning to the Tropicana 400 as its defending champion.

Kevin Harvick also stayed static in the points race, entering Daytona 10th in the standings and, with a 14th-place finish, leaving it in the same spot. The driver of Richard Childress Racing's No. 29 GM Goodwrench Chevrolet held onto the 10th position despite continuing a streak of finishes outside the top 10, which now stood at four. Although he left Daytona 450 points in back of the leader, he was just 17 behind Newman and a healthy 111 in front of 11th-place Kasey Kahne.

From the looks of it, one might say that Gordon was on a "Bud Pole roll." His record lap of 28.886 seconds at 186.942 mph easily eclipsed the old mark of 29.223 seconds at 184.786 mph, set by Stewart a year ago. In fact, aided at least partially by a new, softer tire

*(Above) Jeremy Mayfield (19) keeps his Evernham Motorsports Dodge in front of a charging Jimmie Johnson in the Lowe's Chevrolet. Mayfield led once for 26 laps late in the race but faded a bit near the end and took fifth, while Johnson moved into second to score his 10th top five in the last 11 events.*

*(Left) John Andretti, making his fifth start of the season in the No. 1 Monte Carlo for DEI, races with Kevin Harvick (29), who scored a much-needed top-10 finish to stay among the leaders in the standings.*

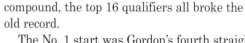 

compound, the top 16 qualifiers all broke the old record.

The No. 1 start was Gordon's fourth straight and fifth of the 2004 season. It was the first time since Bill Elliott did it in 1985 that anyone had earned a consecutive quartet of No. 1 starts, while only two drivers, Bobby Allison (1972) and Cale Yarborough (1980), attained five consecutive pole positions in the sport's modern era (1972-present).

Kahne ran second quickest with a lap speed of 186.871mph, which was a tad quicker than

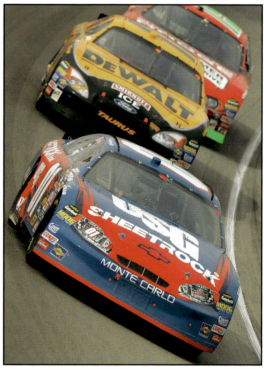

(Above) Sterling Marlin's Coors Light crew is in full swing on pit road, which became a hotbed of activity with nine cautions during the 267-lap event. Marlin picked up a welcome seventh-place finish, just his second top 10 in the last 10 races.

(Far Right) Joe Nemechek keeps his USG Sheetrock Monte Carlo in front of challengers Matt Kenseth (17) and Jeremy Mayfield. Nemechek had a solid performance at Chicago and wound up in eighth at the end of the day.

(Right) Terry Labonte, his team on a role of late, drives a stout Kellogg's Chevrolet to a sixth-place result, his fourth finish of eighth or better in the last six events.

Johnson's effort of 186.290. Rookie Brian Vickers (185.759) and Greg Biffle (185.733) were fourth and fifth quickest in qualifying, while Jeff Burton, Mike Bliss, Newman, Joe Nemechek and Stewart completed the top 10.

En route to his first victory of the season (and 18th in 194 starts), Stewart dominated the event. He had the No. 20 Home Depot Chevrolet out front five times for 160 of 267 laps and was a healthy 2.925 seconds in front of runner-up Johnson's Lowe's Chevrolet at the finish. Dale Jarrett finished third in a Ford, pole-winner Jeff Gordon was fourth and Jeremy Mayfield, who led once for 26 laps but fell off the pace, salvaged fifth place in his Evernham Motorsports Dodge.

Stewart however, already on probation for an incident earlier in the year, was again the center of controversy. On lap 127, following the

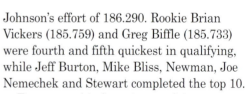

fourth of nine yellow-flag periods, third-running Stewart pulled to the right, bypassed Sterling Marlin and then tapped leader Kasey Kahne's Dodge in the rear. Kahne's Intrepid broke loose and hit the wall, causing an accident that collected seven more cars, while Stewart got by.

A howl went up from Kahne's team. His crew chief, Tommy Baldwin, charged into Stewart's pit, and a brief melee had to be broken up by NASCAR officials. Stewart later said it was a racing accident, nothing more, and NASCAR agreed with him after a thorough review of the incident.

"I don't know what caused him (Kahne) to check up (slow down)," Stewart said. "It could have torn us up as easily as it did him in all reality. It surprised me ... we were boxed in ... that's not a spot where you want to end up having a tangle with somebody."

Stewart eventually took the lead for the last time when he passed Mayfield with seven laps left and scored his first win since October.

Kahne denied "checking up," while Johnson said he thought Stewart's was "the strongest car all day" and "deserved to win the race."

Gordon led the event's first 14 laps and then fell off the pace with a variety of problems and had to work hard for a top-five finish. He was one of 12 drivers (other than the winner) to take brief turns at the front, but once Stewart showed some muscle, the event was just about his for the taking. He completed the race in 3 hours, 5 minutes and 33 seconds at an average speed of 129.507 mph and won $336,803.

Tony Stewart takes the white flag on the way to a very strong win in the Tropicana 400. The Home Depot driver led 160 laps, including the last 27, and scored his first win of the 2004 season.

## Tropicana 400 Presented by Meijer  *final race results*

| Fin. Pos. | Start Pos. | Car No. | Driver | Team | Fin. Pos. | Start Pos. | Car No. | Driver | Team |
|---|---|---|---|---|---|---|---|---|---|
| 1 | 10 | 20 | Tony Stewart | Home Depot Chevrolet | 23 | 40 | 22 | Scott Wimmer | Caterpillar Dodge |
| 2 | 3 | 48 | Jimmie Johnson | Lowe's Chevrolet | 24 | 18 | 6 | Mark Martin | Viagra Ford |
| 3 | 29 | 88 | Dale Jarrett | UPS Ford | 25 | 34 | 4 | Jimmy Spencer | Wide Open Energy Drink Chevrolet |
| 4 | 1 | 24 | Jeff Gordon | DuPont Chevrolet | 26 | 42 | 45 | Kyle Petty | Georgia-Pacific/Brawny Dodge |
| 5 | 19 | 19 | Jeremy Mayfield | Dodge Dealers/UAW Dodge | 27 | 41 | 49 | Ken Schrader | Red Baron Dodge |
| 6 | 24 | 5 | Terry Labonte | Kellogg's Chevrolet | 28 | 38 | 43 | Jeff Green | Cheerios/Betty Crocker Dodge |
| 7 | 32 | 40 | Sterling Marlin | Coors Light Dodge | 29 | 16 | 10 | Scott Riggs | Valvoline Chevrolet |
| 8 | 9 | 01 | Joe Nemechek | USG Sheetrock Chevrolet | 30 | 15 | 77 | Brendan Gaughan | Jasper Eng. & Trans./Kodak Dodge |
| 9 | 39 | 15 | Michael Waltrip | NAPA Chevrolet | 31 | 7 | 80 | Mike Bliss | Slim Jim/Act II Chevrolet |
| 10 | 17 | 29 | Kevin Harvick | GM Goodwrench Chevrolet | 32 | 30 | 21 | Ricky Rudd | "Keep It Genuine" Ford |
| 11 | 20 | 2 | Rusty Wallace | Miller Lite Dodge | 33 | 6 | 99 | Jeff Burton | Comcast High-Speed Internet Ford |
| 12 | 26 | 17 | Matt Kenseth | DeWalt Power Tools Ford | 34 | 8 | 12 | Ryan Newman | Mobil 1/ALLTEL Dodge |
| 13 | 14 | 42 | Jamie McMurray | Texaco/Havoline Dodge | 35 | 21 | 97 | Kurt Busch | Sharpie Ford |
| 14 | 4 | 25 | Brian Vickers | GMAC Chevrolet | 36 | 2 | 9 | Kasey Kahne | Dodge Dealers/UAW Dodge |
| 15 | 12 | 41 | Casey Mears | Target Dodge | 37 | 36 | 30 | Dave Blaney | America Online Chevrolet |
| 16 | 31 | 1 | John Andretti | Kraft Food Chevrolet | 38 | 35 | 32 | Ricky Craven | Tide Chevrolet |
| 17 | 23 | 31 | Robby Gordon | Cingular Wireless Chevrolet | 39 | 43 | 50 | P.J. Jones | Arnold Development Co. Dodge |
| 18 | 11 | 18 | Bobby Labonte | Wellbutrin XL(tm) Chevrolet | 40 | 33 | 02 | Hermie Sadler | The FanZcar Chevrolet |
| 19 | 22 | 0 | Ward Burton | NetZero Hi-Speed Chevrolet | 41 | 28 | 09 | Bobby Hamilton Jr. | Miccosukee Resorts Dodge |
| 20 | 5 | 16 | Greg Biffle | National Guard Ford | 42 | 27 | 51 | Kevin Lepage | negotiationssolution.com Chevrolet |
| 21 | 13 | 38 | Elliott Sadler | M&M's Ford | 43 | 37 | 37 | Chad Blount | Carter Royal Dispos-all Dodge |
| 22 | 25 | 8 | Dale Earnhardt Jr. | Budweiser Chevrolet | | | | | |

# SIEMENS 300

*"I believe our chase for the championship started today ... I thought we had to apply pressure this week and get our 10 races going right now."*

— *Kurt Busch*

The competitors had a rare weekend off between the Tropicana 400 in Joliet, Ill., and the Siemens 300 at Loudon, N.H., and a rested Jimmie Johnson headed to New Hampshire first in points for the fourth consecutive race week. A second-place effort at Chicagoland Speedway upped his points total to 2,720 and also gave him a series-leading 13 top-five finishes in 18 starts. Included were victories at Darlington, S.C., Concord, N.C., and Pocono, Pa., which helped him gain a comfortable 105-point lead on second-place Dale Earnhardt Jr.

Although Little E remained at No. 2 in points for the fourth consecutive week, he continued to lose ground to Johnson. He'd lost 203 points in the previous five races, and complicating his situation were second-degree burns he received July 18 in an accident while practicing for a sports car race in Sonoma, Calif. Although Earnhardt was able to return home to North Carolina the day following the incident, he had Martin Truex Jr., driver of Earnhardt's NASCAR Busch Series car, on hand at New Hampshire to drive in relief if needed.

Following a fourth-place run in Chicago, Jeff Gordon headed to New Hampshire still third in the standings with 2,478 points, 137 in back of Earnhardt Jr. and 242 out of the lead. He entered the second half of the overall racing season with four top-five finishes (and as many Bud Pole Awards) in the last five races. Included were victories at Sonoma and Daytona Beach, his third and fourth wins of the year.

*Ricky Craven's battered Tide Chevrolet rolls toward pit road after one of two incidents that put a disappointing end to the New England native's day. Craven qualified a season-best 10th at his "home" track but was listed 38th at the finish.*

*(Above) This young fan is hoping his favorite driver can continue his winning ways from Chicagoland. Although Tony Stewart did not end up in victory lane at New Hampshire, he still managed to post his seventh top-five finish of the season.*

*(Above Right) Bobby Labonte carries a look of intensity as he prepares to continue a mid-season upward surge in the standings. All didn't go as planned, however; in his first race with new crew chief Brandon Thomas, Labonte was listed 17th in the finishing order and fell one spot to seventh in the points.*

*(Right) Elliott Sadler holds the inside position on Mark Martin (6), with Jeremy Mayfield (19) and Greg Biffle following his lead. All but Biffle, who suffered engine failure, finished among the 29 drivers who completed all 300 laps.*

Tony Stewart won big at Chicago and was hoping to ride the momentum of his first victory in 2004 into continued success at New Hampshire. Ranked fourth in points for the second consecutive week, the Joe Gibbs Racing driver found himself 327 markers behind leader Johnson and 85 in back of Gordon. A year ago at this point in the season, he was ranked eighth in the standings.

Defending series champion Matt Kenseth remained just one of four drivers to be ranked in the top 10 all year long and left the Chicago event still fifth in the standings, 399 out of the lead. Overall, the Roush Racing Ford driver had been ranked among the top 10 for 53 consecutive race weeks, the longest current streak in the series.

Although he had a mediocre finish in the

Tropicana 400, Bobby Labonte held onto sixth place in the standings. With 2,278 markers, he found himself 442 behind leader Johnson but just 43 in back of Kenseth. He headed to New Hampshire with a trio of top-10 finishes in his last five races and was now paired with interim crew chief Brandon Thomas, who had replaced Michael "Fatback" McSwain at that position.

NASCAR Busch Series regular Martin Truex Jr. (left) paced the Budweiser Chevrolet to the third-fastest lap in qualifying for his boss, Dale Earnhardt Jr. (lower left), who was suffering from injuries sustained in a sports-car event a week earlier. Earnhardt started the Siemens 300 and turned the wheel over to Truex during the first caution of the race.

(Below) Truex gets a quick indoctrination to the NASCAR NEXTEL Cup Series, backing the No. 8 Monte Carlo into the first-turn wall on lap 141 after contact with Ken Schrader. All in all, however, Truex had a respectable outing in his first appearance in the series and helped keep Earnhardt Jr. a comfortable second on the point ladder.

Although he finished 21st in Illinois, M&M's Ford driver Elliott Sadler advanced one place in points, from eighth to seventh. Arguably, he'd been one of the biggest surprises of the season's first half, winning at Texas and being one of just four drivers to be ranked among the top 10 all year long. Sadler was now just 26 points behind Labonte but sat 468 in arrears of Johnson.

Kevin Harvick's 10th-place showing in the Tropicana 400 paid off as he advanced two

(Right) Rusty Wallace was hoping for better than this after a top-10 effort in qualifying and what appeared to be a similar showing in the race. But Lady Luck did not smile on the Miller Lite driver and, with just six laps to go, an accidental nudge from Dale Jarrett sent Wallace into the fourth-turn fence.

(Below) Kurt Busch (97), Jeff Gordon (24) and Ryan Newman (12) hook up nose-to-tail in their late-race skirmish for victory. Busch, however, had the best package over the closing laps and the trio of drivers finished in this order, with Busch taking his second win of the year.

spots in points, from 10th to eighth. The GM Goodwrench Chevrolet pilot found himself only 23 points in back of Sadler, but with 2,229 markers, he was 491 behind the leader. Going into New Hampshire, he'd been running at the finish of 57 consecutive races, the longest streak since the advent of the "modern era," which began in 1972.

Kurt Busch came to New Hampshire determined to turn things around with his Roush Racing Ford team. Perhaps the reason he was ready to do so well was that he'd run into problems at Chicagoland Speedway, where he finished 35th and dropped two places in points, from seventh to ninth, 509 behind Johnson. He'd remained in the top 10 for 17 of the season's 18 weeks but had experienced a steady slide since being ranked No. 1 following the race at Texas in April.

An accident at Chicagoland didn't help Ryan Newman, either. He exited the track 10th in the standings with 2,173 points after going into the event ranked ninth. He was looking to get back on track, as three drivers (Jeremy Mayfield, Dale Jarrett and Jamie McMurray) had all closed to within 105 points of his position.

In Bud Pole qualifying, Newman was the last of 46 drivers to make a timed run, and although he didn't beat his own track record of 133.357 mph, he did go fast enough to capture the No. 1 starting spot for the Siemens 300.

His time and speed of 28.776 seconds at 132.360 mph was sufficient to give him his fourth pole of the year, 22nd of his career and his third in five races at New Hampshire.

Johnson was second quickest with an effort of 28.858 seconds at 131.984 mph, while Truex Jr., subbing for a recovering Earnhardt Jr., was a surprising third quickest with a lap speed of 131.660 mph. Michael Waltrip (131.488) took spot No. 4 and McMurray (131.442) was fifth. Qualifying sixth through 10th were Kasey Kahne, Mayfield, Rusty Wallace, Stewart and Ricky Craven.

Driving the No. 97 IRWIN Ford, Busch steered clear of incidents that caused eight of 12 caution-flag periods and almost breezed his way to winning the Siemens 300. He led twice for 110 laps, one of just three drivers to lead the 19th race of the season, and beat runner-up

Jeff Gordon's Hendrick Motorsports Chevrolet to the checkered flag by 0.607 second.

"My car was just really good on long runs. Once we got to the front, we were able to run real strong in clean air," Busch said.

In the event's latter stages, Gordon tried everything he could think of to overcome Busch, culminating in a late-race challenge following the last interruption with three laps left, but he still came up short.

Newman, who finished third in a Penske Racing Dodge, was in front two times for 187 circuits to take the lap-leader bonus for the race. Kenseth and Stewart finished fourth and fifth, while Jimmy Spencer, the only other driver to lead a lap, ended up 23rd in the Morgan-McClure Motorsports Chevrolet.

Earnhardt Jr. wound up running only 61 laps before turning his car over to Truex Jr. during the first caution period. He was credited with 31st place at the end of the event, two laps off the winner's pace but good enough to remain second in the point standings.

In victory lane after his second NASCAR NEXTEL Cup Series victory of the year, Busch sounded remarkably like an office-seeker who had just won a decisive political primary and was now ready to tackle the opposite party's candidate and go for the "real" win in the general election.

"I believe our chase for the championship started today," Busch said. "I thought we had to apply pressure this week and get our 10 races going right now. It started with the first

The IRWIN Industrial Tools Ford and the entire No. 97 Roush Racing team grace New Hampshire's victory lane. The win vaulted Busch from ninth to sixth in the point standings and would become the stage from which the team would attempt to launch a championship challenge.

Loudon instead of the second because of our (sixth-place) points position. It was time to go."

Busch, who moved up several spots in the standings, said he was now ready to return to the flat, one-mile track in September to contest the first of 10 events in the Chase for the NASCAR NEXTEL Cup, which would ultimately determine who would be the 2004 champion.

Busch completed the race in 3 hours, 14 minutes and 36 seconds at an average speed of 97.862 mph and won $227,225.

## Siemens 300 *final race results*

| Fin. Pos. | Start Pos. | Car No. | Driver | Team |
|---|---|---|---|---|
| 1 | 32 | 97 | Kurt Busch | IRWIN Industrial Tools Ford |
| 2 | 24 | 24 | Jeff Gordon | DuPont Chevrolet |
| 3 | 1 | 12 | Ryan Newman | ALLTEL Dodge |
| 4 | 31 | 17 | Matt Kenseth | Smirnoff Ice/DeWalt Ford |
| 5 | 9 | 20 | Tony Stewart | Home Depot Chevrolet |
| 6 | 4 | 15 | Michael Waltrip | NAPA Chevrolet |
| 7 | 5 | 42 | Jamie McMurray | Texaco/Havoline Dodge |
| 8 | 6 | 9 | Kasey Kahne | Dodge Dealers/UAW Dodge |
| 9 | 25 | 88 | Dale Jarrett | UPS Ford |
| 10 | 7 | 19 | Jeremy Mayfield | Dodge Dealers/UAW Dodge |
| 11 | 2 | 48 | Jimmie Johnson | Lowe's Chevrolet |
| 12 | 27 | 99 | Jeff Burton | Roush Racing Ford |
| 13 | 19 | 29 | Kevin Harvick | GM Goodwrench Chevrolet |
| 14 | 26 | 6 | Mark Martin | Viagra Ford |
| 15 | 13 | 38 | Elliott Sadler | M&M's Ford |
| 16 | 11 | 5 | Terry Labonte | Kellogg's Chevrolet |
| 17 | 20 | 18 | Bobby Labonte | Interstate Batteries Chevrolet |
| 18 | 38 | 22 | Scott Wimmer | Caterpillar Dodge |
| 19 | 28 | 09 | Bobby Hamilton Jr. | Miccosukee Dodge |
| 20 | 18 | 01 | Joe Nemechek | U.S. Army Chevrolet |
| 21 | 37 | 40 | Sterling Marlin | Coors Light Dodge |
| 22 | 29 | 77 | Brendan Gaughan | Kodak/Jasper Eng. & Trans. Dodge |
| 23 | 35 | 4 | Jimmy Spencer | Morgan-McClure Motorsports Chevrolet |
| 24 | 30 | 43 | Jeff Green | Cheerios/Betty Crocker Dodge |
| 25 | 21 | 31 | Robby Gordon | Cingular Wireless Chevrolet |
| 26 | 22 | 41 | Casey Mears | Target Dodge |
| 27 | 39 | 45 | Kyle Petty | Georgia-Pacific/Brawny Dodge |
| 28 | 15 | 10 | Scott Riggs | Valvoline Chevrolet |
| 29 | 12 | 0 | Ward Burton | NetZero Hi-Speed Chevrolet |
| 30 | 8 | 2 | Rusty Wallace | Miller Lite Dodge |
| 31 | 3 | 8 | Dale Earnhardt Jr. | Budweiser Chevrolet |
| 32 | 36 | 50 | Mike Wallace | LesCare Kitchens Dodge |
| 33 | 14 | 30 | Dave Blaney | America Online Chevrolet |
| 34 | 23 | 25 | Brian Vickers | GMAC Chevrolet |
| 35 | 16 | 16 | Greg Biffle | National Guard/Subway Ford |
| 36 | 42 | 72 | Ted Christopher | Freddie B's Ford |
| 37 | 17 | 49 | Ken Schrader | Schwan's Home Service Dodge |
| 38 | 10 | 32 | Ricky Craven | Tide Chevrolet |
| 39 | 34 | 21 | Ricky Rudd | Motorcraft Ford |
| 40 | 41 | 89 | Morgan Shepherd | Racing with Jesus/Red Line Oil Dodge |
| 41 | 40 | 98 | Todd Bodine | Lucas Oil Ford |
| 42 | 33 | 46 | Carl Long | Howes Lubricator Dodge |
| 43 | 43 | 02 | Hermie Sadler | The FanZcar Chevrolet |

# PENNSYLVANIA 500

## POCONO RACEWAY
### AUGUST 1, 2004

*"That race car was incredible ... We're definitely bringing this trophy home in memory of Papa Joe."*
— Jimmie Johnson

**M**ark Martin could be the NASCAR NEXTEL Cup Series' ultimate realist. Even after taking the lead about two-thirds of the way through the Pocono 500, he about admitted to himself that he wouldn't win his first race on the 2.5-mile triangle nestled in the scenic Pennsylvania resort area, a track on which he had already posted five runner-up results over his career.

Jimmy Johnson was just too strong. The driver of Hendrick Motorsports' No. 48 Lowe's Chevrolet took the lead for the final time on lap 163 and led the remaining 38 circuits on his way to the checkered flag. It was no contest.

Johnson had arrived at Pocono for the year's 20th race with an already comfortable lead in the point standings. With 2,850 markers, he was 165 in front of second-place pointsman Dale Earnhardt Jr. He'd brought his run of five consecutive top-five finishes to an end with an 11th place in the Siemens 300 at Loudon, N.H., the week before but was still safely in pursuit of the final 10-race Chase for the NASCAR NEXTEL Cup. He headed to Pocono No. 1 in points for the fifth consecutive week.

Earnhardt Jr. was still recovering from injuries he sustained in a non-NASCAR event in California the week before New Hampshire. There, he ran just 61 laps before turning his Budweiser Chevrolet over to relief driver Martin Truex Jr., who finished 31st. While Junior remained No. 2 in points for the fifth straight week, he had lost more ground to Johnson.

*The Lowe's Chevrolet flashes across the start/finish line at Pocono Raceway in front of the field, as it did for most of the 500-mile event. Driver Jimmie Johnson assumed command of the race for the first time on lap 32 and went on to pace the field a total of six times, leading 62 percent of the laps on the way to his fourth win of the season.*

(Above) Joe Nemechek stands ready during pre-race ceremonies after putting the U.S. Army Chevrolet on the front row for the start of the race. Nemechek jumped ahead of pole-winner Casey Mears when the green flag waved and led the first 31 laps.

(Top Right) Fans enjoy the race from atop their RVs and campers in Pocono's infield, where they enjoy a great view of the action on the spacious 2.5-mile triangular layout.

(Right) Michael Waltrip gets a happy good-luck hug from daughter Margaret before going to work in the season's 20th event. Unfortunately, his luck didn't hold out as the engine in the NAPA Chevrolet let go midway through the race.

(Bottom Right) Always a favorite with fans, Kyle Petty takes time to sign autographs outside the Pocono garage, which is named in honor of Kyle's son, Adam.

With a runner-up performance in New Hampshire, Jeff Gordon remained third in the standings for the third week in a row and headed to Pennsylvania with 2,648 points, which put him just 37 behind Earnhardt Jr. and 202 in arrears of teammate Johnson. The run in Loudon was his fourth consecutive top-five finish and fifth in the previous six events.

Riding the momentum of a fifth-place finish in the Pepsi 400 at Daytona and a victory in the Tropicana 400 at Chicagoland, Tony Stewart finished fifth at New Hampshire, thus remaining fourth in points for the third consecutive week. The run at Loudon was his seventh top-five finish of the year and he left the track 100 points behind Gordon and 302 out of the lead.

With just one top-10 finish in his previous six races, defending series champion Matt Kenseth bounced back with a fourth-place run at Loudon and held on to fifth place in points going into Pocono. It was his best effort since finishing third at Charlotte in late May and marked his seventh top-five finish of the year. Although he was 369 points behind Johnson, he trailed Stewart by only 67 and remained just one of four drivers to be ranked in the top 10 all year long.

Kenseth's Roush Racing teammate, Kurt Busch, outdistanced Gordon by 0.607 second in the Siemens 300 for his second victory of the

season and jumped three spots in points, from ninth to sixth. It was a huge boost as far as the "chase" for the title was concerned, and Busch left victory lane with 2,396 points, just 85 behind Kenseth but 454 in arrears of the leader. It was also his highest points ranking since Dover, Del., six races ago.

(Left) Casey Mears holds his Target Dodge on the low side with Chevrolet-driving Robby Gordon (31) looking to gain momentum on the outside. Mears won his first career Bud Pole Award for this event with a lap at nearly 172 miles per hour, while Gordon started 22nd and raced to seventh at the finish.

(Below) Kasey Kahne waits for a set of fresh Goodyears and a load of fuel before heading back into action. Kahne, the Raybestos Rookie of the Year point leader, scored his sixth top-three finish of the season in third.

Bobby Labonte finished 17th at New Hampshire and dropped a spot in points, from sixth to seventh. It marked the third time in the last four races the Chevrolet driver had been unable to crack the top 15, but he extended his run of consecutive weeks in the top 10 in points to 11. Also, he was just six points behind Busch but had to watch Ford-driving Elliott Sadler, who was just 20 markers behind him.

Sadler, because of a 15th-place finish in New Hampshire, also lost a position in points, dropping from seventh to eighth. But the run at Loudon ended a two-race stretch of finishing

(Above) Mark Martin (6) gets some heat from rookie Brendan Gaughan (77) while rounding Pocono's seeping third turn. Martin was better than 41 other cars in this race, but had to face the realization that no one had an answer for Jimmie Johnson.

(Right) Elliott Sadler's M&M's mates swarm into action on the second of nine cautions during the day. Sadler was able to break a string of three straight finishes outside the top 10 and jump up two positions to sixth in the championship standings.

were 11th through 13th in the standings, all within 134 points of the ALLTEL Dodge driver.

Casey Mears' time and speed of 52.411 seconds at 171.720 mph earned him his first Bud Pole in 56 starts and gave his career a needed boost. Team owner Chip Ganassi made it clear that he expected improvements in 2004, and the 26-year-old driver delivered at Pocono.

"We knew we were going to struggle last year. We just didn't know it was going to be that bad," Mears said. "It was apparent by the end (of 2003) that we needed to get our ducks in a row."

Chevrolet driver Joe Nemechek, a tad slower than Mears at 171.654 mph, took the No. 2 spot on the starting grid. Busch (171.540 mph), Sterling Marlin (171.256) and Sadler (171.168) were third through fifth quickest, while Brian Vickers, McMurray, Stewart, Mayfield and Brendan Gaughan rounded out the top 10 qualifiers.

In the race, Mears led once for 17 laps but wasn't able to capitalize on his start from the pole and finished 18th. Johnson, on the other hand, took the lead for the first time on lap 32 and began to rule the day. He went to the front for the final time after pitting under the seventh of nine caution flags and went on to leave Martin a distant 2.38 seconds behind at the finish.

outside the top 20, and he remained as one of the four drivers to be ranked 10th or better in points for the entire season.

The news was much the same for RCR Chevrolet driver Kevin Harvick. He finished 13th at New Hampshire and dropped from eighth to ninth in points. With 2,370 to his credit, he left Loudon trailing the leader by 480 points but was only 17 behind Sadler.

Ryan Newman, who had finished 10th or better in just one of the past seven races, rebounded with a third-place showing at Loudon. It was good enough for him to keep the 10th-place spot in points, with 2,348 in the books. Still, Newman couldn't relax, as Jeremy Mayfield, Dale Jarrett and Jamie McMurray

"I was pretty sure that the '48' was going to be up there pretty soon," said Martin, who led laps 128-138 before Johnson regained the point for the fourth time in the event. "I didn't even run as hard as I could because I knew he was going to get there (and) we needed to save fuel.

"I could have led several more laps had I tried to stretch it out while he was back in traffic, but ... it would just have delayed the inevitable."

Johnson, of course, was elated — and for good reason. Not only did his fourth victory of the year solidify his lead in the points, but he also accomplished the "Pocono sweep" for 2004, becoming the first driver to win both Pocono events in the same season since Bobby Labonte did it in 1999.

"That race car was incredible," said Johnson, who led a total of six times for 124 laps. "I knew by eight laps in the car was going to be strong. I could also tell that whoever was going to win the race would have to be on top of their car, adjusting, because in a five-lap swing the car would really change.

"We're definitely bringing this trophy home in memory of 'Papa Joe,'" Johnson said referring to Joseph R. Hendrick, the father of team owner Rick Hendrick, who passed away in July at age 84. Loved and respected by many, the elder Hendrick also was listed as the owner of rookie driver Brian Vickers' No. 25 Chevrolet.

Kasey Kahne finished third behind Martin, with Greg Biffle fourth ahead of Jeff Gordon and Terry Labonte, who made it an especially

strong day for Hendrick Motorsports by placing three drivers in the top six positions. Robby Gordon, Kenseth, Mayfield and Sadler rounded out the top 10 finishers.

Johnson completed the event in 3 hours, 57 minutes and 35 seconds at an average speed of 126.271 mph and won $276,950.

*Jeremy Mayfield (19) and Greg Biffle try to chase down hot-running Jimmie Johnson and his Lowe's Monte Carlo. Johnson was having none of it, however, and left Mayfield, a two-time Pocono winner, to settle for ninth place, while Biffle was able to finish fourth in his first top-five effort of the season.*

## Pennsylvania 500 *final race results*

| Fin. Pos. | Start Pos. | Car No. | Driver | Team |
|---|---|---|---|---|
| 1 | 14 | 48 | Jimmie Johnson | Lowe's Chevrolet |
| 2 | 21 | 6 | Mark Martin | Viagra Ford |
| 3 | 20 | 9 | Kasey Kahne | Dodge Dealers/UAW Dodge |
| 4 | 19 | 16 | Greg Biffle | National Guard Ford |
| 5 | 13 | 24 | Jeff Gordon | DuPont Chevrolet |
| 6 | 29 | 5 | Terry Labonte | Kellogg's/Team USA Chevrolet |
| 7 | 22 | 31 | Robby Gordon | Cingular Wireless Chevrolet |
| 8 | 15 | 17 | Matt Kenseth | DeWalt Power Tools Ford |
| 9 | 9 | 19 | Jeremy Mayfield | Dodge Dealers/UAW Dodge |
| 10 | 5 | 38 | Elliott Sadler | M&M's Ford |
| 11 | 28 | 22 | Scott Wimmer | Caterpillar Dodge |
| 12 | 33 | 21 | Ricky Rudd | "Keep It Genuine" Ford |
| 13 | 30 | 12 | Ryan Newman | ALLTEL Dodge |
| 14 | 6 | 25 | Brian Vickers | GMAC Chevrolet |
| 15 | 4 | 40 | Sterling Marlin | Aspen Edge Dodge |
| 16 | 2 | 01 | Joe Nemechek | U.S. Army Chevrolet |
| 17 | 12 | 2 | Rusty Wallace | Miller Lite Dodge |
| 18 | 1 | 41 | Casey Mears | Target Dodge |
| 19 | 25 | 45 | Kyle Petty | Georgia-Pacific/Brawny Dodge |
| 20 | 35 | 32 | Ricky Craven | Tide Chevrolet |
| 21 | 39 | 49 | Ken Schrader | Schwan's Home Service Dodge |
| 22 | 26 | 10 | Scott Riggs | Valvoline Chevrolet |
| 23 | 36 | 4 | Jimmy Spencer | Morgan-McClure Motorsports Chevrolet |
| 24 | 24 | 88 | Dale Jarrett | UPS Ford |
| 25 | 16 | 8 | Dale Earnhardt Jr. | Budweiser Chevrolet |
| 26 | 3 | 97 | Kurt Busch | IRWIN Industrial Tools Ford |
| 27 | 31 | 30 | Dave Blaney | America Online Chevrolet |
| 28 | 10 | 77 | Brendan Gaughan | Kodak/Jasper Eng. & Trans. Dodge |
| 29 | 17 | 18 | Bobby Labonte | Interstate Batteries Chevrolet |
| 30 | 7 | 42 | Jamie McMurray | Texaco/Havoline Dodge |
| 31 | 27 | 0 | Ward Burton | NetZero Hi-Speed Chevrolet |
| 32 | 18 | 29 | Kevin Harvick | GM Goodwrench Chevrolet |
| 33 | 32 | 43 | Jeff Green | Cheerios/Betty Crocker Dodge |
| 34 | 23 | 99 | Jeff Burton | Roush Racing Ford |
| 35 | 8 | 20 | Tony Stewart | Home Depot Chevrolet |
| 36 | 11 | 15 | Michael Waltrip | NAPA Chevrolet |
| 37 | 40 | 89 | Morgan Shepherd | Racing with Jesus/Red Line Oil Dodge |
| 38 | 37 | 98 | Todd Bodine | Lucas Oil Ford |
| 39 | 43 | 80 | Carl Long | Commercial Truck and Trailer Ford |
| 40 | 42 | 02 | Jason Jarrett | The FanZcar Chevrolet |
| 41 | 41 | 72 | Kirk Shelmerdine | Freddie B's Ford |
| 42 | 38 | 13 | Greg Sacks | ARC Dehooker/Vita Coco Dodge |
| 43 | 34 | 50 | P.J. Jones | Arnold Development Co. Dodge |

# BRICKYARD 400

*"It feels amazing. I can't compare four (victories) in a stock car to what my heroes like Rick Mears and A.J. Foyt did here."*

— *Jeff Gordon*

The 11th annual Brickyard 400 NASCAR NEXTEL Cup Series race just might go into the record book as one of the most memorable events run at the historic oval located in Speedway, Ind.

The victor, Jeff Gordon, made the race one to remember simply because he became the first driver to win it a record four times. The driver of Hendrick Motorsports' No. 24 DuPont Chevrolet captured the Inaugural Brickyard 400 in 1994 and followed that up with wins in 1998 and 2001.

Overall, Gordon joined Indianapolis 500 champions A.J. Foyt, Rick Mears and Al Unser Sr. as the only four-time winners at the venerable track, which opened in 1909.

"It feels amazing. I can't compare four (victories) in a stock car to what my heroes like Rick Mears and A.J. Foyt did here," Gordon said. "To win at this speedway, I can't even describe the feeling right now."

Going into the race, points leader Jimmie Johnson found himself firmly in the catbird's seat. A victory in the previous week's Pocono 500, his fourth of the year and second straight at Pocono, put the Lowe's Chevrolet driver solidly out front with 3,040 points. The win was his sixth top-five performance in his last seven starts, keeping him in the lead for the sixth consecutive week. Also, his 232-point edge on No. 2-ranked Jeff Gordon was the largest spread of the year to date.

With an event record 13 yellow flags thrown during the race, Indianapolis Motor Speedway's relatively narrow pit road was a very busy — and very hectic — place during the 11th running of the Brickyard 400.

Gordon, Johnson's teammate, mentor and car co-owner, ended up finishing fifth at Pocono, and that bumped him up a spot in points from third to second. It was his highest ranking of the season and marked the 11th time in the past 12 race weeks he'd been fifth or better in the standings. Gordon also moved Dale Earnhardt Jr. from second in the standings to third and had 35 points on Earnhardt going into Indy.

Earnhardt Jr. headed to Indy still recovering from burns he received in a sports car event three weeks earlier in California. He started the Pocono race but had to exit his No. 8 Budweiser Chevrolet after running 51 laps. He turned the car over to relief driver John Andretti, who managed a 25th-place finish. The result cost Earnhardt one place in the point standings, and he left Pocono with 2,773 markers, 267 out of the lead.

Matt Kenseth finished eighth at Pocono, scoring his 12th top-10 effort of the year and second in a row, and subsequently advanced one position in points to fourth after being fifth for the last three weeks. With 2,623 points, the DeWalt Tools Ford driver was 417 out of the lead, 150 behind Earnhardt Jr. but just 17 in front of Tony Stewart.

*Ricky Rudd (21) and Bobby Labonte (18), both former winners of this event, hug the inside line while paired off with Jason Leffler (60) and Ricky Craven (32) in the opening laps of the race. Labonte had to start in the back of the field due to an engine change but, with a 15th-place finish, still managed to pick up one important position in the point standings.*

(Above Left) Track officials replace one of the foam sections that are part of the SAFER energy-absorbing barriers installed at Indianapolis prior to this year's running of the Brickyard 400.

(Above) Casey Mears added another line to the Indianapolis record book under the Mears name with his track-record run of 186.293 mph, capturing his second career and second consecutive Bud Pole. Offering congratulations is team owner Chip Ganassi (left), who also fielded cars for Indianapolis 500 pole winners in 1993 and 2002.

(Left) Tony Stewart's Chevrolet leads the side-by-side Dodge duo of Kasey Kahne (9) and Casey Mears, followed by the Fords of Kurt Busch (97) and Dale Jarrett (88). Stewart overcame an early-race spin and a somewhat ill-handling car to gain a hard-fought fifth place at the finish.

Stewart went into Pocono fourth in points, but an accident in his No. 20 Home Depot Chevrolet and the 35th-place result, his worst of the year, saw him drop from fourth to fifth in the standings after three straight weeks at No. 4. The incident also ended a run of consecutive top-five finishes at three and dropped Stewart to 434 points behind the leader.

Elliott Sadler rallied at Pocono to finish 10th and jumped two places in points from eighth to sixth, tying Ryan Newman for the largest gain in the top 10 for the week. He headed into Indy with 2,504 points, 536 behind Johnson and 102 in back of Stewart with just six races left to determine the participants in the 10-race Chase for the NASCAR NEXTEL Cup.

Coming off a win in New Hampshire, Roush Racing's Kurt Busch ended up 26th at Pocono because of a transmission problem and fell from sixth to seventh in points. Yet, the event marked Busch's 19th consecutive week among the top 10 and put him in the middle of an interesting battle among positions sixth through 10. With 2,481 points, he was 23 behind Sadler but just 61 in front of 10th-ranked Kevin Harvick.

Ryan Newman finished 13th at Pocono, but that was good enough to see him advance to eighth in points from 10th. It marked Newman's fifth top-15 finish in the last six races. With 2,472 markers, he was just 32 out of sixth place but had to keep an eye on ninth-place Bobby Labonte, who was only six points behind him.

(Top) Matt Kenseth (17) blasts away from his pit box sandwiched between Roush teammates Mark Martin (6) and Kurt Busch (97). Although Busch fared best of the three with a 10th-place finish, Greg Biffle (top right) led all five Roush teams with a strong sixth place in the finishing order after starting back in 35th.

(Above) Kasey Kahne (9) takes on Brian Vickers down Indy's cavernous frontstretch in a battle of rookies. Kahne worked his way to third, while Vickers, who was having a strong run, suffered damage in an accident with five laps to go and fell to 29th.

(Right) Jeff Gordon sails through the corner in clean air ahead of (in order) Elliott Sadler, Dale Jarrett, Matt Kenseth and Robby Gordon. Although Sadler proved to be Gordon's toughest competition, Jarrett eventually got around him to finish second, moving his Robert Yates teammate back to third.

Labonte went into Pocono seventh in points, but because of a late-race accident, he finished 29th and exited the track ninth in the running. Still, with 2,466 points, it marked his 12th consecutive race week in the top 10, although it was his lowest spot in the standings since the early-May event at Fontana, Calif.

Going into the Brickyard 400, Harvick had to be just a bit on edge. His GM Goodwrench Chevrolet suffered a blown engine at Pocono, and a 32nd-place finish dropped Harvick from ninth in points to 10th. The misfortune stopped his modern-era record for the most consecutive races running at the finish at 58. Now with 2,420 points, he was just 40 in front of 11th-running Jeremy Mayfield, 69 ahead of 12th-ranked Kasey Kahne and 89 up on 13th-place pointsman Mark Martin.

In Bud Pole qualifying for the Brickyard 400, Casey Mears, the nephew of Rick Mears, smashed the old track record of 184.343 mph set by Harvick a year ago. Mears, in the No. 41 Target Dodge, blistered

the track with a time and speed of 48.311 seconds at 186.293 mph, leading a pack of six drivers who eclipsed Harvick's mark.

Because he won the pole for the previous event at Pocono, Mears also became the first driver to post his first two career No. 1 starts in consecutive races since the late Billy Wade did it in 1964.

"It feels good to (proudly) hold up the name Mears," the sophomore driver said. "This place has created a lot of good fortunes for my family. It's huge."

Ward Burton took the second starting spot in the NetZero Chevrolet with a clocking of 48.546 seconds at 185.391 mph. Sadler (185.162 mph), Joe Nemechek (184.976 mph), Earnhardt Jr. (184.968 mph) and Brian Vickers (184.665 mph) completed the record-breaking sextet. Rounding out the top 10 qualifiers were Newman, Jamie McMurray, Johnson and Sterling Marlin, while Jeff Gordon took the 11th starting spot.

Gordon didn't let that hinder him, though. He took the lead for the first time on lap 27 when he passed Sadler and ended up leading four times for 124 of the event's 161 laps. He was so dominant that he was leading upon completion of nine of the 13 caution periods.

Gordon beat Robert Yates Racing Ford driver Dale Jarrett, winner of this event in 1996 and 1999, to the finish line under caution. Jarrett's teammate, Sadler, was third, Kasey Kahne was fourth in a Dodge, and Tony Stewart was fifth in a Chevrolet.

Several things made the race a bit offbeat. One, it was the first event where NASCAR employed the new green-white-checkered-flag rule to ensure that it wouldn't end under caution. At 161 laps, it did anyway, as the final yellow flag was displayed on the last lap for three drivers whose cars were slowed by flat tires.

A record 13 yellow flags for 47 laps resulted in an average speed of 115.037 mph, making it the slowest Brickyard 400 ever run. Also, a record 16 drivers failed to finish the event.

Gordon may have had a little bit of luck on his side as well. Eighteen laps from the finish, his car hit a piece of debris that damaged the Chevrolet's front air dam. Still, he persevered and won $518,053 for a 3-hour-29-minute-56-second drive.

*Jeff Gordon salutes the huge crowd on hand at Indianapolis after capturing his record fourth Brickyard 400 crown. Gordon was simply the dominant driver in this race, leading four times for 124 of 160 laps, including the final 34.*

## Brickyard 400 *final race results*

| Fin. Pos. | Start Pos. | Car No. | Driver | Team | Fin. Pos. | Start Pos. | Car No. | Driver | Team |
|---|---|---|---|---|---|---|---|---|---|
| 1 | 11 | 24 | Jeff Gordon | DuPont Chevrolet | 23 | 26 | 45 | Kyle Petty | Georgia-Pacific/Brawny Dodge |
| 2 | 17 | 88 | Dale Jarrett | UPS Ford | 24 | 37 | 32 | Ricky Craven | Tide Chevrolet |
| 3 | 3 | 38 | Elliott Sadler | M&M's Ford | 25 | 16 | 6 | Mark Martin | Viagra Ford |
| 4 | 12 | 9 | Kasey Kahne | Dodge Dealers/UAW Dodge | 26 | 1 | 41 | Casey Mears | Target Dodge |
| 5 | 24 | 20 | Tony Stewart | Home Depot Chevrolet | 27 | 5 | 8 | Dale Earnhardt Jr. | Budweiser Chevrolet |
| 6 | 35 | 16 | Greg Biffle | National Guard Ford | 28 | 40 | 21 | Ricky Rudd | "Keep It Genuine" Ford |
| 7 | 8 | 42 | Jamie McMurray | Texaco/Havoline Dodge | 29 | 6 | 25 | Brian Vickers | GMAC Chevrolet |
| 8 | 32 | 29 | Kevin Harvick | GM Goodwrench Chevrolet | 30 | 36 | 23 | Tony Raines | Bill Davis Racing Dodge |
| 9 | 18 | 91 | Bill Elliott | Visteon Dodge | 31 | 7 | 12 | Ryan Newman | ALLTEL Dodge |
| 10 | 15 | 97 | Kurt Busch | Sharpie Ford | 32 | 34 | 22 | Scott Wimmer | Caterpillar Dodge |
| 11 | 13 | 19 | Jeremy Mayfield | Dodge Dealers/UAW Dodge | 33 | 10 | 40 | Sterling Marlin | Coors Light Dodge |
| 12 | 19 | 99 | Jeff Burton | Roush Racing Ford | 34 | 22 | 00 | Kenny Wallace | Aaron's Chevrolet |
| 13 | 29 | 2 | Rusty Wallace | Miller Lite Dodge | 35 | 30 | 77 | Brendan Gaughan | Jasper Eng. & Trans./Kodak Dodge |
| 14 | 14 | 43 | Jeff Green | General Mills/Boxtops for Education Dodge | 36 | 9 | 48 | Jimmie Johnson | Lowe's Chevrolet |
| 15 | 39 | 18 | Bobby Labonte | Interstate Batteries Chevrolet | 37 | 27 | 10 | Scott Riggs | Valvoline Chevrolet |
| 16 | 23 | 17 | Matt Kenseth | Smirnoff Ice/DeWalt Ford | 38 | 21 | 5 | Terry Labonte | Kellogg's/Delphi Chevrolet |
| 17 | 4 | 01 | Joe Nemechek | U.S. Army Chevrolet | 39 | 2 | 0 | Ward Burton | NetZero Hi-Speed Chevrolet |
| 18 | 31 | 49 | Ken Schrader | Schwan's Home Service Dodge | 40 | 43 | 98 | Derrike Cope | America's Most Wanted Ford |
| 19 | 33 | 4 | Jimmy Spencer | Featherlite Trailers Chevrolet | 41 | 41 | 50 | Todd Bodine | Arnold Development Co. Dodge |
| 20 | 28 | 15 | Michael Waltrip | NAPA Chevrolet | 42 | 42 | 09 | Scott Pruett | Miccosukee Resorts Dodge |
| 21 | 38 | 30 | Dave Blaney | America Online Chevrolet | 43 | 25 | 60 | Jason Leffler | Haas Automation Chevrolet |
| 22 | 20 | 31 | Robby Gordon | Cingular Wireless Chevrolet | | | | | |

# SIRIUS AT THE GLEN

*"I don't know how I got to (the winner's circle)."*

— *Tony Stewart*

With just five events left before the crucial start of the 10-race Chase for the NASCAR NEXTEL Cup, points leader Jimmie Johnson headed to Watkins Glen hoping to atone for a damaging 36th-place showing in the previous week's Brickyard 400 at Indianapolis. The Lowe's Chevrolet driver went to Indy 232 points ahead of Jeff Gordon and left with 3,095 markers, or just 97 more than his Hendrick Motorsports teammate. Though it was disappointing for Johnson, it marked the seventh consecutive week he'd been the leader.

Gordon, on the other hand, continued his recent surge with a fourth Brickyard 400 victory. It was his sixth consecutive top-five finish, a stretch that included three of his series-leading five wins. Combined with Johnson's poor showing, Gordon's success allowed him to gain 135 points at Indy alone.

Dale Earnhardt Jr. remained third in the standings for the second consecutive week, 133 points behind Gordon and 240 out of the lead. His 27th place in the Brickyard 400 marked the fourth consecutive race he'd finished outside the top 20, as he continued to recover from his injuries. Earnhardt, however, was able to go the distance at Indianapolis, not requiring relief as he had in the previous two events.

Tony Stewart went into Indy fifth in points and, with a fifth-place showing in the Brickyard 400, emerged in fourth. It was his fourth top-five finish in the last five events, and with 2,761 points, he was 334 behind Johnson and just 94 in back of Earnhardt Jr.

*Sterling Marlin's Coors Light Dodge gets turned around with some help from Greg Biffle (16) in Watkins Glen's first turn, which brought out the second of five cautions 17 laps into the race. Later, both drivers would have to retire to the garage with engine problems.*

(Right) Raybestos Rookie of the Year contenders Brendan Gaughan (left) and Scott Riggs look cheerful before starting the Sirius at The Glen. Gaughan ran well and was able to lead seven laps at the two-thirds mark in the race, but his Kodak Dodge succumbed to transmission failure with 15 laps remaining.

(Below) Ron Fellows (1) paces Scott Riggs (10) and a pack of challengers in his march through the field. Fellows, driving a Chevrolet for DEI, had to start at the back of the field after qualifying was cancelled due to weather, and proceeded to improve 41 positions over the 90-lap event to finish second in an outstanding effort.

Stewart, however, had to keep an eye on Ford-driving Matt Kenseth. Although the defending champion dropped a spot in points after his 16th-place finish at Indy, he was just 23 behind Stewart and remained among the top five in the standings for the 20th consecutive week. He also stayed among a group of four drivers to be ranked in the top 10 all year long and had been 10th or better for 56 consecutive race weeks.

Robert Yates Racing Ford driver Elliott Sadler finished third at Indy in his best showing since winning at Texas in early April and held onto sixth place on the point ladder. He headed to Watkins Glen with 2,674 points, 421 out of the lead and only 64 in arrears of Kenseth. He was also one of the four drivers to be ranked 10th or better all year long.

Due in part to a finish of 10th at Indianapolis, Roush Racing's Kurt Busch held onto seventh place in points for the second straight week. Busch headed to The Glen with 2,615 points, 480 behind Johnson and 59 less than Sadler. The Indy run was Busch's third top-10 showing in the last five races and ninth of the season.

Interstate Batteries Chevrolet-driving Bobby Labonte finished a middling 15th at the Brickyard but advanced a spot in points, from ninth to eighth. Although it was just his second top-15 finish in the last six events, with 2,584 points he closed to 31 behind Busch but had the drivers ranked 9-12 all within 74 points of his position.

Kevin Harvick brought the No. 29 GM Goodwrench Chevrolet home eighth at Indy and advanced from 10th to ninth in standings as a result. The Brickyard 400 marked just his second top-10 performance in the previous eight races and his best effort since finishing third at Talladega, Ala., in April. Although he was 533 points behind Johnson, he was just 22 in back of Labonte and 20 ahead of the 10th-place man, Ryan Newman.

Newman, who was involved in an accident at Indy, finished 31st and dropped two spots in the standings. Going into Watkins Glen, Newman had Kasey Kahne, Jeremy Mayfield and Dale Jarrett all challenging him for a berth in the Chase for the NASCAR NEXTEL Cup.

*(Above) Tony Stewart (20) fends off a challenge for the lead from four-time Watkins Glen winner Jeff Gordon (24), who swapped the lead with Stewart on three occasions before transmission woes rendered the DuPont Chevrolet a non-contender.*

*(Left) Jimmie Johnson puts the power to the pavement while charging through the uphill third turn. That power didn't last however, as a missed shift damaged the engine and sent the points leader to the garage after just 23 laps with his second straight DNF.*

*(Below Left) Ricky Rudd (21) climbs hard on the binders to keep from making matters worse for a spinning Scott Riggs. Rudd emerged from the incident relatively unscathed and continued his climb from a 29th-place start to eighth at the finish.*

(Above) Brendan Gaughan slides across the grass off turn 10 while Casey Mears continues on in the Target Dodge. Mears held the lead late in the race before Stewart regained it for the final time with 15 laps to go, and managed an impressive fourth place despite running out of fuel on the final lap.

(Above Right) Mark Martin, a three-time winner of this event, powers toward the backstretch on the way to a very solid third place, his second top-three finish in the last three events.

(Below Right) Dale Earnhardt Jr. (8) sets his sights on Kevin Harvick's GM Goodwrench Chevrolet. The Budweiser driver eventually caught and passed Harvick to finish fifth and end a three-race slide outside the top 20, while Harvick came home in sixth.

Bud Pole qualifying for the Sirius at the Glen was rained out, so car owner points determined the starting field. That automatically eliminated non-regulars Scott Pruett, Klaus Graff, Stanton Barrett and Boris Said from the field. It also allowed time for Jeff Burton to talk about leaving Roush Racing and the No. 99 Ford after the event at The Glen and move into Richard Childress' No. 30 AOL Chevrolet. Burton, with Jack Roush since 1996, had won 17 races in his career, but none since the 2001 season.

While Burton would replace interim driver Dave Blaney, who had taken over for Johnny Sauter earlier in the season, it appeared the seat in the "99" would go to Roush Racing's NASCAR Craftsman Truck Series driver Carl Edwards.

NASCAR also used the cancelled qualifying session to unofficially announce that its experiment with using rain tires on road courses had ended. Wet-weather tires had never been used in a points race, and NASCAR NEXTEL Cup Series Director John Darby, in noting none had been brought to the track, said: "We reached the point where we were either going at the wet-weather situation full-bore or just disband it.

"I think we are a dry-weather sport and we need to stay that way."

Stay that way it did, as dry conditions prevailed for Sunday's 90-lap event on the 11-turn, 2.45-mile road course in upstate New York. But for Tony Stewart, the weather was the furthest thing from his mind. Stomach cramps can be debilitating enough to send almost anyone

home for the day. Stewart, however, didn't let a severe case of gastric contractions "cramp" his style.

Instead, the driver of the Joe Gibbs Racing Home Depot Chevrolet, who began feeling ill about 17 laps into the season's 22nd NASCAR NEXTEL Cup Series race, toughed it out. A gentle prodding from crew chief Greg Zipadelli seemed to be the tonic Stewart needed to make his second trip to victory lane in 2004. Upon arriving in the coveted place of celebration, though, Stewart exited his car and headed to his team's hauler to try to recover. A few minutes later, the winner returned and talked about his long day at The Glen.

"I let the guys know what the problem was," Stewart explained. "I had to try to find somebody and see if there was something I could do. If there was something I could drink .. a pill I could take ... anything to help. They gave me something. It was the worst tasting thing I've ever had in my life.

"I don't know how I got to (the winner's circle). The best part is I have all these guys (his team) to share it with. They are the reason for our success today."

Boris Said stood by to drive in relief of Stewart, but Zipadelli scotched the idea when he saw that the lanky road racer was just too tall to fit into Stewart's custom-made seat. So Stewart, who led laps 2-13, went on to pace the field three more times. Finally, he took the lead away from Dodge driver Casey Mears on lap 76

and went on to beat road racing specialist Ron Fellows by 1.517 seconds. Fellows, who also finished second in this event in 1999, was driving a Chevrolet for Dale Earnardt, Inc.. Mark Martin finished third in a Ford, Mears almost ran out of fuel but finished fourth, while Earnhardt Jr. came home fifth.

"I don't have any complaints, just a little disappointment," said Fellows, who had to start at the rear of the field after qualifying was rained out. "We certainly worked hard."

As for Stewart, his hard work (and discomfort) over the event that took 2 hours, 23 minutes and 25 seconds to complete was rewarded with a check totaling $195,288.

*(Top) Despite some physical ailments, Tony Stewart had his home Depot Chevrolet flying around the 11-turn road course, pacing the field four times for a race-leading 46 laps to gather his second win of the season. Stewart also won this event in 2002, the year he won the championship.*

*(Above) Jason Shapiro prepares road-racing ace Boris Said for a possible stint in relief of Tony Stewart. As it turned out, Stewart remained in the car and was able to make it to the end.*

## Sirius at The Glen  *final race results*

| Fin. Pos. | Start Pos. | Car No. | Driver | Team | Fin. Pos. | Start Pos. | Car No. | Driver | Team |
|---|---|---|---|---|---|---|---|---|---|
| 1 | 4 | 20 | Tony Stewart | Home Depot Chevrolet | 23 | 31 | 10 | Scott Riggs | Valvoline Chevrolet |
| 2 | 43 | 1 | Ron Fellows | Nutter Butter/Nilla Wafer Chevrolet | 24 | 27 | 30 | Dave Blaney | America Online Chevrolet |
| 3 | 15 | 6 | Mark Martin | Viagra Ford | 25 | 17 | 2 | Rusty Wallace | Kodak/Miller Lite Dodge |
| 4 | 16 | 41 | Casey Mears | Target Dodge | 26 | 10 | 12 | Ryan Newman | ALLTEL Dodge |
| 5 | 3 | 8 | Dale Earnhardt Jr. | Budweiser Chevrolet | 27 | 13 | 88 | Dale Jarrett | UPS Ford |
| 6 | 9 | 29 | Kevin Harvick | GM Goodwrench Chevrolet | 28 | 32 | 49 | Ken Schrader | Schwan's Home Service Dodge |
| 7 | 12 | 19 | Jeremy Mayfield | Dodge Dealers/UAW Dodge | 29 | 37 | 72 | Tom Hubert | Freddie B's Ford |
| 8 | 29 | 21 | Ricky Rudd | "Keep It Genuine" Ford | 30 | 22 | 25 | Brian Vickers | GMAC Chevrolet |
| 9 | 5 | 17 | Matt Kenseth | DeWalt Power Tools Ford | 31 | 42 | 80 | Tony Ave | Lamers Motor Racing Chevrolet |
| 10 | 7 | 97 | Kurt Busch | IRWIN Industrial Tools Ford | 32 | 34 | 32 | Ricky Craven | Tide Chevrolet |
| 11 | 8 | 18 | Bobby Labonte | Interstate Batteries Chevrolet | 33 | 41 | 02 | Hermie Sadler | SCORE Motorsports Chevrolet |
| 12 | 24 | 99 | Jeff Burton | Roush Racing Ford | 34 | 30 | 77 | Brendan Gaughan | Kodak/Jasper Eng. & Trans. Dodge |
| 13 | 14 | 42 | Jamie McMurray | Texaco/Havoline Dodge | 35 | 21 | 16 | Greg Biffle | Subway/National Guard Ford |
| 14 | 11 | 9 | Kasey Kahne | Dodge Dealers/UAW Dodge | 36 | 19 | 40 | Sterling Marlin | Coors Light Dodge |
| 15 | 6 | 38 | Elliott Sadler | M&M's Ford | 37 | 28 | 0 | Ward Burton | NetZero Chevrolet |
| 16 | 23 | 31 | Robby Gordon | Cingular Wireless Chevrolet | 38 | 40 | 89 | Morgan Shepherd | Racing with Jesus/Red Line Oil Dodge |
| 17 | 35 | 43 | Jeff Green | Cheerios/Betty Crocker Dodge | 39 | 20 | 5 | Terry Labonte | Kellogg's Chevrolet |
| 18 | 33 | 45 | Kyle Petty | Georgia-Pacific/Brawny Dodge | 40 | 1 | 48 | Jimmie Johnson | Lowe's Chevrolet |
| 19 | 26 | 22 | Scott Wimmer | Caterpillar Dodge | 41 | 36 | 50 | Todd Bodine | Arnold Development Co. Dodge |
| 20 | 18 | 15 | Michael Waltrip | NAPA Chevrolet | 42 | 38 | 4 | Jimmy Spencer | Lucas Oil/77sports.com Chevrolet |
| 21 | 2 | 24 | Jeff Gordon | DuPont Chevrolet | 43 | 39 | 98 | Larry Gunselman | Mach 1 Racing Ford |
| 22 | 25 | 01 | Joe Nemechek | U.S. Army Chevrolet | | | | | |

# GFS MARKETPLACE 400

### MICHIGAN INTERATIONAL SPEEDWAY
#### AUGUST 22, 2004

*"We've got our team where we need it. ... I feel totally confident and I think we'll win another race this season."*

— *Greg Biffle*

Following the season's 23rd event, Jack Roush, the patriarch of a series-leading five separate race teams, compared himself to a mythical figure in children's literature.

"I liken myself to the nursery rhyme about the old lady who lives in a shoe and has so many children she doesn't know what to do," Roush quipped following driver Greg Biffle's first win of the year and second of his NASCAR NEXTEL Cup Series career.

Usually, when one or two of Roush's teams do well, the others turn in performances that have him removing his trademark hat to scratch quizzically at a nagging mental itch.

Not here, though, at the two-mile track located not all that far from Roush Industries' base in Livonia, Mich. Not only did Biffle put his No. 16 Ford out front a race-leading six times for 73 laps, he also beat the No. 2 finisher by a whopping 8.216 seconds. The runner-up was none other than Mark Martin, who has been with Roush since the team's founding in 1988. Roush's three remaining drivers also fared well, with Kurt Bush finishing sixth, Matt Kenseth in eighth, and Carl Edwards taking 10th in his first run for Roush in a NASCAR NEXTEL Cup Series car.

In short, the "Man in the Hat" saw all of his teams end up in the top 10. "This was a banner day for me," he said. "Racing in front of the home crowd here is always one of my favorite things."

*Greg Biffle's Roush Racing Ford sports a paint scheme featuring The Flash at Michigan. And, at least on this day in this race, Biffle truly was "the fastest man alive," leading all drivers in laps led (73) and positions gained in the race (23).*

*Tony Stewart breaks the pre-race tension by clowning around on pit road, giving Jamie McMurray, Sterling Marlin and Casey Mears a good laugh while the TV camera looks on. Also amused is Kevin Harvick (far left), who stands by for an interview on TNT.*

As the teams headed to Michigan International Speedway, Jimmie Johnson was looking back on a second bad week after ending up 40th at Watkins Glen, N.Y., because of engine failure. However, the Hendrick Motorsports driver was still leading in points for the eighth straight week. With 3,143 markers, he was just 40 up on teammate Jeff Gordon after losing 57 at The Glen.

Johnson had lost 192 of a 232-point lead in just two races since Pocono, Pa., but was still 511 in front of 11th-place Kasey Kahne. Still, the Sirius at The Glen was his fourth DNF of the year and marked the first time he had ever dropped out of two consecutive events.

Gordon's day at Watkins Glen was almost as dismal as Johnson's. He finished 21st but retained second place in the standings. Like Johnson, he was coming closer to attaining a lock on being one of the 10 drivers to begin the final Chase for the NASCAR NEXTEL Cup following the year's 26th race at Richmond in September.

Apparently, Dale Earnhardt Jr. had put the injuries he sustained in a June sports car event behind him. He ran strong on the Watkins Glen road course and finished fifth, marking just his second top-10 showing in the last eight races. He also held onto third place in the standings and left New York with 3,015 points, just 128

He headed to Michigan 192 points behind the leader and just 75 in front of fifth-place Kenseth.

Kenseth remained fifth in points, thanks to a ninth-place run at Watkins Glen, and approached Michigan 267 in back of Johnson. The finish on the serpentine road course was his third top-10 finish in the previous four races and his 13th of the year.

M&M's Ford driver Elliott Sadler had a mediocre day in New York with a 15th-place finish, but he did not relinquish the sixth spot in NASCAR's top 10. He was still safely in contention for a place in the Chase for the NASCAR NEXTEL Cup, and with 2,792 points he was 160 in front of the 11th-place man but only 38 in front of seventh-place Busch.

With a 10th-place run at Watkins Glen for his third top-10 finish in the last four races and 10th of the year overall, Busch maintained seventh place in the standings and left the track with 2,754 points. He was another driver who had to keep an eye on 11th-place Kahne, who was just 122 points behind Busch.

Finishing sixth at Watkins Glen paid a bit

behind Johnson and 88 in back of Gordon.

Tony Stewart fought illness all day long at The Glen but went the entire distance without relief and ended up winning his second race of the year. His 12th top-10 finish of the season and fifth top five in the last six events allowed him to hold onto fourth place in the standings.

*(Left) Mark Martin (6) shows the way for fellow Roush mates (in order) Kurt Busch and Greg Biffle. Martin, who led five times for 46 laps, may have had the fastest car but had to battle back after a pit violation and wound up second.*

*(Below) Jack Roush called on Carl Edwards to fill the vacant seat in the No. 99 Roush Ford, and Edwards made an impressive series debut with a 10th-place effort in the race.*

*(Above) Jamie McMurray (42) tries to outpace Matt Kenseth (17) along Michigan's frontstretch. McMurray was the fastest of the Dodge drivers and posted a fourth place for his fifth top five of the season, while Kenseth brought his Ford home in eighth.*

*(Above Right) Dale Jarrett gets fresh rubber from his UPS crew during one of nine caution periods in the race. Jarrett, who traditionally fares well at MIS, continued a recent surge and picked up his fourth top 10 in the last six events.*

*(Right) Jeff Gordon pushes the nose of his DuPont Chevrolet to the inside of Kasey Kahne's Dodge. Gordon paced the race in the early going and then settled in for yet another top 10, while Kahne led twice in the late going and grabbed fifth place at the finish.*

of a dividend to Richard Childress Racing's Kevin Harvick. His second top-10 effort in a row allowed him to move up a spot in points, from ninth to eighth. With 2,717 points, he was just 37 in back of Busch, but he had just 85 on 11th-place Kahne.

Following the Sirius at The Glen, Bobby Labonte dropped from eighth to ninth in the standings, while Jeremy Mayfield, who was 12th, jumped two spots and found himself in the coveted top 10. Labonte finished 11th in New York, while Mayfield came home seventh and became the first driver to move into the top 10 since Labonte jumped from 12th to 10th following the ninth race of the year at Talladega, Ala.

Crew chief Michael "Fatback" McSwain, released from Joe Gibbs Racing after the Tropicana 400 in July, was back on the job at Michigan. McSwain signed on with Wood Brothers Racing, replacing Ben Leslie, thus reuniting with driver Ricky Rudd. McSwain and Rudd had worked together previously at Robert Yates Racing for three years and won as many races there.

Leslie took a position with Ford Motorsports as its field manager and replaced Robin Pemberton, who joined NASCAR's technical staff.

Several days before the Michigan event, NASCAR announced a new "gear rule" for 2005, which would affect its top three divisions. The rule would restrict gear ratios to those determined by NASCAR in an attempt to cut research and development costs and would apply to races at all tracks except Daytona and Talladega, where restrictor plates limit horsepower.

In a related announcement, in 2005, NASCAR said it would reduce spoiler heights to 4-1/2 inches (down an inch from this year).

The rule would apply to all tracks except Daytona and Talladega, the idea being to promote more passing during races.

Bud Pole qualifying at Michigan was rained out for the second straight week, and the starting lineup was based on car owner points. That put Biffle's Ford 24th on the grid, but it didn't stay there long. Jeff Gordon immediately took the lead from teammate Jimmie Johnson, led the first 30 laps, and also led laps 32-38 before ceding the flagship spot to Busch, who led through lap 42.

Biffle revealed his car's strength early on and went to the front by passing Busch and leading through lap 46. In a race that was interrupted by a track record-tying nine caution-flag periods, Biffle went to the front once more during the race's first half (100 laps) and four more times during the second. Superior handling and horsepower, plus fresher tires at the end, did it for Biffle. He took the lead for the final time 18 laps from the finish and sailed away to the victory.

Martin, who led five times for 46 laps, overcame a call that was almost disastrous. Following a stop under the last caution (laps 130-135), Martin was recalled to the pits because race officials said they had spotted a loose lug nut. Martin restarted 28th but rallied back.

Biffle raced to victory at Michigan in 2 hours, 52 minutes and 35 seconds at an average speed of 139.063 mph and won $190,180. Seventeen drivers went the entire 200-lap distance, among them Jeff Burton, who finished 12th in his debut with Richard Childress Racing.

*(Top) Greg Biffle launches from his pit box and heads back into action. Driver and crew were outstanding on pit road, which helped Biffle lead the field on the final restart of the race. From there he led 52 of the final 66 laps.*

*(Above) The Flash joins Greg Biffle and team owner Jack Roush (right) in Michigan's victory lane to celebrate Biffle's second career win. It was a banner day for Roush, with all five of his teams finishing among the top 10.*

## GFS Marketplace 400 *final race results*

| Fin. Pos. | Start Pos. | Car No. | Driver | Team | Fin. Pos. | Start Pos. | Car No. | Driver | Team |
|---|---|---|---|---|---|---|---|---|---|
| 1 | 24 | 16 | Greg Biffle | National Guard/The Flash Ford | 23 | 34 | 43 | Jeff Green | Cheerios/Betty Crocker Dodge |
| 2 | 13 | 6 | Mark Martin | Viagra/Batman Ford | 24 | 27 | 21 | Ricky Rudd | Motorcraft/Wonder Woman Ford |
| 3 | 14 | 88 | Dale Jarrett | UPS Ford | 25 | 19 | 31 | Robby Gordon | Cingular Wireless Chevrolet |
| 4 | 15 | 42 | Jamie McMurray | Texaco/Havoline Dodge | 26 | 9 | 18 | Bobby Labonte | Wellbutrin XL Chevrolet |
| 5 | 11 | 9 | Kasey Kahne | Dodge Dealers/UAW Dodge | 27 | 21 | 5 | Terry Labonte | Kellogg's/Delphi Chevrolet |
| 6 | 7 | 97 | Kurt Busch | Sharpie/Superman Ford | 28 | 33 | 49 | Ken Schrader | Schwan's Home Service Dodge |
| 7 | 2 | 24 | Jeff Gordon | DuPont Chevrolet | 29 | 32 | 45 | Kyle Petty | Georgia-Pacific/Brawny Dodge |
| 8 | 5 | 17 | Matt Kenseth | DeWalt Power Tools Ford | 30 | 29 | 0 | Ward Burton | NetZero Chevrolet |
| 9 | 4 | 20 | Tony Stewart | Home Depot/USA Olympics Chevrolet | 31 | 38 | 4 | Jimmy Spencer | Lucas Oil Chevrolet |
| 10 | 23 | 99 | Carl Edwards | Green Lantern Ford | 32 | 6 | 38 | Elliott Sadler | M&M's Ford |
| 11 | 10 | 19 | Jeremy Mayfield | Dodge Dealers/UAW Dodge | 33 | 30 | 77 | Brendan Gaughan | Kodak/Jasper Eng. & Trans. Dodge |
| 12 | 28 | 30 | Jeff Burton | America Online Chevrolet | 34 | 40 | 89 | Morgan Shepherd | Racing with Jesus/Red Line Oil Dodge |
| 13 | 25 | 01 | Joe Nemechek | U.S. Army Chevrolet | 35 | 35 | 32 | Ricky Craven | Tide Chevrolet |
| 14 | 12 | 12 | Ryan Newman | ALLTEL/Justice League Dodge | 36 | 18 | 2 | Rusty Wallace | Miller Lite Dodge |
| 15 | 20 | 40 | Sterling Marlin | Coors Light Dodge | 37 | 37 | 72 | Kirk Shelmerdine | Freddie B's Ford |
| 16 | 8 | 29 | Kevin Harvick | GM Goodwrench Chevrolet | 38 | 41 | 09 | Bobby Hamilton Jr. | Miccosukee Resort Dodge |
| 17 | 17 | 15 | Michael Waltrip | NAPA Chevrolet | 39 | 43 | 80 | Carl Long | Commercial Truck & Trailer Ford |
| 18 | 26 | 22 | Scott Wimmer | Caterpillar Dodge | 40 | 1 | 48 | Jimmie Johnson | Lowe's Chevrolet |
| 19 | 31 | 10 | Scott Riggs | Valvoline Chevrolet | 41 | 39 | 98 | Derrike Cope | America's Most Wanted Ford |
| 20 | 16 | 41 | Casey Mears | Target Dodge | 42 | 42 | 02 | Hermie Sadler | Zapf Creation Chevrolet |
| 21 | 3 | 8 | Dale Earnhardt Jr. | Budweiser Chevrolet | 43 | 36 | 50 | Todd Bodine | Arnold Development Co. Dodge |
| 22 | 22 | 25 | Brian Vickers | GMAC Chevrolet | | | | | |

# SHARPIE 500

*"This team is as tough as nails! Man, we needed this. This is one of the biggest wins of my career."*

— Dale Earnhardt Jr.

Four years ago, when Dale Earnhardt Jr. was in his rookie NASCAR NEXTEL Cup Series season, his father, Dale Earnhardt Sr., was trying to show him the best way to negotiate the high banks of Bristol Motor Speedway. "Junior" knew enough to pay attention to his dad, who had won there nine times, but he wasn't quite sure if he understood what he was being told.

The advice was simply this: Just after going past the flagstand, let off the gas pedal, roll through the corner without excessive use of the brakes, and then punch the accelerator coming out of the turn.

It took a while, but Earnhardt Jr., who had never won anything at Bristol, finally caught on. He captured the Food City 250 NASCAR Busch Series event. Then, the following evening, he undoubtedly earned his Bristol "diploma" by soundly thrashing the competition in the Sharpie 500.

A few days earlier as the teams headed to Bristol for the 24th race of the season, Jimmie Johnson was still feeling the sting of yet another problem-plagued performance, this time in the GFS Marketplace 400 at Michigan. Once again, a sour engine dropped the Lowe's Chevrolet driver to the bottom of the finishing order, this time in 40th place, and that, combined with a solid seventh-place finish for teammate Jeff Gordon, resulted in the two Hendrick drivers swapping positions in the standings.

A crowd estimated at 160,000 packs the grandstands that enclose the 0.533-mile oval for Saturday night racing in the mountains of eastern Tennessee.

Gordon left the Michigan superspeedway with 3,254 points and the top spot on the point ladder for the first time since he won the championship in 2001. Gordon, who had been ranked No. 2 for the previous three weeks, trailed Johnson by 40 points going into Michigan and came out 68 in front.

The fact was, however, that going into Bristol, it appeared as though the drivers in at least the first six or seven spots in points had a "lock" on a spot in the coveted 10-race Chase for the NASCAR NEXTEL Cup, which would begin with race No. 27 in September at New Hampshire.

Earnhardt Jr., coming off a strong fifth-place finish at Watkins Glen, N.Y., finished 21st at Michigan for his fifth finish outside the top 20 in the previous six events. Yet, with 3,115 points he held onto third in the standings for the fourth consecutive race week. However, fourth-place Tony Stewart had closed to within 26 points of Earnhardt with a ninth-place run in the GFS Marketplace 400.

With 3,089 points, the Home Depot Chevrolet driver was 165 out of the lead but was closing the gap. Stewart's Michigan performance was his sixth top 10 in his last seven starts, allowing him to remain in fourth place for the third consecutive week.

With an eighth-place run at Michigan, Matt Kenseth headed to Bristol fifth in points for the third week in a row and the sixth time in the past seven weeks. It was also his second consecutive top-10 finish and 14th of the season. The DeWalt Tools Ford driver now trailed Stewart by just 71 points and was 236 behind the leader.

By finishing sixth at Michigan, registering his third consecutive top-10 finish and fourth in the last five events, Kenseth's teammate, Kurt Busch, moved up a spot in points, from seventh to sixth. He moved 45 points ahead of Elliott Sadler, who was ranked sixth going into Michigan, but left in seventh place. With 2,909 points, Busch was 345 out of the lead and 109 behind Kenseth.

At Michigan, Sadler's run of consecutive top-15 finishes ended at four when he finished 32nd, his worst showing of the year, due to problems with the M&M's Ford. Sadler now was looking over his shoulder as the three remaining drivers in the top 10 were all within just 72 points of his position.

Kevin Harvick brought the GM Goodwrench Chevrolet home 16th at Michigan, but with 2,832 points, held onto eighth place in the standings for the second straight week. Harvick also ended a modest two-race streak of top-10 finishes, marking just the second time in the last eight races he'd landed outside the top 15.

Bobby Labonte had a precarious hold on a top-10 ranking heading into Bristol. He rode into Michigan with back-to-back top-15 efforts but skidded to a finish of 26th. That was good enough to retain the ninth spot in points, 33 behind Harvick, but with 2,799 markers he was just seven ahead of Kasey Kahne, 13 in front of No. 11 Jeremy Mayfield and 40 up on Mark Martin.

Bristol Motor Speedway's 36-degree banking — steepest in NASCAR — allows for lap speeds in excess of 120 miles per hour on the concrete bullring. Don't blink; you might miss something!

*(Above) The Budweiser team was on top of its game at Bristol, keeping Junior among the leaders on stops under caution and out front while pitting under green. The dominating win was truly an all-around team effort.*

*(Above Right) Jeff Burton dives into the turn in the Richard Childress-owned AOL Chevrolet. In just his second start with the new team, Burton picked up a very welcome fourth-place finish to match his only other top-five result this season, that coming at Dover in June.*

*(Right) Joe Nemechek slams the outside wall in turn one, the result of being caught up in another driver's accident on lap 33. The incident brought out the second caution on a relatively quiet night for Bristol that saw a total of nine yellow flags.*

By finishing fifth at Michigan, Kahne moved up a position in points from 11th to 10th and bounced Mayfield out of the top 10. Things, for sure, were getting edgy.

Gordon didn't better Ryan Newman's Bristol track record speed of 128.709 mph in Bud Pole qualifying, but his time and speed of 14.930 seconds at 128.520 mph was good enough to put him on the pole for the Sharpie 500. It was his sixth No. 1 start of the year and his fourth pole at Bristol, his third for the night race.

"We wanted the pole really bad," Gordon said. "I ran the first lap and thought it was good, but I didn't know if it was enough. I was pushing so hard on the second lap, I almost wrecked."

Kahne joined Gordon on the front row with an effort of 13.060 seconds at 127.410 mph, while Sterling Marlin, Ryan Newman and Jamie McMurray completed the top five in time trials. Johnson ran 11th quickest but added to his troubles of late when he wrecked his car in

a practice session and was forced to the rear of the field for the start of the race.

In winning the Sharpie 500, Earnhardt Jr. broke a six-week slump. Also, his victory came in a Bristol race that was odd in that there were just nine caution flags for 63 laps — the last of which ended 102 laps before the race did — and few frayed tempers. Also unlike the usual Bristol slugfest was Earnhardt Jr.'s sizeable 4.390-second margin of victory over Penske Dodge driver Newman, who, in turn was well in front of third-running Johnson and fourth-place Jeff Burton.

It was also obvious that Earnhardt Jr.'s car and pit crew were in tip-top shape. He started 30th and ended up leading the race more than anyone else — six times for 295 of 500 laps. He took the lead for the first time on lap 64 when

he passed Rusty Wallace (also a nine-time Bristol winner) and led through lap 104. He paced laps 119-131, 191-215, 240-355 and 376-390. Then, when he caught up to Burton's No. 30 AOL Chevrolet and passed him on lap 416, the race was his.

Not only did his victory come exactly five years after his late father had won his final Bristol event, but Earnhardt Jr. also became the first NASCAR driver to win NASCAR NEXTEL Cup Series and NASCAR Busch Series events on the same NASCAR weekend.

"This team is as tough as nails! Man, we needed this. This is one of the biggest wins of my career." Earnhardt Jr. said in victory lane. "We were struggling. You have to say that."

Rusty Wallace was disappointed that he hadn't done better at Bristol — he started 13th, led three times for 79 laps but ended up 26th at the end — as two days after the race he announced that he would compete in 2005 and then retire. Wallace, 48, ran his first NASCAR NEXTEL Cup Series race in 1980, was named Raybestos Rookie of the Year in 1984 and won the championship in 1989. His first victory came on April 6, 1986, at Bristol.

"This is something I've thought long and hard about," Wallace said of his decision to retire. "I want to go out at the top of my game ... a front runner."

Earnhardt Jr. was at the top of his game in the Sharpie 500. He completed the event in 3 hours and 36 seconds at an average speed of 88.538 mph and won $322,443.

*(Above) Dale Earnhardt Jr. brings out the broom after sweeping the weekend's competition at Bristol. Junior won the NASCAR Busch Series event on Friday night, then "cleaned up" the competition on Saturday by leading 295 of 500 laps in the Sharpie 500, 216 of those in the last half of the race alone.*

*(Left) Nine-time Bristol winner Rusty Wallace takes his turn at the front of the field, one of three times the Miller Lite driver paced the field before a multi-car accident took him from contention. Days after the race, Rusty announced that the 2005 season would be his last.*

## Sharpie 500 *final race results*

| Fin. Pos. | Start Pos. | Car No. | Driver | Team | Fin. Pos. | Start Pos. | Car No. | Driver | Team |
|---|---|---|---|---|---|---|---|---|---|
| 1 | 30 | 8 | Dale Earnhardt Jr. | Budweiser Chevrolet | 23 | 40 | 50 | Todd Bodine | Arnold Development Co. Dodge |
| 2 | 4 | 12 | Ryan Newman | ALLTEL Dodge | 24 | 21 | 29 | Kevin Harvick | RealTree/GM Goodwrench Chevrolet |
| 3 | 11 | 48 | Jimmie Johnson | Lowe's Chevrolet | 25 | 28 | 00 | Kenny Wallace | Aaron's Chevrolet |
| 4 | 15 | 30 | Jeff Burton | America Online Chevrolet | 26 | 13 | 2 | Rusty Wallace | Miller Lite Dodge |
| 5 | 8 | 38 | Elliott Sadler | M&M's Ford | 27 | 36 | 15 | Michael Waltrip | NAPA Chevrolet |
| 6 | 3 | 40 | Sterling Marlin | Coors Light Dodge | 28 | 41 | 09 | Mike Wallace | Miccosukee Resorts Dodge |
| 7 | 5 | 42 | Jamie McMurray | Texaco/Havoline Dodge | 29 | 27 | 43 | Jeff Green | Cheerios/Betty Crocker Dodge |
| 8 | 24 | 97 | Kurt Busch | Sharpie Retractable Ford | 30 | 22 | 41 | Casey Mears | Energizer Dodge |
| 9 | 23 | 17 | Matt Kenseth | DeWalt Power Tools Ford | 31 | 38 | 4 | Jimmy Spencer | Food City Supreme Clean Chevrolet |
| 10 | 14 | 88 | Dale Jarrett | UPS Ford | 32 | 26 | 49 | Ken Schrader | Schwan's Home Service Dodge |
| 11 | 10 | 16 | Greg Biffle | National Guard Ford | 33 | 25 | 99 | Carl Edwards | RoundUp Ford |
| 12 | 18 | 31 | Robby Gordon | Cingular Wireless Chevrolet | 34 | 35 | 32 | Ricky Craven | Tide Chevrolet |
| 13 | 7 | 6 | Mark Martin | Viagra Ford | 35 | 17 | 77 | Brendan Gaughan | Kodak/Jasper Eng. & Trans. Dodge |
| 14 | 1 | 24 | Jeff Gordon | DuPont Chevrolet | 36 | 34 | 22 | Scott Wimmer | Caterpillar Dodge |
| 15 | 12 | 5 | Terry Labonte | Kellogg's Chevrolet | 37 | 31 | 45 | Kyle Petty | Georgia-Pacific/Brawny Dodge |
| 16 | 19 | 18 | Bobby Labonte | Interstate Batteries Chevrolet | 38 | 42 | 98 | Derrike Cope | America's Most Wanted Ford |
| 17 | 39 | 10 | Scott Riggs | Valvoline Chevrolet | 39 | 33 | 51 | Tony Raines | Marathon Oil/Chase Chevrolet |
| 18 | 16 | 0 | Ward Burton | NetZero Chevrolet | 40 | 32 | 21 | Ricky Rudd | "Keep It Genuine" Ford |
| 19 | 6 | 20 | Tony Stewart | The Home Depot Chevrolet | 41 | 43 | 89 | Morgan Shepherd | Racing with Jesus/Red Line Oil Dodge |
| 20 | 20 | 25 | Brian Vickers | GMAC Chevrolet | 42 | 37 | 01 | Joe Nemechek | U.S. Army Chevrolet |
| 21 | 2 | 9 | Kasey Kahne | Dodge Dealers/UAW Dodge | 43 | 29 | 37 | Kevin Lepage | Carter's Royal Dispos-all Dodge |
| 22 | 9 | 19 | Jeremy Mayfield | Dodge Dealers/UAW Dodge | | | | | |

# POP SECRET 500

*"The cautions were definitely helping me ... but my car was unbelievable the last 10 laps. My team deserves this."*

— *Elliott Sadler*

With a 14th-place finish in the Sharpie 500 at Bristol, Tenn., Jeff Gordon headed toward his home-state track leading the point standings for the second straight week. The Bristol run marked just the second time in the last nine races he'd been unable to finish seventh or better, and with 3,380 points, he was now a slim 24 points up on teammate Jimmie Johnson.

Johnson snapped a drought of three consecutive finishes of 36th or worse (all due to engine failure) with a third-place finish at the Tennessee short track. With 3,356 markers, he remained second in the standings for the second consecutive week and had been either second or better for 16 weeks in a row.

After a decisive victory in the Sharpie 500, it looked as though Dale Earnhardt Jr. might have put a stop to a recent slide that showed him finishing outside the top 20 in five of the last six events. Bristol was his fourth win of the year and allowed him to close to within 51 points of Johnson and 75 of Gordon and keep the third position in the standings.

At Bristol, Tony Stewart saw his streak of top-10 finishes end at three. Although he ended up 19th at Bristol, he held onto the fourth spot in points for the fourth consecutive week, and with 3,195 he was 185 points out of the lead and 110 behind Earnhardt Jr.

Kasey Kahne's Dodge receives a fresh set of tires and fuel under one of 11 cautions during the Pop Secret 500. Although Kahne's bid for the win came up a bit short in his fifth runner-up finish of the season, he did exactly what he needed to do to bounce back into the top 10 in the point standings.

*(Below) J.J. Yeley poses with his mount, fielded by Joe Gibbs Racing, before making his NASCAR NEXTEL Cup Series debut at California. Yeley, who had made 12 NASCAR Busch Series starts for Gibbs this year, had an early-race accident that ended his race in the garage.*

*(Bottom Left) Like Yeley, NASCAR Craftsman Truck Series regular Shane Hmiel came to California to make his first big-league start in a Bill Davis-owned Dodge, which ultimately suffered transmission problems.*

*(Bottom Right) Team owner Cal Wells (right) chose Bobby Hamilton Jr. (left) to take the wheel of the Tide Chevrolet at California. The race would mark his seventh start of the season and the ninth of his young career.*

Matt Kenseth had a decent run to ninth place in the Sharpie 500, which was his third consecutive top-10 finish and fifth in his last six starts. He remained fifth in the points race for the fourth week in a row, and with 3,156, he was now 39 points behind Stewart.

Kenseth's teammate, Kurt Busch, finished eighth in the Bristol 500-lapper for his fourth straight top-10 finish and fifth in the last six weeks. It was also his 12th top-10 run of the year and kept him sixth in the rankings for the second week in a row.

Elliott Sadler finished fifth at Bristol and held onto spot No. 7 in the rankings. His Bristol performance was just his third top-10 finish in the last eight races, but it allowed him to close in on Busch, as well as provide a small cushion between him and Kevin Harvick. A total of 3,019 points put Sadler 361 behind the leader and 32 in arrears of Busch.

Harvick held onto his eighth-place ranking for a third straight week, but a 24th-place showing in the Sharpie 500 opened the door for a host of drivers attempting to earn a berth in

the Chase for the NASCAR NEXTEL Cup. Although he'd been among the top 10 for 19 consecutive weeks, Harvick now could look over his shoulder and see Bobby Labonte and Ryan Newman nipping at his heels.

Labonte left Bristol with a 16th-place finish and 2,919 points, just four less than Harvick. The Bristol race marked the seventh consecutive time he had not posted a top-10 finish, and

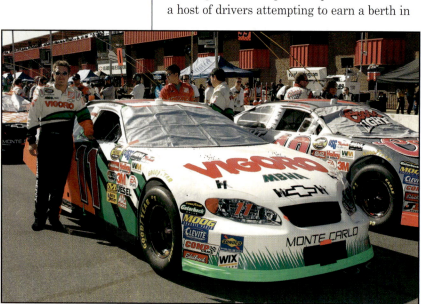

the gap between him and those outside the top 10 continued to narrow. Although Labonte trailed Harvick by just four points heading into California, 10th-place Ryan Newman had just one point less than he did, while Kasey Kahne, Mark Martin, Jeremy Mayfield, Dale Jarrett and Jamie McMurray all posed potential threats to his ranking among the top 10.

Also, Newman, by finishing second at Bristol, leapt from 13th to 10th in points, displacing Kahne in the process. The performance, which was only his second top-10 finish over the last nine races, allowed him to return to the top 10 after a two-race absence. However, with 2,918 points, his cushion over Kahne wasn't that much — just 26 points with one race left to decide who would compete for the NASCAR NEXTEL Cup Series championship.

(Below) The starting field of 43 rounds turn four led by Bud Pole winner Brian Vickers (his second of the year) and outside front-row starter Jeremy Mayfield (19). Bill Elliott, making his fifth start of the season, took the third spot in his McDonald's-sponsored Dodge.

(Above) Carl Edwards (99) runs alongside Roush Racing team-mate Matt Kenseth (17). Edwards was again impressive in this, his third career start, by bringing home a sixth place, his second top-10 finish.

(Right) Mark Martin (6) leads Elliott Sadler (38) and Ryan Newman (12) during the first half of the race. Martin eventually led 65 circuits to take the lap-leader bonus and then finished in third, which moved him into the top 10 for the first time this year.

(Far Right) Scott Riggs (10) hugs the bottom with Robby Gordon (31) lurking up high. Riggs had a very nice run to seventh place for his second top-10 finish of the season, while Gordon finished ninth.

Pop Secret 500 with a time and speed of 38.417 seconds at 187.417 mph, which was just a tick off the record lap of 38.414 seconds at 187.432 mph, set by Newman in April 2002. Mayfield was second quickest in Bud Pole qualifying with an effort of 38.634 seconds at 186.364 mph, but neither of the front-row starters could capitalize on their positions in the race itself. Vickers led four times for 44 laps but finished 13th, while Mayfield led once for nine laps and ended up 16th.

Bill Elliott started his fifth race of the year by qualifying his own McDonald's-sponsored Dodge third quickest. The fast-food giant backed Elliott's self-owned team from 1995 through 2000, and this year planned to sponsor him again at Atlanta in October. Unfortunately, Elliott ran into mechanical problems and limped home 25th in the Pop Secret 500.

It took a lot more than incredibly hot race-day weather and a so-called "near miss" during a practice session to keep Elliott Sadler from accomplishing two goals at Fontana, Calif., in the first Labor Day weekend NASCAR NEXTEL Cup Series race staged west of the Mississippi River.

The Virginian's aims were simple: Come as close as possible to notching his second victory of the year; assure himself and his Robert Yates Racing team a coveted spot in the final 10-race Chase for the NASCAR NEXTEL Cup, which would commence in two weeks at New Hampshire International Speedway.

The driver of the No. 38 M&M's Ford attained both in dramatic fashion. Sadler started 17th in a 43-car field, led eight times for 59 of 250 laps and, 3 hours, 53 minutes and 47

Although terms were not specified, Chip Ganassi Racing announced a day before the Pop Secret 500 that Casey Mears' contract had been renewed and he would be in the No. 41 Target-sponsored Dodge in 2005. And most likely, according to Dodge and NASCAR, that car would be the new Charger.

Brian Vickers put his No. 25 Hendrick Motorsports Chevrolet on the Bud Pole for the

seconds after taking the green flag, found himself in victory lane for the third time in his career and the first since April 4 at Texas Motor Speedway.

More important, however, was that now all Sadler had to do to really clinch a spot in the privileged top 10 was to take the starting flag in the upcoming Chevrolet Rock & Roll 400 at Richmond, Va. Good pit stops and being in contention led to his victory. Luck, however, played a role when he spun his car during a practice run the day before the race. Sadler kept away from the wall, narrowly missed a collision with another car, and after his crew inspected his mount, it was found to be undamaged and fit for competition.

The Pop Secret 500 was fraught with interruptions — there were 11 caution flags for 51 laps — but Sadler managed to stay away from

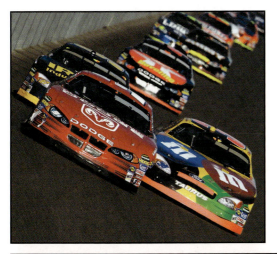

trouble. He took the lead for the final time on lap 224 (following the ninth yellow flag) and beat rookie Kasey Kahne to the checkered flag by 0.263 second. Kahne, who finished second for the fifth time this season, also found himself among the top 10 in points after the race, as did third-running Mark Martin.

"The cautions were definitely helping me," Sadler said, adding, "but my car was unbelievable the last 10 laps. My team deserves this.

"I told Robert, 'This is a dream come true. This is the reason I came to Robert Yates Racing.'"

One could easily understand Sadler's outlook, as he was all but assured of a trip to New York City in December and a place on the stage at the Waldorf=Astoria.

*(Above) M&M's Ford team members leap onto pit road as Elliott Sadler takes the checkered flag in his second victory of the season. The win was significant for the entire team in that it virtually guaranteed them a spot in the Chase for the NASCAR NEXTEL Cup.*

*(Left) Elliott Sadler (38) peeks to the inside of Kasey Kahne (9) with Kurt Busch tucked in behind as the field enters turn three. In fourth place is the Texaco Dodge with Jamie McMurray, who finished in fourth to continue his late-season surge toward the top 10.*

## Pop Secret 500 *final race results*

| Fin. Pos. | Start Pos. | Car No. | Driver | Team | Fin. Pos. | Start Pos. | Car No. | Driver | Team |
|---|---|---|---|---|---|---|---|---|---|
| 1 | 17 | 38 | Elliott Sadler | M&M's Ford | 23 | 21 | 15 | Michael Waltrip | NAPA Chevrolet |
| 2 | 5 | 9 | Kasey Kahne | Dodge Dealers/UAW Dodge | 24 | 18 | 84 | Kyle Busch | CarQuest Chevrolet |
| 3 | 11 | 6 | Mark Martin | Viagra Ford | 25 | 3 | 98 | Bill Elliott | McDonald's Dodge |
| 4 | 23 | 42 | Jamie McMurray | Texaco/Havoline Dodge | 26 | 31 | 40 | Sterling Marlin | Coors Light Dodge |
| 5 | 14 | 12 | Ryan Newman | Sony/ALLTEL Dodge | 27 | 13 | 43 | Jeff Green | Pop Secret Dodge |
| 6 | 19 | 99 | Carl Edwards | Shop Rat Ford | 28 | 27 | 29 | Kevin Harvick | GM Goodwrench Chevrolet |
| 7 | 9 | 10 | Scott Riggs | Valvoline Chevrolet | 29 | 6 | 41 | Casey Mears | Target House Dodge |
| 8 | 25 | 88 | Dale Jarrett | UPS Ford | 30 | 36 | 36 | Boris Said | Centrix Chevrolet |
| 9 | 35 | 31 | Robby Gordon | Cingular Wireless Chevrolet | 31 | 39 | 0 | Ward Burton | NetZero/Fear Factor Chevrolet |
| 10 | 26 | 2 | Rusty Wallace | Miller Lite Dodge | 32 | 41 | 4 | Jimmy Spencer | Lucas Oil Chevrolet |
| 11 | 4 | 97 | Kurt Busch | IRWIN Industrial Tools Ford | 33 | 40 | 49 | Ken Schrader | Schwan's Home Service Dodge |
| 12 | 10 | 01 | Joe Nemechek | U.S. Army Chevrolet | 34 | 12 | 8 | Dale Earnhardt Jr. | Budweiser Chevrolet |
| 13 | 1 | 25 | Brian Vickers | GMAC Chevrolet | 35 | 28 | 45 | Kyle Petty | Georgia-Pacific/Brawny Dodge |
| 14 | 16 | 48 | Jimmie Johnson | Lowe's Chevrolet | 36 | 7 | 16 | Greg Biffle | National Guard Ford |
| 15 | 34 | 30 | Jeff Burton | America Online Chevrolet | 37 | 8 | 24 | Jeff Gordon | DuPont Chevrolet |
| 16 | 2 | 19 | Jeremy Mayfield | Dodge Dealers/UAW Dodge | 38 | 24 | 32 | Bobby Hamilton Jr. | Tide Chevrolet |
| 17 | 20 | 21 | Ricky Rudd | "Keep It Genuine" Ford | 39 | 29 | 23 | Shane Hmiel | Bill Davis Racing Dodge |
| 18 | 33 | 20 | Tony Stewart | The Home Depot Chevrolet | 40 | 43 | 96 | Derrike Cope | Mach 1 Inc. Ford |
| 19 | 15 | 5 | Terry Labonte | Kellogg's Chevrolet | 41 | 32 | 11 | J.J. Yeley | Vigoro/The Home Depot Chevrolet |
| 20 | 37 | 18 | Bobby Labonte | Wellbutrin XL Chevrolet | 42 | 22 | 77 | Brendan Gaughan | Kodak/Jasper Eng. & Trans. Dodge |
| 21 | 38 | 22 | Scott Wimmer | Caterpillar Dodge | 43 | 42 | 50 | Jeff Fuller | Arnold Development Co. Dodge |
| 22 | 30 | 17 | Matt Kenseth | Smirnoff Ice/DeWalt Ford | | | | | |

# CHEVY
# ROCK & ROLL 400

## RICHMOND INTERNATIONAL RACEWAY
### SEPTEMBER 11, 2004

*"We had no choice but to try to win the race and lead the most laps. We focused all week on that."*

— Jeremy Mayfield

Jeremy Mayfield (19) streaks past the battered Chevrolet of Jimmie Johnson (48), which was damaged in a mid-race, multi-car accident. Mayfield, who led the race five times for a total of 151 laps, was on his way to an emotional win and a spot in the field of championship contenders.

Almost ironically, it was Jeremy Mayfield who seemed to set the tone for the pivotal NASCAR NEXTEL Cup Series race of the 2004 season.

The day before the fastest 43 drivers were to go "under the lights" at the capital city's 0.75-mile track, the driver of Ray Evernham's No. 19 Dodge had this to say about the circuit's final event before the 10-race Chase for the NASCAR NEXTEL Cup: "We've got to go all out and run as hard as we can. That doesn't mean going out there and taking somebody out and causing a lot of wrecks. It just means racing hard, and that's what we've all been pretty much doing anyway."

Mayfield more than heeded his own advice. Starting seventh, he went into the lead for the first of five times on the 99th circuit, led 151 of 400 laps, beat Dale Earnhardt Jr. to the checkered flag by a healthy 4.928 seconds and went into victory lane for the first time in over four years.

The victory, however, was almost secondary. By winning, Mayfield, who started the event 14th in the standings, became one of the select group of 10 drivers who would now compete for the 2004 NASCAR NEXTEL Cup Series championship.

*(Above) Mike Bliss, the 2002 NASCAR Craftsman Truck Series champion and current NASCAR Busch Series competitor, climbs aboard a Chevrolet fielded by Joe Gibbs Racing before making his second NASCAR NEXTEL Cup Series start of the season, the 31st of his career.*

*(Above Right) In the race, Bliss (80) fends off a challenge from Ward Burton (0). Bliss, who started 33rd, picked up 29 positions during the race, many after falling out of pit sequence with the rest of the leaders, and came home in fourth, the best finish of his career in the series.*

*(Right) Mark Martin (6), Jimmie Johnson (48) and Kurt Busch (97) attack the turns together using three different lines. Johnson and Busch were already assured a place in the final 10-race chase, while Martin secured his spot with a hard-fought fifth place in the race.*

Mayfield's destiny was fulfilled eight laps from the end. When race-leader Kurt Busch's Roush Racing Ford ran out of gas, Mayfield took the lead and sailed away for good. Jeff Gordon came home third in the Hendrick Motorsports Chevrolet, Mike Bliss drove a Joe Gibbs Racing Chevrolet to fourth, while Mark Martin, in another Roush Ford, finished fifth.

"We had no choice but to try to win the race and lead the most laps," Mayfield said. "We focused all week on that.

"I couldn't believe it (when Busch faltered)," added Mayfield. "The way my luck has been … there was no way he was going to run out of gas. I'm standing here now thinking, 'What the heck just happened?'"

What happened is that the native son of Owensboro, Ky., now had a chance to win the 2004 NASCAR NEXTEL Cup Series championship. What also occurred is that the tables were turned on the bookmakers, as far as Evernham Motorsports was concerned. Going into the Chevy Rock & Roll 400, the odds were on Mayfield's teammate, Kasey Kahne, getting into the 10-race chase. Following the Pop Secret 500 at Fontana, Calif., Kahne stood ninth in the standings, while Mayfield was trailing Martin, Jamie McMurray, Bobby Labonte and Dale Jarrett, going into Richmond 14th in points.

Instead, Kahne got bumped by Earnhardt Jr. on the 207th lap, which brought out the ninth of 10 caution-flag periods for 57 laps. Kahne was able to stay in the race, but a 24th-place finish did him in. He left the track 12th in overall points and lost a potential spot in the "big 10."

"We didn't get in the deal," Kahne said. "I thought we were going to have a good enough car to get in, but it just didn't happen. It stinks, running as bad as we did."

Jamie McMurray went into the event 11th in points and finished ninth in the Texaco/Havoline Dodge. That wasn't good enough, though, and he exited Richmond still 11th in the overall rankings and didn't make the cut.

"The motor just blew up again with about 25 laps to go, and there wasn't a whole lot we could do," McMurray said. "We don't deserve to be in it."

The only other drivers who stood any chance at all of getting into the ultimate chase were Kevin Harvick, Jarrett and Bobby Labonte. They went into Richmond 15th, 13th and 12th in points, respectively, and after finishing the race in 12th, 26th and 16th, in that order, left the track 14th, 15th and 13th in the standings.

"We looked like we weren't prepared for that," said Jarrett, the driver of Robert Yates Racing's UPS-sponsored Ford. "We ran terrible, just terrible."

With the completion of the Chevy Rock & Roll 400, points for the top 10 drivers were revised, with the leader assigned 5,050 and the remaining drivers assigned point totals down to 5,005 on a sliding scale of five points per position.

Drivers 11th and lower in the standings retained their point totals from the first 26 races of the season, and all drivers would now continue to accrue points according to the same system in place since the start of the season, beginning with the next event on the schedule.

Gordon went into Richmond second in points

and, with a third-place finish emerged as the new leader with 5,050 markers to his credit. His teammate, Jimmie Johnson, was the leader going into Richmond, but got caught up in an accident on the 179th lap. He finished the event in the 36th position and dropped to second in points with 5,045.

Earnhardt Jr., Tony Stewart, Matt Kenseth, Elliott Sadler and Busch left the event at Fontana, Calif., third through seventh in points, respectively, and emerged from Richmond in the same order. Earnhardt Jr. survived two incidents in the Chevy Rock & Roll 400 and finished second, while Stewart could do no better than come home 19th, a lap down.

*(Above) Kasey Kahne (9) takes a wild ride through the second turn after a bump from Dale Earnhardt Jr. in an incident that brought out the ninth of 10 cautions in the race. This was just part of a frustrating night for Kahne, who finished 24th and fell from ninth to 12th in the standings.*

*(Below) Dale Earnhardt Jr. (8), Mike Wallace (09) and Matt Kenseth (17) take on the frontstretch three wide in a Chevy-Dodge-Ford fight for position. Wallace held the lead for 45 laps and came away with a season-high seventh place in his fifth start of the year.*

(Above) Jimmie Johnson's Lowe's Chevrolet shows damage suffered in an incident that started when Jimmy Spencer and Casey Mears got together in front of the field near the halfway point in the race. Jeff Gordon, in the DuPont Chevrolet, barely escaped hitting Johnson and went on to finish third, taking over the points lead in the process.

(Right) Pole-winner Ryan Newman holds the inside in his ALLTEL Dodge with Jamie McMurray (42) on his right. Newman's 20th-place finish was not what he had hoped for but was just good enough to keep him among the top 10 at night's end. McMurray, who was battling to get into the top 10, finished ninth in the race but wound up 15 points shy of the field that would contend for the championship.

Defending champion Kenseth ended up 28th in the Richmond 400-lapper (mainly because of two error-ridden pit stops). Sadler started 20th and finished 17th, but he was already guaranteed a spot in the top 10. It was the same for Busch, who went from leading the race to finishing 15th, a lap down, because of a miscue that saw his Ford's fuel cell run dry in the waning laps.

Martin ran his heart out at Richmond — he started second and finished fifth — and that moved him from 10th to eighth in points,

while Mayfield's victory was, of course, rewarding, and he ended up ninth in the standings. Ryan Newman was eighth in points after California, and a 20th-place run at Richmond saw him drop two spots, but that was still good enough to join the others in the Chase for the NASCAR NEXTEL Cup.

Newman captured his fifth Bud Pole of the year and 23rd of his career by lapping the Richmond track in 20.979 seconds at 128.700 mph, which was quite a bit quicker than Martin's effort of 21.192 seconds at 127.407 mph,

while Johnson, Joe Nemechek and Jeff Burton rounded out the five fastest qualifiers.

"Not knowing how the race is going to start, it could be the most important pole we've had if there's a big crash in the middle of the field on the first lap, or something crazy like that," Newman said.

"I know for positive that we are going to run good," added Martin before the race. "I am tired of all this talking about it (10-race chase). I want to go race."

During the entire Richmond weekend, most of the chatter concerned the year's last 10 events and who might do what. One "study" concluded that Stewart would emerge as the 2004 champion. Other racing touts said the odds favored either Gordon (a four-time champion) or Johnson (whose team is partially owned by Gordon). And of course, don't rule out Earnhardt Jr., who is beginning to resemble his late father.

But for a while, Mayfield was the center of attention. He took 3 hours, 1 minute and 55 seconds to complete the race at an average speed of 98.946 mph and win $211,120.

Veteran driver Terry Labonte is normally quiet and unassuming. Maybe that's why the announcement by team owner Rick Hendrick

that Labonte had decided to begin some sort of partial "retirement" in 2005 almost got lost in all the hoopla. Labonte, 47, ran his first series race in 1978, won for the first time two years later and captured the championship in 1984 and 1996.

"I know Terry will run at least 10 races (next year)," Hendrick said. "That's all we know right now."

(Above) Jeremy Mayfield (19) assumes the lead with a handful of laps remaining as Kurt Busch fades to the inside, out of fuel. Dale Earnhardt Jr. (8) follows Mayfield past Busch but could not catch the red Dodge and finished second.

(Below) Two-time NASCAR champion Terry Labonte announced that 2004 would be his last season running the full series schedule, opting to race in selected events over the next two years before his retirement.

## Chevy Rock & Roll 400 *final race results*

| Fin. Pos. | Start Pos. | Car No. | Driver | Team |
|---|---|---|---|---|
| 1 | 7 | 19 | Jeremy Mayfield | Dodge Dealers/UAW Dodge |
| 2 | 14 | 8 | Dale Earnhardt Jr. | Budweiser Chevrolet |
| 3 | 9 | 24 | Jeff Gordon | DuPont Chevrolet |
| 4 | 33 | 80 | Mike Bliss | Conagra/Hunt's Ketchup Chevrolet |
| 5 | 2 | 6 | Mark Martin | Viagra Ford |
| 6 | 13 | 99 | Carl Edwards | Roush Racing Ford |
| 7 | 41 | 09 | Mike Wallace | Miccosukee Resorts Dodge |
| 8 | 8 | 16 | Greg Biffle | National Guard/Subway Ford |
| 9 | 36 | 42 | Jamie McMurray | Texaco/Havoline Dodge |
| 10 | 12 | 2 | Rusty Wallace | Miller Lite Dodge |
| 11 | 22 | 32 | Bobby Hamilton Jr. | Tide Chevrolet |
| 12 | 27 | 29 | Kevin Harvick | GM Goodwrench Chevrolet |
| 13 | 19 | 15 | Michael Waltrip | NAPA Chevrolet |
| 14 | 24 | 40 | Sterling Marlin | Coors Light Dodge |
| 15 | 17 | 97 | Kurt Busch | IRWIN Industrial Tools Ford |
| 16 | 18 | 18 | Bobby Labonte | Wellburtin XL(tm) Chevrolet |
| 17 | 20 | 38 | Elliott Sadler | M&M's Ford |
| 18 | 23 | 5 | Terry Labonte | Kellogg's Chevrolet |
| 19 | 15 | 20 | Tony Stewart | The Home Depot Chevrolet |
| 20 | 1 | 12 | Ryan Newman | ALLTEL Dodge |
| 21 | 6 | 21 | Ricky Rudd | U.S. Air Force/Motorcraft Ford |
| 22 | 4 | 01 | Joe Nemechek | U.S. Army Chevrolet |

| Fin. Pos. | Start Pos. | Car No. | Driver | Team |
|---|---|---|---|---|
| 23 | 5 | 30 | Jeff Burton | America Online Chevrolet |
| 24 | 11 | 9 | Kasey Kahne | Dodge Dealers/UAW Dodge |
| 25 | 10 | 43 | Jeff Green | Grand Biscuits Dodge |
| 26 | 25 | 88 | Dale Jarrett | UPS Ford |
| 27 | 37 | 77 | Brendan Gaughan | Kodak/Jasper Eng. & Trans. Dodge |
| 28 | 16 | 17 | Matt Kenseth | DeWalt Power Tools Ford |
| 29 | 30 | 23 | Shane Hmiel | Bill Davis Racing Dodge |
| 30 | 32 | 49 | Ken Schrader | Schwan's Home Service Dodge |
| 31 | 34 | 27 | David Green | Timberwolf Chevrolet |
| 32 | 28 | 31 | Robby Gordon | Cingular Wireless Chevrolet |
| 33 | 39 | 4 | Jimmy Spencer | Lucas Oil Chevrolet |
| 34 | 31 | 45 | Kyle Petty | Georgia-Pacific/Brawny Dodge |
| 35 | 29 | 41 | Casey Mears | Target Dodge |
| 36 | 3 | 48 | Jimmie Johnson | Lowe's Chevrolet |
| 37 | 26 | 25 | Brian Vickers | GMAC Chevrolet |
| 38 | 21 | 22 | Scott Wimmer | Caterpillar Dodge |
| 39 | 35 | 10 | Scott Riggs | Valvoline Chevrolet |
| 40 | 38 | 0 | Ward Burton | NetZero Chevrolet |
| 41 | 43 | 72 | Kirk Shelmerdine | Freddie B's Ford |
| 42 | 42 | 98 | Derrike Cope | Mach 1 Racing Ford |
| 43 | 40 | 50 | Todd Bodine | Arnold Development Co. Dodge |

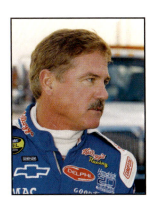

# And Then There Were Ten

## The Chase for the NASCAR NEXTEL Cup 2004

### Chase for the NASCAR NEXTEL Cup 2004

| Pos. | Driver | Points |
|------|--------|-------:|
| 1 | Jeff Gordon | 5050 |
| 2 | Jimmie Johnson | 5045 |
| 3 | Dale Earnhardt Jr. | 5040 |
| 4 | Tony Stewart | 5035 |
| 5 | Matt Kenseth | 5030 |
| 6 | Elliott Sadler | 5025 |
| 7 | Kurt Busch | 5020 |
| 8 | Mark Martin | 5015 |
| 9 | Jeremy Mayfield | 5010 |
| 10 | Ryan Newman | 5005 |

*After 26 races, 7,487 laps and 10,354.4 miles, 10 drivers earned the right to participate in the Inaugural Chase for the NASCAR NEXTEL Cup, the final 10-race stretch to determine the 2004 NASCAR NEXTEL Cup Series champion. Shown here with the NASCAR NEXTEL Cup trophy, they are (front row from left) Jeremy Mayfield, Kurt Busch, Mark Martin, Ryan Newman, (back row from left) Matt Kenseth, Dale Earnhardt Jr., Jeff Gordon, Jimmie Johnson, Tony Stewart and Elliott Sadler.*

The format for the pursuit of the 2004 NASCAR NEXTEL Cup Series championship seemed to prove true the old adage: "The cream rises to the top."

The 10 drivers who qualified for the first ever Chase for the NASCAR NEXTEL Cup accounted for victories in 24 of the year's first 26 races. Four each drove Chevrolets and Fords, and two were in Dodges. Roush Racing's Kurt Busch, Matt Kenseth and Mark Martin represented Ford along with Elliott Sadler from Robert Yates Racing. Jeff Gordon and Jimmie Johnson were in Hendrick Motorsports Chevrolets, joining Dale Earnhardt Jr. (DEI) and Tony Stewart (Joe Gibbs Racing) in the "Bowtie Brigade," while Jeremy Mayfield (Evernham Motorsports) and Ryan Newman (Penske Racing South) put the Dodge marque in the field.

Jeff Gordon started the season seventh in points after an eighth-place finish in the Daytona 500 and started moving up until an accident in race No. 5 at Darlington, S.C., caused him to drop to 13th. He improved one spot with a ninth-place effort at Bristol, Tenn., the next weekend and followed that with a strong third-place effort at Texas, which put him back into the top 10, where he remained from then on. Five wins over the next 15 races helped Gordon inch upward in the standings until August, when a seventh-place finish at Michigan put him in first place for the first time in the season. Engine failure at Fontana, Calif., in September dropped him to second, but finishing third in race No. 26 at Richmond, Va., put him back on top for the final 10-race Chase for the NASCAR NEXTEL Cup.

In addition to his series-leading five wins, Gordon collected 13 more top-10 finishes, dropped out of just three races and, with four series championships to his credit already, had to be considered a strong contender to win his fifth title.

Jimmie Johnson, in just his third full year of NASCAR NEXTEL Cup Series competition, tied Dale Earnhardt Jr. in victories with four over the 26 races contested so far. Eleven more top-five finishes more than offset five DNFs (did not finish), and Johnson ended up second in points. But for him it was a strange season.

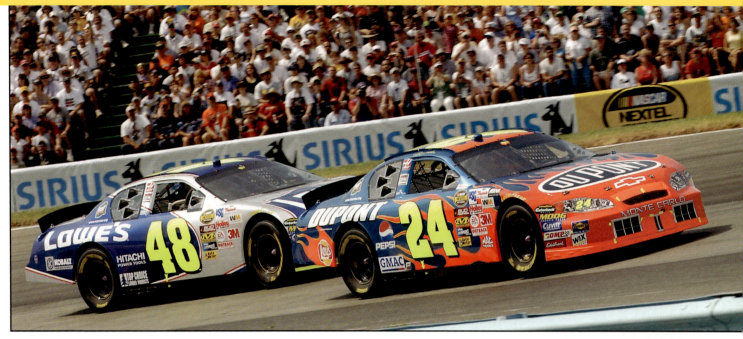

Johnson finished fifth in the Daytona 500, but an accident in the next event at Rockingham, N.C., dropped him to 25th place in the standings. He moved up six spots with a 16th-place effort at Las Vegas and then started marching forward. By the ninth race of the season, at Talladega, Ala., in April, he had moved all the way to second in points, where he stayed for five more races until a fourth-place finish at Michigan in June put him first. He remained on top of the standings through the next eight races, but engine failure in the second Michigan event (his third in a row) dropped him into second. Johnson regained the lead after the second race at Fontana, Calif., but finishing 36th at Richmond dropped him to second behind Gordon.

Johnson's past record and the resources and talent at Hendrick Motorsports would make him one of the favorites to take the title, but he would likely have to contend with his teammate and car co-owner to do it.

Dale Earnhardt Jr., who won nine times in his first four years of competition (2000-2003), started 2004 off by winning the Daytona 500. A fifth-place run at Rockingham kept him first in points, but he fell to seventh after dropping out of race No. 3 at Las Vegas. Winning at Atlanta in the next event moved him up to third in points, and he'd never go below that mark in the next 22 races. He regained the lead with a third-place run at Martinsville, Va., in April, and held it for the next six races before falling to second after the first

Michigan event. Running 25th at Pocono, Pa., in July, dropped him to third in points, where he remained through the 26th race of the season.

Aside from his four wins, Earnhardt Jr. collected another 11 top-10 finishes with just one DNF. Many felt that his ambition and drive could spell his first championship, and there's also the matter of perhaps desiring to honor his late father, himself a seven-time titlist.

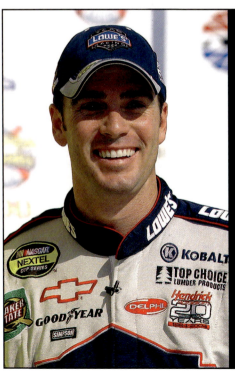

Jeff Gordon (above) and Jimmie Johnson (far left) made team owner Rick Hendrick (left) proud by taking the top two positions for the start of the Chase for the NASCAR NEXTEL Cup. Four-time champion Gordon, leading all drivers in wins, dubbed the final 10 events his "Drive for Five." Johnson's spectacular string of 13 top fives in 17 races gave him a lead so large that it took three straight DNFs just to knock him down to second in the points.

*Dale Earnhardt Jr. (right) started his season by winning twice in the first four events. He spent a total of nine race weeks at the top of the standings but eventually fell to third after injuries suffered in a non-NASCAR practice accident in late June forced him to use relief drivers in three of four straight races that produced finishes no better than 22nd.*

*Matt Kenseth (below) put up a strong defense of his series title by winning the second and third races of the season and then showing the kind of consistency that he and longtime crew chief Robbie Reiser (bottom, at right) have become known for.*

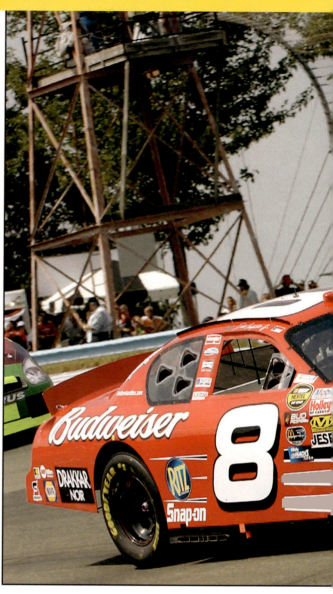

When Joe Gibbs created the No. 20 team in 1999 specifically for Tony Stewart, he took a gamble that paid off. Stewart was the Raybestos Rookie of the Year in 1999 and captured the series championship three years later. Though he never led in 2004 points, he never dropped lower than eighth in the standings and entered the Chase for the NASCAR NEXTEL Cup in fourth place with two victories, seven additional top fives, four more between sixth and 10th, and had just one DNF, an accident at Pocono in July.

Stewart's record from the start of his career, along with his philosophy of racing hard and letting the points take care of themselves, make him a credible threat to win his second series crown.

Defending series champion Matt Kenseth had an up-and-down season leading into the Chase for the NASCAR NEXTEL Cup. He started the year ninth in points, which became his low point, but jumped to second in the standings the following week with a win at Rockingham. Kenseth led the field in the next four events before finishing eighth at Texas and dropping to second. He never fell lower than fifth in points but stalled there after a mid-pack finish at Indianapolis in early August.

Kenseth won twice, had 13 more top-10 finishes and failed to finish three times. He won his first championship by running consistently well while winning just one race, and that consistency, along with another win or two, could just lead to Kenseth's second consecutive title.

Elliott Sadler (sixth in points) and Kurt Busch (seventh) each won two races over the first 26 events, while Mark Martin (eighth), Jeremy Mayfield (ninth) and Ryan Newman captured one win apiece.

Sadler labored for his spot in the Chase for the NASCAR NEXTEL Cup, but he was just one of four drivers (Earnhardt Jr., Kenseth and Stewart were the others) to never fall below 10th in points the entire season. He started out eighth, fell to 10th on three occasions and was in seventh after the second Michigan event. Winning at Fontana, Calif., in September meant that all he had to do at Richmond was take the green flag. Eleven top 10s while never failing to finish any of the season's first 26 events was good enough to place him among those who would contend for the championship.

Teammates Busch and Martin each earned a dozen finishes in the top 10, while Mayfield and Newman came away with 10 and 11, respectively. Busch started the year 16th in points,

It took 2002 champion Tony Stewart 18 races to post his first win of the season, that coming at Chicagoland in July. He followed that up with another win four weeks later at Watkins Glen (above) and spent the 16 race weeks leading up to the start of the Chase for the NASCAR NEXTEL Cup hovering between fourth and fifth in the standings.

*(Above) Like Tony Stewart did in 2002, Mark Martin started the season 43rd in points after a last-place finish in the season-opening Daytona 500. But he and crew chief Pat Tryson (left) never lost sight of the larger goal and finally cracked the top 10 at California in the season's 25th race. A top five in the next event at Richmond solidified his place among the championship contenders.*

*(Right) Elliott Sadler was among the group of four drivers who never dropped out of the top 10 in points. His win at California in September, the second of the season for the M&M's driver, all but assured his spot among those who would compete for the title.*

steadily moved up and took the lead after finishing sixth at Texas, the year's seventh race. From there, though, he continued losing spots and then gaining them back. After the race at Chicago in July, Busch had fallen to ninth in the standings and was only a little over 100 points out of 11th. Winning the first New

Hampshire race elevated him to sixth and, thanks to four more top 10s, he entered the Chase for the NASCAR NEXTEL Cup in seventh place.

Martin's story is one of perseverance. He finished last in the Daytona 500 and, from there, began a long climb through the standings.

A win at Dover, Del., in June placed him 13th in points, and with two races left before the field of contenders would be finalized, he was listed in 12th. It that event, at Fontana, Martin's third-place finish finally saw him crack the top 10, and a strong run at Richmond, where he started second and finished fifth, landed him in the Chase for the NASCAR NEXTEL Cup.

Mayfield and Newman both began the year "in the hole" (the former finished 25th in the Daytona 500 and the latter 31st) and each had to claw his way toward the top. Mayfield cracked the top 10 in points for the first time after the event in Watkins Glen, N.Y. Following race No. 25 at Fontana, he was listed 14th, but a stirring victory at Richmond did the trick. By squeaking onto the final list of championship contenders, he knocked teammate Kasey Kahne out of the running.

Newman was in the top 10 more than he was out over the 25 races that led up to Richmond, but five DNFs (four due to accidents) meant he had to work all that much harder as the schedule wore on. That he did. With two top-five finishes in the last three races, even a 20th-place finish in the Richmond event couldn't keep him from missing the final cut.

With the field set, everyone turned their attention to New Hampshire International Speedway for the first of 10 races that would decide who would become the 2004 NASCAR NEXTEL Cup Series champion.

(Top Left) Fourth-year driver Kurt Busch (left) and veteran crew chief Jimmy Fennig (center) created a formidable combination for powerhouse team owner Jack Roush (right) and entered the 10-race "Chase" in seventh place, one of three Roush-owned teams to earn a shot at the title.

(Middle Left) In their third season together, 2002 Raybestos Rookie of the Year Ryan Newman and crew chief Matt Borland (right) put together 11 top-10 finishes, including a win at Michigan in June, and took the 10th spot in points after Richmond.

(Bottom) Jeremy Mayfield (19), racing with Mike Wallace (09) and Kurt Busch (97), entered Richmond, the 26th race of the year, 14th in the standings after an up-and-down season. He did exactly what was needed to do by leading the most laps and taking the win, which vaulted him up to ninth in points and into the championship-contending field.

# SYLVANIA 300

---

### RACE NO.1

## NEW HAMPSHIRE INTERNATIONAL SPEEDWAY
### SEPTEMBER 19, 2004

---

For a while, it looked as if the start of the final pursuit of the 2004 NASCAR NEXTEL Cup Series championship just might be postponed, for a wee bit anyway.

The remnants of Hurricane Ivan swept through the eastern United States up into New England, producing heavy rains that washed out Bud Pole qualifying for the Sylvania 300 at the one-mile Loudon, N.H., facility. Two days later, though, the weather became more than cooperative, and with the starting field lined up according to car-owner points, 43 drivers were ready to contest the 27th race of the year.

This event, however, was different. For the top 10 drivers in points, it signaled the beginning of the 2004 season's 10-race Chase for the NASCAR NEXTEL Cup. Following the 400-lap race at Richmond International Raceway, the points for the top 10 had been adjusted and now just five points separated each member of the select group. The points remained the same for everyone else, and the goal for those in the second group was to finish 11th in the overall standings at season's end and collect a guaranteed $1 million bonus.

*(Above Left) Roush teammates Mark Martin and Kurt Busch discuss strategy in the New Hampshire garage during the Sylvania 300 weekend.*

*Robby Gordon's Cingular Chevrolet begins a spin in turn one after receiving some help from Greg Biffle's National Guard Ford on lap 17. The incident triggered a chain of events that would play out over the afternoon, severely affecting the championship hopes of two other drivers.*

The starting field takes the initial green flag for the Sylvania 300 led by Jeff Gordon (24) and his Hendrick teammate, Jimmie Johnson (48). After weather caused the cancellation of Bud Pole qualifying, the Chase for the NASCAR NEXTEL Cup contenders were lined up in the first 10 positions.

"I've always taken the approach that we really don't think about No. 7, which is to tie Richard and Dale; we think about the next one," Gordon said. "I'm amazed and blown away that we have four under our belt, and it's awesome for us to be talking about the 'Drive for Five,' which is the motto we have going around our shop.

"We can't think about No. 6 until we get No. 5 (and) we can't think about No. 7 until we get to No. 6. Right now, I know we've got a great opportunity this year. My race team is at the top of its game. ... I think we've got a great opportunity to win another championship."

Earnhardt Jr. was just as confident prior to the Sylvania 300. The driver of the No. 8 Budweiser Chevrolet had been in the mix for much of the season. Even injuries he received in an accident while practicing for a sports car event during a rare summer weekend between NASCAR races couldn't keep him from being a contender. Briefly on the sidelines, yes. Out of commission, no.

"We have a real shot at winning the championship," Earnhardt Jr. said. "We're a team that has been up and down, but if you look back on

*(Right, Above) Kevin Harvick is all smiles and ready to go during driver introductions. He was also smiling later after posting his 10th top-10 finish of the season.*

*(Right, Below) Matt Kenseth observes preparations on his DeWalt Tools Ford. Due to poor weather on Friday and Saturday, teams were forced to figure out their setups without the benefit of the usual practice sessions.*

So, at the beginning of the Sylvania 300, the lineup for the front of the field looked like this: Jeff Gordon, Jimmie Johnson, Dale Earnhardt Jr., Tony Stewart, Matt Kenseth, Elliott Sadler, Kurt Busch, Mark Martin, Jeremy Mayfield and Ryan Newman.

Going into New Hampshire, it was clear that for those drivers, all eyes were on the grand prize. Each competitor had something left to prove, and for Gordon, it was something he was calling the "Drive for Five." The DuPont Chevrolet driver had captured the series championship in 1995, 1997, 1998 and 2001 and was looking for a fifth title, which would give him two less than seven-time champs Richard Petty and Dale Earnhardt.

In the New Hampshire race, though, it turned out the man and car to watch were Busch and the No. 97 Roush Racing Ford. Starting seventh, Busch waited until well into the event to bare his fangs. When he did, though, he became too much for anyone else to handle and ended up winning his third race of the year and 11th of his career while completing a season sweep at New Hampshire.

Busch, who ended up leading three times for 155 of 300 laps, went to the front for the first time on lap 135 when he moved past Kasey Kahne and led the field through lap 183 when Earnhardt Jr. took over. Busch, however, went back to the front of the pack two laps later and paced the pack through lap 255 before pitting and ceding the lead to Ryan Newman.

Jamie McMurray, Kevin Harvick and Johnson each led laps late in the running, but when Johnson made his final green-flag pit stop on lap 264, the way was paved for Busch. He went to the front for the last time and beat

*(Left) Kasey Kahne brings his Dodge to a stop on pit road during one of seven cautions during the 300-lapper. Kahne's crew got him out first for the second restart, one of two times he led the race before posting a solid fourth-place finish.*

*(Below) Elliott Sadler brings his M&M's Ford around the corner in front of Jamie McMurray's Texaco Dodge, with Joe Nemechek on the inside in his USG Chevrolet. All three drivers added top 10s to their season scorecards, with McMurray finishing fifth ahead of Nemechek in sixth, while Sadler came home eighth to stay in the championship hunt.*

our NASCAR Busch Series days, we've always finished really strong in the last third of each season.

"We have a lot of tests coming up, and I believe the races at Kansas (October 10) and Homestead (November 21) are going to decide our championship chances. We've struggled at those places. ... If we get those figured out, we're going to be tough to beat."

his teammate, Kenseth, to the checkered flag by a healthy 2.488 seconds. Earnhardt Jr., Kahne and McMurray rounded out the top five, while Joe Nemechek, Jeff Gordon, Sadler, Michael Waltrip and Harvick were sixth through 10th, respectively.

Wet weather on Friday and more rain on Saturday had curtailed practice, so when it came to gearing and chassis adjustments, guesswork was the order of the day. Jimmy Fennig, Busch's crew chief, ended up making the right calls, which allowed Busch to take advantage of that "instant engineering."

"For us to be able to do this, a lot had to fall into place," Busch said with a smile. "To bring (the car) out and be able to make just a couple

*Robby Gordon goes spinning down the backstretch (above), bringing out the fifth caution of the day on lap 114. While Gordon was looping his car on the track, those of Jeremy Mayfield (right) and Tony Stewart (below) were behind the wall, being repaired after they became victims of Gordon's earlier retaliation against Greg Biffle. Stewart suffered the most, dropping four positions in the standings when the day was done.*

quick changes really played in our favor."

"I knew we probably weren't going to catch him," Kenseth noted. "Kurt had a great car. I just couldn't get in (the turns) like he did, so I tried to keep up with him as long as I could."

Spread throughout the race were seven yellow-flag periods for 30 laps, the first coming on the 17th circuit when Robby Gordon spun his RCR Chevrolet in the first turn after making contact with Greg Biffle's Ford. The second came on lap 36 when NASCAR officials called for a competition caution to check on racing and car conditions. The third caution period emerged on the 64th circuit and was the cause of much controversy.

## Chase for the NASCAR NEXTEL Cup Standings
*(With 9 Races Remaining)*

| Pos. | Driver | Points | Behind | Change |
|------|--------|--------|--------|--------|
| 1 | **Dale Earnhardt Jr.** | 5210 | — | +2 |
| 2 | Kurt Busch | 5210 | — | +5 |
| 3 | Jeff Gordon | 5201 | -9 | -2 |
| 4 | Matt Kenseth | 5200 | -10 | — |
| 5 | Jimmie Johnson | 5180 | -30 | -3 |
| 6 | Elliott Sadler | 5172 | -38 | — |
| 7 | Mark Martin | 5139 | -71 | +1 |
| 8 | Tony Stewart | 5086 | -124 | -4 |
| 9 | Ryan Newman | 5074 | -136 | +1 |
| 10 | Jeremy Mayfield | 5068 | -142 | -1 |

## Sylvania 300  *final race results*

| Fin. Pos. | Start Pos. | Car No. | Driver | Team |
|-----------|-----------|---------|--------|------|
| 1 | 7 | 97 | Kurt Busch | IRWIN Industrial Tools Ford |
| 2 | 5 | 17 | Matt Kenseth | DeWalt Power Tools Ford |
| 3 | 3 | 8 | Dale Earnhardt Jr. | Budweiser Chevrolet |
| 4 | 12 | 9 | Kasey Kahne | Dodge Dealers/UAW Dodge |
| 5 | 11 | 42 | Jamie McMurray | Texaco/Havoline Dodge |
| 6 | 25 | 01 | Joe Nemechek | U.S.G. Sheetrock Chevrolet |
| 7 | 1 | 24 | Jeff Gordon | DuPont Chevrolet |
| 8 | 6 | 38 | Elliott Sadler | M&M's Ford |
| 9 | 16 | 15 | Michael Waltrip | NAPA Chevrolet |
| 10 | 14 | 29 | Kevin Harvick | GM Goodwrench Chevrolet |
| 11 | 2 | 48 | Jimmie Johnson | Lowe's Chevrolet |
| 12 | 19 | 40 | Sterling Marlin | Coors Light Dodge |
| 13 | 8 | 6 | Mark Martin | Viagra Ford |
| 14 | 17 | 2 | Rusty Wallace | Miller Lite Dodge |
| 15 | 26 | 30 | Jeff Burton | America Online Chevrolet |
| 16 | 33 | 49 | Ken Schrader | Schwan's Home Service Dodge |
| 17 | 35 | 32 | Ricky Craven | Tide Chevrolet |
| 18 | 13 | 18 | Bobby Labonte | Interstate Batteries Chevrolet |
| 19 | 31 | 43 | Jeff Green | Cheerios/Betty Crocker Dodge |
| 20 | 21 | 99 | Carl Edwards | Roush Racing Ford |
| 21 | 34 | 45 | Kyle Petty | Georgia-Pacific/Brawny Dodge |
| 22 | 24 | 25 | Brian Vickers | GMAC Chevrolet |
| 23 | 36 | 50 | Todd Bodine | Yale Cancer Center Dodge |
| 24 | 23 | 5 | Terry Labonte | Kellogg's Chevrolet |
| 25 | 29 | 0 | Ward Burton | NetZero Chevrolet |
| 26 | 30 | 10 | Scott Riggs | Valvoline Chevrolet |
| 27 | 15 | 88 | Dale Jarrett | UPS Ford |
| 28 | 20 | 16 | Greg Biffle | National Guard Ford |
| 29 | 18 | 41 | Casey Mears | Target Dodge |
| 30 | 32 | 77 | Brendan Gaughan | Kodak/Jasper Eng. & Trans. Dodge |
| 31 | 42 | 02 | Hermie Sadler | SCORE Motorsports Chevrolet |
| 32 | 22 | 31 | Robby Gordon | Cingular Wireless Chevrolet |
| 33 | 10 | 12 | Ryan Newman | Mobil 1/ALLTEL Dodge |
| 34 | 41 | 09 | Mike Wallace | Miccosukee Resort Dodge |
| 35 | 9 | 19 | Jeremy Mayfield | Dodge Dealers/UAW Dodge |
| 36 | 27 | 22 | Scott Wimmer | Caterpillar Dodge |
| 37 | 28 | 21 | Ricky Rudd | Motorcraft Ford |
| 38 | 38 | 4 | Jimmy Spencer | Lucas Oil Dodge |
| 39 | 4 | 20 | Tony Stewart | The Home Depot Chevrolet |
| 40 | 40 | 89 | Morgan Shepherd | Racing with Jesus/Red Line Oil Dodge |
| 41 | 39 | 98 | Geoffrey Bodine | Mach 1 Racing Ford |
| 42 | 37 | 72 | Kirk Shelmerdine | Vote for Bush Ford |
| 43 | 43 | 80 | Ted Christopher | Commercial Truck & Trailer Ford |

*Kurt Busch (97) stretches his lead over (in order) Matt Kenseth, Jamie McMurray and Dale Earnhardt Jr. Busch took his third lead of the day on lap 265 and padded it into a two-and-a-half second margin of victory over Kenseth, while Earnhardt moved into third for the finish.*

Robby Gordon, who had threatened to "get" Biffle for the 17th-lap fracas, did just that and whacked Biffle, spinning both cars. The trouble was, they took championship contenders Jeremy Mayfield and Tony Stewart with them.

Stewart's team replaced the radiator in his No. 20 Chevrolet and got him back in the event, but he was eventually black-flagged for going too slow and finished 39th. Mayfield managed to coax a 35th-place finish out of his No. 19 Evernham Motorsports Dodge.

Gordon, who spun out again on lap 114, causing the fifth caution period, was penalized two laps and left the teams of Mayfield and Stewart fuming.

Well after the event's end, Gordon ended up issuing two public apologies for his behavior, but it wasn't good enough for Richard Childress, his car owner. Three days after the race, Childress put his driver on probation for the rest of the year.

"If there is one positive, I think this can make Robby understand that there is more to racing than just being aggressive," Childress said.

Busch, who said he was trying not to be overly concerned with the incident that may have removed two top-10 drivers from contention, directed his attention to festivities in victory lane. After completing the event in 2 hours, 53 minutes and 31 seconds at an average speed of 109.753 mph, he gratefully accepted the winner's check for $237,225.

# MBNA AMERICA 400

---
### RACE NO.2
### DOVER INTERNATIONAL SPEEDWAY
#### SEPTEMBER 26, 2004
---

Dale Earnhardt Jr. and Kurt Busch had gone into the Sylvania 300 at New Hampshire International Speedway — the first event of the 10-race Chase for the NASCAR NEXTEL Cup — third and seventh in points, respectively, and emerged tied at the top of the standings, each with 5,210 points. Although Busch won the race and Earnhardt finished third, Earnhardt was listed first and Busch second because of the tie-breaker rule: Earnhardt Jr. had won four races during the season compared to Busch's three.

"It's kind of nice to be leading the points again, even though I'd prefer to be up there by myself," Earnhardt Jr. said.

Added Busch: "Before the (New Hampshire) race, I joked about us coming out with the points lead. I didn't think it was possible, but we're really excited to kick this thing off with a win."

Jeff Gordon went into the Loudon event first in points, but a seventh-place finish dropped him to third, a loss of two spots. Matt Kenseth also had a good day in Loudon, finishing second to his teammate and moving up a slot in points from fifth to fourth. He entered the race with 5,030 points and came away with 5,200, just a single marker behind Gordon.

(Above Left) Ryan Newman celebrates his second victory of the season after thoroughly thrashing the field at Dover International Speedway.

Jeremy Mayfield's Dodge Dealers/UAW crew steps back as Mayfield prepares to launch out of his stall at the end of pit road, there by virtue of the fact that he won his second pole of the season, both of them coming at Dover.

To illustrate just how competitive the new points format is, Jimmie Johnson, Gordon's teammate, was sitting second in points (5,045) going into the Sylvania 300 but came away fifth, with 5,180, because of an 11th-place finish. And an eighth-place run didn't do much for Ford-driving Elliott Sadler. He went into the event sixth in points and emerged in the same spot. But with 5,172 points, he found himself trailing Johnson by just eight.

Yet Sadler left the track in an upbeat mood, noting, "Everything went our way. We did lead a lap (actually he led 20) and got five bonus points. So that will count at the end."

Although he wound up 13th in the Sylvania 300, Mark Martin's day ended on the plus side. With 5,015 points going into the event, he came away with 5,139 and moved from eighth to seventh in the standings.

*(Above) Dale Earnhardt Jr. (left) and Elliott Sadler discuss their setups in the garage. Sadler had a strong run going in the race until an unscheduled late-race stop for tires and a subsequent speeding penalty dropped him to 20th in the finishing order.*

*(Right) Tony Stewart wears his game face before 400 grueling laps on Dover's one-mile oval. After starting back in 23rd, the two-time Dover winner fought off handling problems and emerged with a sixth-place effort on the day.*

*(Far Right) A pensive Jeremy Mayfield considers his chances for a strong Dover run. Although he started from the pole, he never led the race but still grabbed a top-10 finish to keep his championship hopes alive.*

*(Below Right) Mark Martin (6) runs alongside Brian Vickers' GMAC Monte Carlo as he works toward the leaders. Martin, a three-time winner at Dover, stayed out of trouble and posted a runner-up finish for his fifth top five in the last seven events.*

Joe Gibbs Racing driver Tony Stewart wasn't as fortunate, though. He started the New Hampshire event fourth in points, with 5,035, and came away eighth with just 5,086. Stewart got caught up in an accident, the result of a clash involving Greg Biffle and Robby Gordon, and while his crew tried to repair his Chevrolet, he was eventually black-flagged and finished 39th.

"Well, it wasn't but two years ago that we left Daytona 43rd and came back and won (the championship)," Stewart said of the incident. "I can promise you one thing: This team has never given up, and they're not going to give up now."

Ryan Newman was simply the victim of a blown engine at New Hampshire that put him 33rd in the final running order. He led once for four laps, picking up five bonus points, and actually gained a spot in the

*(Left) The front end of Matt Kesneth's Ford sits outside the garage while the DeWalt crew hurriedly affects repairs to the race car that was damaged in the incident below.*

*(Below) Shane Parsnow, rear tire changer for Jimmie Johnson, comes to the aid of Matt Kenseth after he lost control of the car trying to enter pit road and landed on top of a water-filled tire barrier. The accident was costly for Kenseth as he fell to 32nd in the finishing order and dropped three positions in the championship standings.*

(Above) Ryan Newman must be feeling kind of lonely on the Dover concrete, but surely he doesn't mind! Newman, who swept the events here last season, put all but seven cars at least one lap down while leading 325 of the event's 400 circuits (that's 81.25%) and finished with an almost unheard-of 8.149-second margin of victory.

(Right) Dale Jarrett's team springs into action on the UPS Ford, helping their driver stay among the fray. Jarrett did just that, staying on the lead lap and finishing fourth to gain his seventh top 10 in the last 11 races.

(Opposite page) Brian Vickers' up-and-down weekend comes to an abrupt end on the Monster Mile. After wrecking his primary mount in practice, Vickers posted the third-fastest qualifying speed in his backup machine, but he lasted only 46 laps after the green flag fell before contact with the wall ended his day early.

standings, going from 10th to ninth. But that was at the expense of Mayfield, who was also involved in the Biffle-R. Gordon dust up. He went into the race ninth in points, with 5,010, and after finishing 35th, came away in 10th with 5,068.

In Bud Pole qualifying at Dover, Mayfield didn't beat the track record time and speed of 22.288 seconds at 161.522 mph, but his effort of 22.584 seconds at 159.405 mph was what it

took to give him the No. 1 starting spot in the MBNA America 400. Mayfield, however, would have had to beat himself, as it was he who had run the record lap earlier in the season.

"Hopefully, that's (starting first) going to keep us out of trouble. You have a better shot to stay out of a wreck," Mayfield noted. "Any time you have a race track you run pretty good at, you're confident."

The last driver to sweep both Bud Poles in a

## Chase for the NASCAR NEXTEL Cup Standings
*(With 8 Races Remaining)*

| Pos. | Driver | Points | Behind | Change |
|------|--------|--------|--------|--------|
| **1** | **Jeff Gordon** | **5371** | — | **+2** |
| 2 | Kurt Busch | 5370 | -1 | — |
| 3 | Dale Earnhardt Jr. | 5353 | -18 | -2 |
| 4 | Jimmie Johnson | 5314 | -57 | +1 |
| 5 | Mark Martin | 5314 | -57 | +2 |
| 6 | Elliott Sadler | 5275 | -96 | — |
| 7 | Matt Kenseth | 5272 | -99 | -3 |
| 8 | Ryan Newman | 5264 | -107 | +1 |
| 9 | Tony Stewart | 5236 | -135 | -1 |
| 10 | Jeremy Mayfield | 5214 | -157 | — |

## MBNA America 400 *final race results*

| Fin. Pos. | Start Pos. | Car No. | Driver | Team |
|-----------|------------|---------|--------|------|
| 1 | 2 | 12 | Ryan Newman | ALLTEL Dodge |
| 2 | 12 | 6 | Mark Martin | Viagra Ford |
| 3 | 21 | 24 | Jeff Gordon | DuPont Chevrolet |
| 4 | 11 | 88 | Dale Jarrett | UPS Ford |
| 5 | 13 | 97 | Kurt Busch | Sharpie Ford |
| 6 | 23 | 20 | Tony Stewart | Home Depot Chevrolet |
| 7 | 1 | 19 | Jeremy Mayfield | Dodge Dealers/UAW Dodge |
| 8 | 10 | 42 | Jamie McMurray | Texaco/Havoline Dodge |
| 9 | 16 | 8 | Dale Earnhardt Jr. | Budweiser Chevrolet |
| 10 | 9 | 48 | Jimmie Johnson | Lowe's Chevrolet |
| 11 | 19 | 16 | Greg Biffle | National Guard/Subway Ford |
| 12 | 14 | 21 | Ricky Rudd | "Keep It Genuine" Ford |
| 13 | 7 | 2 | Rusty Wallace | Miller Lite Dodge |
| 14 | 6 | 18 | Bobby Labonte | MBNA Chevrolet |
| 15 | 34 | 40 | Sterling Marlin | Coors Light Dodge |
| 16 | 5 | 15 | Michael Waltrip | NAPA Chevrolet |
| 17 | 27 | 45 | Kyle Petty | Georgia-Pacific/Brawny Dodge |
| 18 | 15 | 99 | Carl Edwards | Roush Racing Ford |
| 19 | 30 | 29 | Kevin Harvick | GM Goodwrench Chevrolet |
| 20 | 4 | 38 | Elliott Sadler | M&M's Ford |
| 21 | 28 | 43 | Jeff Green | Cheerios/Betty Crocker Dodge |
| 22 | 25 | 77 | Brendan Gaughan | Kodak/Jasper Eng. & Trans. Dodge |
| 23 | 29 | 22 | Scott Wimmer | Caterpillar Dodge |
| 24 | 26 | 41 | Casey Mears | Target Dodge |
| 25 | 31 | 49 | Ken Schrader | Schwan's Home Service Dodge |
| 26 | 36 | 4 | Jimmy Spencer | Lucas Oil Chevrolet |
| 27 | 38 | 5 | Terry Labonte | Kellogg's Chevrolet |
| 28 | 37 | 51 | Tony Raines | Buddy Lee Dungarees Chevrolet |
| 29 | 22 | 32 | Bobby Hamilton Jr. | Tide Chevrolet |
| 30 | 32 | 31 | Robby Gordon | Cingular Wireless Chevrolet |
| 31 | 18 | 10 | Scott Riggs | Valvoline Chevrolet |
| 32 | 8 | 17 | Matt Kenseth | DeWalt Power Tools Ford |
| 33 | 33 | 30 | Jeff Burton | America Online Chevrolet |
| 34 | 42 | 89 | Morgan Shepherd | Racing with Jesus/Red Line Oil Dodge |
| 35 | 24 | 01 | Joe Nemechek | U.S. Army Chevrolet |
| 36 | 35 | 37 | Kevin Lepage | Carter's-Royal Dispos-all Dodge |
| 37 | 17 | 0 | Ward Burton | NetZero Chevrolet |
| 38 | 3 | 25 | Brian Vickers | GMAC Chevrolet |
| 39 | 41 | 98 | Geoffrey Bodine | Mach 1 Racing Ford |
| 40 | 43 | 72 | Kirk Shelmerdine | Vote for Bush Ford |
| 41 | 40 | 09 | Joe Ruttman | Miccosukee Resorts Dodge |
| 42 | 20 | 9 | Kasey Kahne | Dodge Dealers/UAW Dodge |
| 43 | 39 | 50 | Jeff Fuller | Arnold Development Co. Dodge |

season at Dover was Cale Yarborough in 1980. Before him, David Pearson did it in 1973 and was the first driver to accomplish a Dover pole sweep. The track hosted its first "Cup" race in 1969 and, two years later, started hosting two annual events.

Newman went through the traps in 22.639 seconds at 159.018 mph, while Raybestos Brakes Rookie of the Year contender Brian Vickers was third quickest at 158.436 mph. The feat was heartening in that Vickers had wrecked his primary Chevrolet in a practice session and had to go to a backup machine before qualifying.

In the MBNA 400, Newman more than made up for a disastrous 33rd-place finish at New Hampshire by roaring back to win on the "Monster Mile." The driver of Penske Racing South's ALLTEL Dodge immediately grabbed the lead from pole-winner Mayfield, led 325 of 400 laps and breezed to a whopping 8.149-second victory over runner-up Martin. But with just eight races left in the fight for the 2004 NASCAR NEXTEL Cup Series championship, almost no one in the elite top 10 let any grass grow under his tires.

Eight of them finished 10th or better in the 400-mile event on the high-banked one-mile track. Included were: Gordon (third), Busch (fifth), Stewart (sixth), Mayfield (seventh), Earnhardt Jr. (ninth) and Johnson (10th).

The race winner led the first 32 laps, lap 49, 93-184, 196-260 and 266-400. Of the five caution-flag periods in the race, Newman was running first when four of them came to an end. When the race went green for the final time on lap 336, Martin found himself behind Newman, but he just didn't have a car that was equal to Newman's Dodge. By the time he'd reached the third turn on lap 336, Newman was about five car-lengths in front of Martin.

"I would have liked to have given Ryan a run for his money on the last restart," Martin noted. "I thought we could, but boy was I wrong."

"We've got to forget about today right now. If you're spending time celebrating, you're not spending time working," Newman said about his second win of 2004 and his third at Dover, where he swept both events a year earlier. "If we can finish in the top five in the last nine races, I can pretty much guarantee us a championship.

"But we can't finish 33rd, first and then 33rd. We'll just do the best we possibly can, and if we don't deserve it, then we won't get it."

Newman completed the event in 3 hours, 21 minutes and 34 seconds at an average speed of 119.067 mph and won $195,477.

# EA SPORTS 500

─── RACE NO.3 ───
**TALLADEGA SUPERSPEEDWAY**
OCTOBER 3, 2004

(Left) Just havin' some fun. Dale Earnhardt Jr. cracks a smile while doing post-race donuts in the Talladega grass after notching his fifth win of the year.

The field fans out five wide at nearly 200 mph through Talladega's frontstretch during the EA Sports 500, a race that featured 47 lead changes over the 188-lap distance.

D ale Earnhardt Jr. approached the EA Sports 500, the year's 29th NASCAR Cup Series event and third in the 10-race Chase for the NASCAR NEXTEL Cup, seemingly with everything in his favor.

The driver of the No. 8 Budweiser Chevrolet prepared for his 10th career start at the 2.66-mile speedway already carrying an impressive record there. It included four victories between October 2001 and April 2003 and runner-up finishes in his last two starts. Also, he went into Talladega leading all active drivers in victories and with a finishing average of 8.0.

"Talladega is so much fun," Earnhardt said. "It's not at all physically tough to race there, but the mental strain is extremely exhausting. You have to be aware at all times about where you are and where everybody else is.

"You're using every bit of your peripheral vision while trying to watch the guys behind you in the mirror and not running into the guy in front of you."

And sure enough, "Junior" disappointed no one. He started 10th, led nine times for 78 of 188 laps and bested Kevin Harvick, the second-place finisher, by 0.117 second at the finish.

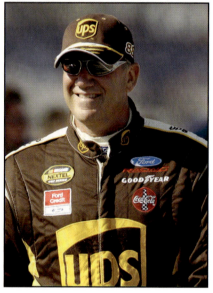

(Top) Pole-winner Joe Nemechek (01) moves up on the inside of Rusty Wallace (2), who's busy racing with Kerry Earnhardt. Earnhardt started his third race of the year at Talladega driving a Chevrolet fielded by Richard Childress.

(Above Left) Rookie Brendan Gaughan put together a career-best race, leading twice for seven laps and finishing in fourth for his first top five of the season.

(Above Right) Dale Jarrett wears a confident smile before the start of the EA Sports 500. After turning the third-fastest lap in qualifying, Jarrett held onto that spot and finished third to continue his team's strong performances over the second half of the season.

markers he was in third place, just 39 ahead of fourth-place Jimmie Johnson. The winner of four races in 2004, Johnson finished 10th at Dover and moved up a spot in points.

While Johnson and Mark Martin each had 5,314 points after the MBNA 400, Johnson was listed fourth in the standings ahead of Martin in fifth, by virtue of the tie-breaker rule. Johnson had four wins for the year as opposed to just one for Martin. Yet, Martin managed to move up two positions in points from seventh to fifth by virtue of his runner-up finish at Dover.

Elliott Sadler had a rough time of it at Dover but managed to hold onto the sixth spot in the top 10. During the race, he made a green-flag pit stop, thinking he had a soft tire, and he was caught speeding out of the pit lane after his stop was completed. The resulting penalty dropped Sadler back in the field where he eventually finished in 20th place and left the race with 5,275 points, 96 behind leader Gordon.

It was an especially tough day at the "Monster Mile" for defending series champion Matt Kenseth. While attempting to make a green-flag pit stop, he lost control of his Ford

One idea behind revamping the points system and having the top 10 in the standings duke it out over the year's final 10 events was to keep the competition close. And following the MBNA 400 at Dover, Del., close it was. Jeff Gordon, who went into that event third in points, finished third in the race and emerged as the new leader headed to Talladega.

But not by much. Kurt Busch came home fifth at Dover and left with 5,370 points, just one less than Gordon to preserve his No. 2 spot. For the year, Gordon had 20 top-10 finishes, including five victories, while Busch had claimed three wins and 11 more finishes of 10th or better. With just a single point separating Busch and Gordon, it was the closest margin between first and second with eight races still to be run since 1982.

Earnhardt Jr. corralled his 17th top-10 finish of the year with a ninth-place run at Dover but dropped two places in points. With 5,353

and slammed into a tire barrier. After taking the car into the garage for repairs, he re-entered the race and finished 32nd.

Kenseth blamed himself, saying he lost control. But he dropped three spots in the top 10, from fourth to seventh, and left the race with three points fewer than Sadler but just eight ahead of eighth-place Ryan Newman.

Newman, of course, couldn't have had a better race. He won the MBNA 400 and advanced one spot in the standings. The victory was his second of the 2004 season, but he would have to work hard continue to climb up the points ladder.

Although he finished sixth at Dover, Tony Stewart actually dropped a position in points, falling from eighth to ninth, while Jeremy Mayfield held onto 10th. Stewart left Dover with 5,236 points, 22 ahead of Mayfield.

In the race for 11th place, which at year's end would see the top driver take home a $1 million bonus, Jamie McMurray held onto the position and left Dover 99 points ahead of 12th-place Kevin Harvick and 106 up on 13th-place Bobby Labonte.

*Robby Gordon (31) and Scott Wimmer (22) chase Brendan Gaughan (77), with Mark Martin creeping up on the inside, all in a blur past the frontstretch grandstands.*

In Bud Pole qualifying, Joe Nemechek became the 11th different inside front-row starter of the year. He put the U.S. Army Chevrolet on the pole with a time and speed of 50.202 seconds at 190.749 mph. It was the Florida native's seventh career pole and his first in 133 races. His last No. 1 start came on Oct. 13, 2000, also at Talladega.

"It's about the car," Nemechek said. "The car has to be right and the engine has to be right. When the race comes, that's when the driver makes a difference."

Ricky Rudd, in the Wood Brothers' No. 21 Ford, was second quickest with a clocking of 50.239 seconds at 190.609 mph, while Dale Jarrett, Scott Riggs and Jeff Gordon rounded out the top five qualifiers.

In the race, 20 drivers swapped the lead 47 times. Earnhardt Jr. wasted no time showing he'd be the man to beat by taking the lead initially on lap four and leading through lap 22.

He then laid back, not pouncing again until the 98th circuit, when he went to the front after

*(Top) Kevin Harvick's crew prepares to launch the GM Goodwrench Chevrolet during a late-race gas-and-go. Harvick held the point briefly with a handful of laps remaining, but couldn't hold off the charging Earnhardt Jr. and finished a season-best second.*

*(Above) Kurt Busch (97) holds the inside edge against Rusty Wallace (2) and Elliott Sadler (38), while Ryan Newman looks for an opening for his ALLTEL Dodge. Busch took fifth place at the finish and would wind up on top of the championship standings.*

(Above) Elliott Sadler finishes, but it ain't pretty! Reminiscent of a ride he took down the backstretch in this event one year ago, Sadler takes another tumble, this time with the finish line in sight. The M&M's Ford rode briefly on the hood before landing on its wheels and taking the checkered flag ahead of four other lead-lap finishers.

(Below Right) With drafting help from Ricky Rudd (21), Dale Earnhardt Jr. (8) goes for the lead on Kevin Harvick (29) with a dozen laps left. Trailing the pack is Tony Stewart (20), who took the lead two laps later but finished sixth, while Robby Gordon (31) fell to ninth.

(Far Right) Dale Earnhardt Jr. celebrate his fifth career Talladega win after charging through the top 10 in the closing laps. It also gave him the lead in points, at least temporarily.

a series of green-flag pit stops. From there, Earnhardt led 59 of the remaining 91 laps, going to the front on seven more occasions. But it is after the final restart with five laps to go that he really got everyone's attention.

The victim of an untimely caution during final green-flag stops for fuel, Earnhardt sat 11th as the green flag waved for the last time in the race. Reminiscent of his dad's seemingly uncanny ability to defy the laws of restrictor-plate physics, Dale Jr. began a stirring charge, slicing his way through traffic. It took just two laps around the giant 2.66-mile tri-oval before the red-and-white Monte Carlo bearing the name "Earnhardt" steamed past then-leader Kevin Harvick and emerged at the front of the field. Once in front, the outcome was never in doubt, as Junior surged ahead to lead the final three laps on his way to the popular win.

"He just got up on the outside and got so much momentum ... he just drove by us," Harvick said afterwards.

The race was interrupted just five times for 22 laps, and this time around there were no massive accidents. Earnhardt Jr. completed the event in 3 hours, 11 minutes and 12 seconds at an average speed of 156.929 mph and took home $305,968, including the $90,000 NASCAR NEXTEL Cup leader bonus.

Earnhardt Jr. was absolutely jubilant in victory lane, but his ebullience would also put a damper on the day. When asked by a TV reporter how it felt to win five times at Talladega, Earnhardt replied by saying, compared to his late father who won 10 times there, it really didn't signify that much. But the scatological term he used on live television to emphasize his point was a definite no-no.

## Chase for the NASCAR NEXTEL Cup Standings
*(With 7 Races Remaining)*

| Pos. | Driver | Points | Behind | Change |
|------|--------|--------|--------|--------|
| 1 | **Kurt Busch** | **5530** | — | +1 |
| 2 | Dale Earnhardt Jr. | 5518 | -12 | +1 |
| 3 | Jeff Gordon | 5482 | -48 | -2 |
| 4 | Mark Martin | 5432 | -98 | +1 |
| 5 | Matt Kenseth | 5393 | -137 | +2 |
| 6 | Tony Stewart | 5391 | -139 | +3 |
| 7 | Ryan Newman | 5384 | -146 | +1 |
| 8 | Elliott Sadler | 5377 | -153 | -2 |
| 9 | Jimmie Johnson | 5371 | -159 | -5 |
| 10 | Jeremy Mayfield | 5263 | -267 | — |

## EA SPORTS 500   *final race results*

| Fin. Pos. | Start Pos. | Car No. | Driver | Team |
|-----------|-----------|---------|--------|------|
| 1 | 10 | 8 | Dale Earnhardt Jr. | Budweiser Chevrolet |
| 2 | 15 | 29 | Kevin Harvick | GM Goodwrench Chevrolet |
| 3 | 3 | 88 | Dale Jarrett | UPS Ford |
| 4 | 26 | 77 | Brendan Gaughan | Kodak/Jasper Eng. & Trans. Dodge |
| 5 | 8 | 97 | Kurt Busch | Sharpie Ford |
| 6 | 30 | 20 | Tony Stewart | Home Depot Chevrolet |
| 7 | 1 | 01 | Joe Nemechek | U.S. Army Chevrolet |
| 8 | 34 | 41 | Casey Mears | Target Dodge |
| 9 | 36 | 31 | Robby Gordon | Cingular Wireless Chevrolet |
| 10 | 28 | 0 | Ward Burton | NetZero/Shark Tale Chevrolet |
| 11 | 4 | 10 | Scott Riggs | Zerex/Valvoline Chevrolet |
| 12 | 2 | 21 | Ricky Rudd | Rent-A-Center/Motorcraft Ford |
| 13 | 13 | 30 | Jeff Burton | America Online Chevrolet |
| 14 | 7 | 17 | Matt Kenseth | Smirnoff Ice/DeWalt Ford |
| 15 | 17 | 6 | Mark Martin | Viagra Ford |
| 16 | 19 | 12 | Ryan Newman | ALLTEL Dodge |
| 17 | 24 | 42 | Jamie McMurray | Texaco/Havoline Dodge |
| 18 | 41 | 09 | Mike Wallace | Miccosukee Resorts Dodge |
| 19 | 5 | 24 | Jeff Gordon | DuPont Chevrolet |
| 20 | 37 | 49 | Ken Schrader | Schwan's Home Service Dodge |
| 21 | 38 | 5 | Terry Labonte | Kellogg's/Delphi Chevrolet |
| 22 | 6 | 38 | Elliott Sadler | M&M's Ford |
| 23 | 11 | 02 | Hermie Sadler | East Tennessee Trailers Ford |
| 24 | 22 | 33 | Kerry Earnhardt | Bass Pro Shops/Tracker Chevrolet |
| 25 | 14 | 15 | Michael Waltrip | NAPA Chevrolet |
| 26 | 33 | 2 | Rusty Wallace | Miller Lite Dodge |
| 27 | 23 | 9 | Kasey Kahne | Dodge Dealers/UAW Dodge |
| 28 | 12 | 16 | Greg Biffle | National Guard/Subway Ford |
| 29 | 35 | 45 | Kyle Petty | Georgia-Pacific/Brawny Dodge |
| 30 | 20 | 11 | Ricky Craven | Old Spice Chevrolet |
| 31 | 29 | 22 | Scott Wimmer | Caterpillar Dodge |
| 32 | 43 | 1 | Kenny Wallace | Aaron's Chevrolet |
| 33 | 42 | 98 | Larry Gunselman | Mach 1 Racing Ford |
| 34 | 32 | 40 | Sterling Marlin | Coors Light Dodge |
| 35 | 27 | 18 | Bobby Labonte | Interstate Batteries Chevrolet |
| 36 | 21 | 25 | Brian Vickers | GMAC Chevrolet |
| 37 | 16 | 48 | Jimmie Johnson | Lowe's Chevrolet |
| 38 | 9 | 19 | Jeremy Mayfield | Dodge Dealers/UAW Dodge |
| 39 | 18 | 43 | Jeff Green | Cheerios/Betty Crocker Dodge |
| 40 | 40 | 4 | Jimmy Spencer | Lucas Oil Chevrolet |
| 41 | 31 | 06 | Chad Blount | Mobil 1 Dodge |
| 42 | 25 | 99 | Carl Edwards | Roush Racing Ford |
| 43 | 39 | 32 | Bobby Hamilton Jr. | Tide Chevrolet |

Earnhardt was docked $10,000 and 25 championship points. That meant he fell from leading the standings by 13 points to becoming the runner-up, 12 points behind Busch. His team appealed, but NASCAR had no choice. Earlier in the year, it had fined two other drivers for the same offense, and the precedent had been set.

Earnhardt and his crew, though upset, took the penalty in stride. At his "surprise" 30th birthday party a few days later, crew chief Tony Eury Sr. gave him a gift-wrapped box. In it was a muzzle.

"A muzzle for my dog?" he asked.

"No," Eury replied. "That ain't for your dog!"

# BANQUET 400

## RACE NO.4
### KANSAS SPEEDWAY
#### OCTOBER 10, 2004

Sure, anyone who knows at least something about the geography of the United States is aware that Kansas is a landlocked state in the nation's heartland. But where was the U.S. Navy in the 2004 season's 30th NASCAR NEXTEL Cup Series race?

At least that was the joke circulating at the end of the 267-lap event, the fourth of 10 in the Chase for the NASCAR NEXTEL Cup, after Joe Nemechek, in the U.S. Army Chevrolet, had taken his fourth career victory. In doing so, he had to out-duel Ricky Rudd on the final lap. Rudd was 0.081 second behind in a Wood Brothers Ford sponsored by the Air Force, while Greg Biffle came home third in a Roush Racing Ford that sported the colors of the National Guard.

In a race that saw just four of the 10 drivers pursuing the championship finish in the top 10, Nemechek led only twice. Starting on the Bud Pole, he paced the first four laps, and then after taking the lead from Elliott Sadler, he led the final 37. Biffle led four times for 64 laps, while Rudd picked up five bonus points for leading once for two laps.

Championship contenders Sadler, Jeremy Mayfield (who went to the front five times for 72 laps) and Kurt Busch were fourth through sixth, respectively, at the checkered flag, while Jamie McMurray, Dale Jarrett, contender Dale Earnhardt Jr. and Brendan Gaughan completed the top 10.

*(Left) Joe Nemechek (left) and crew chief Ryan Pemberton enjoy the moment in victory lane after winning the Banquet 400 at Kansas Speedway. Nemechek's fourth career win was the first for Pemberton and the MB2 Motorsports team.*

*Greg Biffle attacks Joe Nemechek's flank in a battle of the armed forces at Kansas. Biffle's National Guard Ford led four times for 64 laps, but the Army conquered in the end with Nemechek leading the final 37 circuits on the way to victory. Biffle held on to finish third.*

(Above) A young fan offers his No. 9 seat cushion for an autograph by Kasey Kahne. The driver of the Evernham Motorsports Dodge would start on the front row and lead the event four times before a late-race spin down the backstretch forced him to salvage a 12th-place finish.

(Above Right) Kyle Busch (left) gets some advice from "big" brother Kurt, who just happened to be leading the championship chase. Kyle, sitting second in NASCAR Busch Series points at the time, was making his fourth start of the season driving a Chevrolet fielded by Hendrick Motorsports.

(Right) Jeremy Mayfield (19) leads the way, something he did for 72 total laps, more than any other driver during the race. A fifth-place finish, however, still left him 10th in the points.

(Below) Ryan Newman (12) spins toward the infield grass after slapping the frontstretch wall, while Tony Stewart (20) and Jamie McMurray scoot past unharmed. The biggest hit of the day for Newman, however, was the resulting 33rd-place finish that all but crushed his championship hopes.

For Nemechek, it was a heady fortnight. He'd taken the pole for the previous week's EA Sports 500 at Talladega, Ala., and then capped his second straight No. 1 start by winning the Saturday NASCAR Busch Series race at Kansas, and then the main event on Sunday. It was his first win since 2003, his first for the team and first for crew chief Ryan Pemberton.

"Deep in my heart, I know my team is capable of being in the top 10," Nemechek said. "This team has run strong; we've been strong all year.

"Incredible! What a day. This is cool. A sweep at Kansas."

Going into the weekend, Dale Earnhardt Jr. should have been leading in championship points, but he wasn't. After winning the EA Sports 500 at Talladega, a slip of the tongue on national television ended up costing him 25 points. That put Busch, who finished fifth in the race, first in the standings with 5,530 points and Earnhardt Jr. in second with 5,518.

Yet, both drivers still came out ahead. Busch moved from second in points to first, while Earnhardt advanced to second from third.

Jeff Gordon went into Talladega leading in

points, with 5,371, but late in the race was a victim of bad timing. He pitted for service just before the caution flag was displayed and, five laps from the finish, was stuck in 19th place. He ended up with 5,482 points, dropping him to third in the title chase.

Mark Martin slogged his way to a 15th-place showing at Talladega, but that was good enough to bump him up a notch in points from fifth to fourth. He came into the EA Sports 500 with 5,314 points and left with 5,432.

Martin's teammate, Matt Kenseth, also could have had a better time of it at Talladega but headed to Kansas a bit better off anyway. Losing the lead draft cost him — he finished 14th — but he advanced two spots in points and headed into Kansas fifth in the running with 5,393 markers.

Considering the fact that Tony Stewart's Chevrolet had a malfunctioning transmission at Talladega, he was lucky to come out of the event with a sixth-place finish. His 15th top 10 of the season saw him advance from ninth to sixth in points. But it was tight. With 5,391 markers, he was two behind Kenseth but just seven in front of seventh-place Ryan Newman.

As for Newman, he noted he was pleased to come out of the Talladega event with a 16th-place showing and a whole race car. He said he'd avoided several "potential big crashes" and headed to Kansas up a notch in the standings, from eighth to seventh, and 5,384 points.

Elliott Sadler, however, wasn't quite as lucky as Newman. On the final lap at Talladega, his Ford went airborne and he "flipped" to a 22nd-place finish. For Sadler, who dropped from sixth in points to eighth, it was "deja vu all over again." He also took a wild ride in the 2003 version of the event. The good news, though, was that he left the track just seven points behind Newman.

An incident on pit road with Kasey Kahne damaged Jimmie Johnson's Chevrolet, and the end result was a 37th-place finish. He also dropped five places in points, from fourth to ninth, and headed to Kansas with 5,371, putting him six behind Sadler and just eight in front of 10th-place Jeremy Mayfield.

Mayfield went to Talladega 10th in points, crashed out of the event, and remained in the same spot.

In the "race" for the million-dollar 11th-place position in final points, the standings following Talladega looked like this: Jamie McMurray, 11th (3,585 points); Kevin Harvick, 12th (3,549); Dale Jarrett, 13th (3,507) and Bobby Labonte, 14th (3,425).

When it came to qualifying for the Banquet 400, "Front Row Joe" appeared to have made a comeback. Nemechek lapped the 1.5-mile Kansas track in 29.974 seconds at a speed of 180.156 mph for his second consecutive Bud Pole and eighth of his career. The Florida native picked up the nickname in 1999 when he won three poles and his first race.

"We're on a roll, man," said Nemechek, who

had never before won back-to-back poles. "Right now, we're just communicating well."

Kahne couldn't come close to Nemechek's effort, but his run of 30.125 seconds at 179.253 mph put him next to Nemechek for the start of the race. Mayfield, Johnson and Bobby Labonte were third through fifth quickest, while Greg Biffle, Newman, Earnhardt Jr., Jarrett and McMurray rounded out the top 10.

In the Banquet 400, Nemechek steered clear of problems that brought out nine yellow flags for 39 laps. Others were not so lucky. Busch spun and brought out the fourth caution, and Johnson was then hit from behind and spun, as well. Newman slapped the wall and spun into the infield, interrupting the event on lap 210, and Johnson looped his car again four laps later and smacked into the wall.

## Chase for the NASCAR NEXTEL Cup Standings
*(With 6 Races Remaining)*

| Pos. | Driver | Points | Behind | Change |
| --- | --- | --- | --- | --- |
| **1** | **Kurt Busch** | **5685** | — | — |
| 2 | Dale Earnhardt Jr. | 5656 | -29 | — |
| 3 | Jeff Gordon | 5606 | -79 | — |
| 4 | Elliott Sadler | 5542 | -143 | +4 |
| 5 | Mark Martin | 5535 | -150 | -1 |
| 6 | Tony Stewart | 5512 | -173 | — |
| 7 | Matt Kenseth | 5505 | -180 | -2 |
| 8 | Ryan Newman | 5453 | -232 | -1 |
| 9 | Jimmie Johnson | 5438 | -247 | — |
| 10 | Jeremy Mayfield | 5428 | -257 | — |

## BANQUET 400  *final race results*

| Fin. Pos. | Start Pos. | Car No. | Driver | Team |
| --- | --- | --- | --- | --- |
| 1 | 1 | 01 | Joe Nemechek | U.S. Army Chevrolet |
| 2 | 12 | 21 | Ricky Rudd | "Keep It Genuine" Ford |
| 3 | 6 | 16 | Greg Biffle | National Guard/Subway Ford |
| 4 | 11 | 38 | Elliott Sadler | Pedigree/Wizard of Oz Ford |
| 5 | 3 | 19 | Jeremy Mayfield | Dodge Dealers/UAW Dodge |
| 6 | 22 | 97 | Kurt Busch | Sharpie Ford |
| 7 | 10 | 42 | Jamie McMurray | Texaco/Havoline Dodge |
| 8 | 9 | 88 | Dale Jarrett | UPS Ford |
| 9 | 8 | 8 | Dale Earnhardt Jr. | Budweiser Chevrolet |
| 10 | 13 | 77 | Brendan Gaughan | Kodak/Jasper/Wizard of Oz Dodge |
| 11 | 26 | 15 | Michael Waltrip | NAPA Chevrolet |
| 12 | 2 | 9 | Kasey Kahne | Dodge Dealers/UAW Dodge |
| 13 | 30 | 24 | Jeff Gordon | DuPont Chevrolet |
| 14 | 24 | 20 | Tony Stewart | The Home Depot Chevrolet |
| 15 | 17 | 30 | Jeff Burton | America Online Chevrolet |
| 16 | 5 | 18 | Bobby Labonte | Interstate Batteries Chevrolet |
| 17 | 15 | 17 | Matt Kenseth | DeWalt Power Tools Ford |
| 18 | 36 | 2 | Rusty Wallace | Miller Lite Dodge |
| 19 | 25 | 25 | Brian Vickers | GMAC Chevrolet |
| 20 | 18 | 6 | Mark Martin | Viagra Ford |
| 21 | 19 | 5 | Terry Labonte | Kellogg's Chevrolet |
| 22 | 16 | 99 | Carl Edwards | Roush Racing Ford |
| 23 | 31 | 32 | Bobby Hamilton Jr. | Tide Chevrolet |
| 24 | 38 | 23 | Shane Hmiel | Bill Davis Racing Dodge |
| 25 | 33 | 4 | Jimmy Spencer | Lucas Oil Chevrolet |
| 26 | 14 | 10 | Scott Riggs | Valvoline/Wizard of Oz Chevrolet |
| 27 | 32 | 49 | Ken Schrader | Schwan's Home Service Dodge |
| 28 | 23 | 31 | Robby Gordon | Cingular Wireless Chevrolet |
| 29 | 27 | 43 | Jeff Green | Cheerios/Betty Crocker Dodge |
| 30 | 35 | 0 | Ward Burton | NetZero Chevrolet |
| 31 | 21 | 41 | Casey Mears | Target/Energizer Dodge |
| 32 | 4 | 48 | Jimmie Johnson | Lowe's Chevrolet |
| 33 | 7 | 12 | Ryan Newman | ALLTEL Dodge |
| 34 | 28 | 40 | Sterling Marlin | Coors Light Dodge |
| 35 | 29 | 29 | Kevin Harvick | GM Goodwrench Chevrolet |
| 36 | 37 | 22 | Scott Wimmer | Caterpillar Dodge |
| 37 | 34 | 84 | Kyle Busch | CarQuest Chevrolet |
| 38 | 39 | 45 | Kyle Petty | Georgia-Pacific/Brawny Dodge |
| 39 | 20 | 50 | Todd Bodine | Arnold Development Co. Dodge |
| 40 | 41 | 02 | Hermie Sadler | SCORE Motorsports Chevrolet |
| 41 | 43 | 94 | Stanton Barrett | AmericInn/Racer's Edge Ford |
| 42 | 40 | 98 | Larry Gunselman | Mach 1 Inc. Ford |
| 43 | 42 | 72 | Kirk Shelmerdine | Vote for Bush Ford |

When caution period number eight ended on lap 246, Nemechek was still in control of the lead but wasn't ready for a surprise rally by Rudd.

"There at the end I was trying to save gas and here comes Ricky out of nowhere," Nemechek said. "I was like 'Holy Moley!' I had to get back on it. He got beside me one time, but I wasn't going to let it happen.

"It worked out just perfect for us."

Nemechek completed the event in 3 hours, 7 minutes and 39 seconds at an average speed of 128.058 mph, walked away with $310,725 and was the day's leading headline. Others, however, were also making the news.

Two days after finishing 21st at Kansas, Hendrick Motorsports driver Terry Labonte made a low-key announcement: This would be his last full season in the NASCAR NEXTEL Cup Series. He would step down gradually, running 10 races each in the next two seasons, saying he planned to make his final series start at Texas Motor Speedway in late 2006.

Born in Corpus Christi, Texas, in 1956, Labonte made his first series start in 1978 and won his first race two years later.

Several days later, fellow veteran competitor Mark Martin said he was going to make 2005 his final complete season in the series. Martin ran his first race in 1981 and was Roush Racing's "founding driver" when the team was formed in 1988. He noted he would not retire completely, saying his plans were yet incomplete, but said as far as NASCAR's top series went, that he'd "had enough of this battle."

# UAW-GM QUALITY 500

---
### RACE NO.5
### LOWE'S MOTOR SPEEDWAY
OCTOBER 16, 2004
---

The 31st race of the 2004 NASCAR NEXTEL Cup Series season should go into the annals of the circuit's history as being unforgettable, but for just what reason might be open for discussion. Would the event be remembered because:

• its winner made a clean sweep of all three of the speedway's major-league NASCAR events in 2004?

• the drivers ranked first and third in points for the Chase for the NASCAR NEXTEL Cup going into the event, both survived potential disasters to emerge in the same positions?

• or, one of the series' most promising rookie drivers was almost without dispute certain to win the event until a failed tire put him into the wall and out of action for the night?

It was a no-holds-barred contest that had 11 yellow-flag periods for 53 laps — the first coming on just the second trip around the 1.5-mile oval — and featured several gut-wrenching surprises. In the end, it was Jimmie Johnson who made the trip to victory lane after taking the lead from Joe Nemechek on the 318th of 334 laps. At the checkered flag, he was a comfortable 1.727 seconds in front of his Hendrick Motorsports teammate, Jeff Gordon, while Dale Earnhardt Jr., Kurt Busch and Nemechek rounded out the top five finishers. All but Nemechek were championship contenders in the Chase for the NASCAR NEXTEL Cup.

(Left) Jimmie Johnson (48) slips past Bobby Hamilton Jr. (32) on his way to completing a season sweep at Lowe's Motor Speedway.

The green flag waves as the field gets underway in the UAW-GM Quality 500, held under the lights for the first time in the event's 44-year history.

*(Right) Crew members attend to Scott Wimmer's Caterpillar Dodge in the Lowe's Motor Speedway garage. Qualifying and some practice sessions were held at night to help teams prepare for actual race conditions.*

*(Below) An enthusiastic crowd estimated at 140,000 packed the massive grandstands for the huge, Saturday night event.*

*(Below Right) Kevin Harvick's GM Goodwrench Chevrolet sports a yellow-and-blue paint scheme reminiscent of the mid-1980s, when team owner Richard Childress fielded similar-colored cars for Dale Earnhardt and sponsor Wrangler.*

"It's unbelievable to win at this track as much as we have. To sweep here is huge," said Johnson, who also won the Coca-Cola 600 in May and the NASCAR NEXTEL All-Star Challenge the week before that. The last driver to win both points-paying events at Lowe's Motor Speedway in the same year was Dale Earnhardt Sr. in 1986, and no one had ever swept all three events in a single season.

Kurt Busch and Jeff Gordon went into the event first and third in points, respectively, and somewhat miraculously emerged in the same spots. On the first lap, Greg Biffle's Ford hit the wall and involved five other cars, including those of Busch and Gordon. They, however, were able to continue, but when Gordon spun in the fourth corner on the 76th lap, his Chevrolet was hit by Rusty Wallace's Dodge, interrupting the race for the fourth time.

The two contenders soldiered on, though. When the race went green for the last time on lap 323, following the last caution, Johnson was

in the lead, Gordon was second and Busch was setting himself up for a top-five finish.

"That was the greatest comeback and second-place comeback in my career," Gordon noted. "The last pit stop the guys made was phenomenal. Then I thought we might have a shot at winning it."

For the longest time, it appeared as though Dodge-driving rookie Kasey Kahne, the owner of five runner-up finishes in 2004, would capture his first series win. Kahne started in second, took the lead for the first time on lap 42 and paced the next 83 circuits. He also led laps 130-176, 187-215 and then grabbed the lead again on lap 220.

Then the worst happened. On the 268th lap, a tire let go and he smacked the wall. In an

instant, he went from hero status to the garage with a 32nd-place finish.

"This was the best car I've ever had in my life," Kahne said. "I don't know what happened. It just ... went straight into the wall."

Busch had caught another lucky break the week before when he spun out during the Banquet 400 at Kansas Speedway but still managed to finish sixth. He went into Kansas first in points and came away still in the lead with 5,685. That put him 29 up on Earnhardt Jr., who finished ninth at Kansas for his 19th top-10 finish of the season.

Gordon, who said he "couldn't get a handle" on his car, was the 13th-place man at Kansas. He did, however, remain third in the race for the title, heading to Lowe's Motor Speedway

*(Above) Kasey Kahne and his Evernham Motorsports Dodge were simply dominant for most of the race, leading four times for 207 laps before an equipment failure sent him into the wall while leading on lap 268.*

*(Left) Kurt Busch (97) leads the way for Terry Labonte, who's ahead of Kurt's younger brother Kyle. The night was eventful for Busch, beginning with an early-race spin when Greg Biffle (16) got loose and hit the wall (below left), which produced the first caution on lap two. Busch recovered and later had a few more close calls, but battled back to a fourth-place finish and retained his lead in the championship fight.*

*(Right) With 11 yellow flags spread throughout the 334-lap contest, pit road was a very busy — and very crowded — place. The abundance of cautions also led to 14 cars finishing on the lead lap, with eight of those leading the race at least once.*

*(Below) In the final charge toward the checkered flag, Jimmie Johnson (48) keeps his Lowe's Chevrolet in front of Jeff Gordon's DuPont machine, Joe Nemechek's U.S. Army Monte Carlo and the Budweiser Chevrolet of Dale Earnhardt Jr. That Gordon was even this close was quite a feat, considering his car was damaged in an accident before the 100-lap mark.*

*(Opposite Page) Jimmie Johnson hoists yet another trophy earned at the speedway that bears his team sponsor's name. This one would make three in his last four regular starts, not counting this year's NASCAR NEXTEL All-Star Challenge.*

with 5,606 points, 50 behind Earnhardt Jr. and 64 ahead of Elliott Sadler, who, in part because of a fourth-place run in the Banquet 400, jumped four spots in the rankings from eighth place to fourth.

"Kurt Busch and his guys are doing a great job," Sadler noted. "We've got to try and beat him every week."

Although Mark Martin, with 5,535 points, was just seven in arrears of Sadler, he had a troublesome day in Kansas and fell from fourth

to fifth in points. Tony Stewart also struggled in the Kansas event and, after running in the top 10, ultimately fell to a 14th-place finish. But with 5,512 points, he remained sixth in the standings.

"We've still got six more races to get this done," Stewart said. "We can still do it."

Matt Kenseth had a "car number" finish at Kansas — 17th. Kenseth, who said he didn't "have a good car" and it was "difficult to drive," lost two spots in points and headed into the

UAW-GM Quality 500 seventh in the running with 5,505 markers.

Both Ryan Newman and Johnson left Kansas hoping for better days to come. Each was victimized by an accident and finished the race 33rd and 32nd, respectively. Newman fell one spot in points from seventh to eighth, while Johnson remained ninth. They were separated by just 15 points (5,453-5,438).

Just 10 points behind Johnson was Jeremy Mayfield. Although he came away with a fifth-place finish in the Banquet 400, he remained 10th in championship points.

In the race for 11th place, Jamie McMurray remained on top with 3,736 points. That put him 82 up on 12th-place Dale Jarrett, while Kevin Harvick (3,607), Kahne (3,549) and Bobby Labonte (3,540) were 13th through 15th, respectively.

After Bud Pole qualifying for the UAW-GM Quality 500 was over, Newman was definitely in an upbeat mood. He lapped the track in 28.590 seconds at 188.877 mph and set a track record in taking his sixth pole of the season, tying Gordon for the top spot in that category. Newman's lap broke the old record of 187.052 mph, set by Johnson in May for the Coca-Cola 600, when he took the record away from Newman!

"That was pretty close to a perfect lap," Newman said, adding that he'd told his wife he wanted the Lowe's Motor Speedway pole record back. "I came off turn four for the white flag, and I thought, 'Man, this is fun!'"

Fellow Dodge driver Kahne was second fastest with a time and speed of 28.820 seconds at 187.311 mph. Casey Mears, Scott Riggs and Sadler were third through fifth quickest in time trials, while Michael Waltrip, Kevin Harvick, Nemechek, Johnson and Carl Edwards rounded out the top 10.

Nine drivers failed to make the field. Among them were Kenny and Mike Wallace, Larry Foyt, Hermie Sadler, Geoffrey Bodine and Kirk Shelmerdine.

Johnson completed the event in 3 hours, 50 minutes and 51 seconds at an average speed of 130.214 mph and won $191,450. While in a celebratory mood, he said he knew his chances of winning the championship were, at best, slim. Three bad finishes in August, plus trouble in October at Talladega, Ala., along with his accident at Kansas had put a serious dent in his team's program.

"Maybe a top-five finish (in points) is a realistic goal," he said. "If these guys bobble up front, then we have a chance."

When team owner Chip Ganassi held a grand opening at his new shop in Concord, N.C., two days before the race, he also announced that Texaco/Havoline, the sponsor of McMurray's No. 42 Dodge, had signed a long-term agreement to continue backing the team. Ganassi had also exercised an option on McMurray's contract, keeping him in the car through 2005.

## Chase for the NASCAR NEXTEL Cup Standings
*(With 5 Races Remaining)*

| Pos. | Driver | Points | Behind | Change |
|---|---|---|---|---|
| 1 | **Kurt Busch** | **5850** | — | — |
| 2 | Dale Earnhardt Jr. | 5826 | -24 | — |
| 3 | Jeff Gordon | 5776 | -74 | — |
| 4 | Elliott Sadler | 5693 | -157 | — |
| 5 | Mark Martin | 5664 | -186 | — |
| 6 | Tony Stewart | 5646 | -204 | — |
| 7 | Matt Kenseth | 5635 | -215 | — |
| 8 | Jimmie Johnson | 5623 | -227 | +1 |
| 9 | Ryan Newman | 5579 | -271 | -1 |
| 10 | Jeremy Mayfield | 5501 | -349 | — |

## UAW-GM QUALITY 500 *final race results*

| Fin. Pos. | Start Pos. | Car No. | Driver | Team |
|---|---|---|---|---|
| 1 | 9 | 48 | Jimmie Johnson | Lowe's Chevrolet |
| 2 | 23 | 24 | Jeff Gordon | DuPont Chevrolet |
| 3 | 25 | 8 | Dale Earnhardt Jr. | Budweiser Chevrolet |
| 4 | 21 | 97 | Kurt Busch | IRWIN Industrial Tools Ford |
| 5 | 8 | 01 | Joe Nemechek | GI Joe/U.S. Army Chevrolet |
| 6 | 39 | 88 | Dale Jarrett | UPS Ford |
| 7 | 5 | 38 | Elliott Sadler | Combos Ford |
| 8 | 24 | 42 | Jamie McMurray | Texaco/Havoline Dodge |
| 9 | 35 | 30 | Jeff Burton | America Online Chevrolet |
| 10 | 15 | 20 | Tony Stewart | The Home Depot Chevrolet |
| 11 | 36 | 17 | Matt Kenseth | DeWalt Power Tools Ford |
| 12 | 31 | 40 | Sterling Marlin | Prilosec Dodge |
| 13 | 12 | 6 | Mark Martin | Viagra Ford |
| 14 | 1 | 12 | Ryan Newman | ALLTEL Dodge |
| 15 | 11 | 32 | Bobby Hamilton Jr. | Tide Chevrolet |
| 16 | 41 | 21 | Ricky Rudd | "Keep It Genuine" Ford |
| 17 | 34 | 18 | Bobby Labonte | Interstate Batteries Chevrolet |
| 18 | 19 | 31 | Robby Gordon | Cingular Wireless Chevrolet |
| 19 | 43 | 0 | Ward Burton | NetZero Chevrolet |
| 20 | 3 | 41 | Casey Mears | Target Dodge |
| 21 | 30 | 49 | Ken Schrader | Schwan's Home Service Dodge |
| 22 | 20 | 14 | John Andretti | VB/A Plus Sunoco Ford |
| 23 | 16 | 77 | Brendan Gaughan | Jasper Eng. & Trans./Kodak Dodge |
| 24 | 29 | 09 | Johnny Sauter | Miccosukee Resorts Dodge |
| 25 | 40 | 5 | Terry Labonte | Kellogg's Chevrolet |
| 26 | 42 | 22 | Scott Wimmer | Caterpillar Dodge |
| 27 | 32 | 45 | Kyle Petty | Georgia-Pacific/Brawny Dodge |
| 28 | 6 | 15 | Michael Waltrip | NAPA Chevrolet |
| 29 | 22 | 4 | Jimmy Spencer | Lucas Oil Chevrolet |
| 30 | 13 | 19 | Jeremy Mayfield | Dodge Dealers/UAW Dodge |
| 31 | 14 | 2 | Rusty Wallace | Miller Lite Dodge |
| 32 | 2 | 9 | Kasey Kahne | Dodge Dealers/UAW Dodge |
| 33 | 18 | 16 | Greg Biffle | National Guard Ford |
| 34 | 38 | 84 | Kyle Busch | CarQuest Chevrolet |
| 35 | 33 | 43 | Jeff Green | Cheerios/Betty Crocker Dodge |
| 36 | 7 | 29 | Kevin Harvick | GM Goodwrench Chevrolet |
| 37 | 10 | 99 | Dave Blaney | Canteen Vending/Kraft Foods Ford |
| 38 | 4 | 10 | Scott Riggs | Valvoline Chevrolet |
| 39 | 27 | 37 | Kevin Lepage | Carter's-Royal Dispos-all Dodge |
| 40 | 17 | 25 | Brian Vickers | GMAC Chevrolet |
| 41 | 37 | 13 | Greg Sacks | ARCDehooker/Vita Coco Dodge |
| 42 | 26 | 50 | Jeff Fuller | Arnold Development Co. Dodge |
| 43 | 28 | 51 | Tony Raines | Marathon/Chase Chevrolet |

# SUBWAY 500

---

### RACE NO.6
### MARTINSVILLE SPEEDWAY
#### OCTOBER 24, 2004

When the teams arrived at Martinsville Speedway to prepare for the Subway 500, five races away from the conclusion of the 2004 NASCAR NEXTEL Cup Series season, nobody knew exactly what was going to shake out. A lot of racing yardbirds, however, had a fairly good idea what kind of race to expect.

In effect, the competitors were facing a brand-new track. The 0.526-mile "paper clip" had been totally repaved with new concrete in the corners and fresh asphalt on the straightaways. Except for the previous afternoon's Kroger 200 NASCAR Craftsman Truck Series event, no one had run competitive laps at Martinsville since April.

"This has always been a track I enjoyed coming to," said Jamie McMurray, driver of Ganassi Racing's No. 42 Texaco/Havoline Dodge. "The fortunate thing is, I've gotten a chance to race in really good equipment. You can't really do it without that."

Of course, McMurray might have been a bit biased; he'd just captured the Kroger 200 NASCAR Craftsman Truck Series race, making him only the eighth driver to find victory in all three of NASCAR's top divisions. He'd also won five NASCAR Busch Series races and, in 2002, the 500-mile NASCAR Cup Series event at Lowe's Motor Speedway.

Jeff Gordon had five Martinsville wins to his credit, including both races last year. But he said, "It's not the same track, and we don't have the same edge."

(Left) The Lowe's crew finishes their service for Jimmie Johnson. Their day was busy, continually working on the car to help Johnson drive toward the front, which he did and took the lead with less than 100 laps to go.

Brian Vickers (25) holds position in Martinsville's tight corners with a challenge on his left by Sterling Marlin (40) and on his right by Ryan Newman (12).

(Above) Reigning NASCAR Craftsman Truck Series champion Travis Kvapil was at Martinsville to make his NASCAR NEXTEL Cup Series debut driving a Dodge fielded by Penske Racing South.

(Above Right) Kvapil (06) holds his position on the outside of Jeff Burton (30) through Martinsville's tight corners while getting a real taste of how it's done in the big league. The 28-year-old Wisconsin native handled himself quite well; he qualified strongly in fifth place and finished the race on the lead lap in 21st position.

(Right) Jamie McMurray wears a confident smile while preparing for the Subway 500. The day before, he won Martinsville's NASCAR Craftsman Truck Series race, and he would carry that momentum over for a runner-up finish in the main event.

Jimmie Johnson actually compared Martinsville, the shortest track in the series, with Talladega Superspeedway, the longest. "You can't get away from everyone or anyone," Johnson said. "You're going to have people around you, and if somebody makes a mistake, you're going to get caught up in it."

"With this surface, it's a whole new look and a whole new feel. The track surface definitely is better, (but) it still has its little quirks," noted Kurt Busch. The Roush Racing Ford driver won at Martinsville in October 2002 and was currently leading in the points after a fourth-place finish in the UAW-GM Quality 500, held the week before at Lowe's Motor Speedway.

Although Busch headed to Martinsville still with the lead, it wasn't by much. He was just 24 points up on Dale Earnhardt Jr. (5,850-5,826), who came home third at Lowe's Motor Speedway and retained the No. 2 spot in points. Earnhardt Jr. actually had more victories than Busch over the season so far (5-3) as well as more top-10 finishes (20-17), but Busch was the more consistent finisher of the two.

"It's very difficult to gain points when everyone else is running in the top five each week," Busch noted. "It's one thing to be lucky and another to be good."

Also with five 2004 victories, Gordon finished second to teammate Johnson the week before Martinsville and came away with 5,776 points, 50 in arrears of Earnhardt Jr. and 74 out of the lead. In fact, the top seven drivers in points before the UAW-GM Quality 500 came out of that event in the same positions.

Elliott Sadler's seventh-place run at the Concord, N.C., track was his 14th top-10 run, and with 5,693 points, he was 157 behind Busch and 83 away from Gordon.

Mark Martin, although remaining fifth in the points chase, was not pleased with his effort in the UAW-GM Quality 500. While running second late in the event, he was swept into an accident not of his making. Although he recovered to finish 13th, he left the track still fifth in points but just 18 up on sixth-place Tony Stewart (5,664-5,646) and 186 out of the lead.

"We did everything we could do," Martin said

after the race. "We had a shot, but it didn't work out."

Stewart ended up 10th at Lowe's Motor Speedway for his 16th top-10 finish of the year, but he had Matt Kenseth nipping at his heels. The defending NASCAR Cup Series champion lost control of his Ford and damaged his car after cutting a tire, but rallied back to finish 11th in the 500-miler and hold onto seventh place in the standings. He headed to Martinsville with 5,635 markers, 11 less than Stewart and with only 12 more than Johnson, who won the race and advanced from ninth to eighth in points.

Ryan Newman, who started first in the UAW-GM Quality 500, seemed to have a good

*(Right) Brendan Gaughan loops the Kodak Dodge in front of Jeremy Mayfield and Bobby Labonte, while Kevin Harvick (29), Scott Wimmer (22) and Jeff Gordon (24) take evasive action up high.*

*(Below) Cars leaving pit road get the "GO" sign as they prepare to rejoin traffic along the back-stretch. The NASCAR official controlling the flow had a busy day, as 17 caution flags flew over the 500-lap event.*

*(Bottom) Sterling Marlin (40) challenges Kurt Busch (97) off the corner in a battle for the lead. Marlin and Busch traded the point twice over a 23-lap stretch in the early going and then found each other at the end, with Marlin taking fourth place ahead of Busch in fifth.*

shot at victory. He, however, was involved in the same late-race accident as Martin but somehow managed a 14th-place finish. Still, he lost eighth place in points to Johnson, trailing him by 44 and 271 out of the lead.

Jeremy Mayfield also had an off-night at Lowe's Motor Speedway, running well at times, but then spinning out once and getting caught in the pits. He finished 30th, 57 laps off the pace, and left the track 349 points out of the lead.

Newman won the Bud Pole at Martinsville, his seventh of the season, second straight and 25th of his career, an that put him in the overall lead for the season-ending Bud Pole Award. With a time and speed of 19.513 seconds at 97.043 mph, he was one of 17 drivers to break the old track record of 19.855 seconds at 95.371 mph, set by Stewart in September 2000.

The packed house on hand for the Subway 500 was treated to a race with 22 lead changes among 12 drivers and 17 caution-flag periods for a record-breaking 125 laps — 25 percent of the race. More than a few drivers ran into trouble, but Johnson wasn't one of them. He kept his No. 48 Hendrick Motorsports Chevrolet out of the way as much as possible, took the lead from Sterling Marlin on lap 440 and drove to a 1.225-second victory over McMurray for his second straight win and his sixth of the year.

Starting 18th, Johnson took advantage of the mayhem and worked his way through it.

He led laps 405-410 before passing the lead to McMurray when he pitted under the 12th caution. When the race went green on lap 417, Marlin was in the lead, and he held it until Johnson made his move.

In an effort to win a second straight Martinsville race, Rusty Wallace took off after Johnson following the last restart on lap 494, but instead was punted back to a 10th-place finish after coming out second best in an on-track "spat" with teammate Ryan Newman, who ended up third. Marlin held on for fourth place, and Busch, who led four times for 120 laps, was fifth. Championship contenders Mayfield and Gordon finished sixth and ninth, respectively.

Johnson's victory celebration consisted of spinning his tires in front on the main grandstand crowd. But that came to a halt when he and everyone else at Martinsville were informed of a tragedy. En route to the Subway 500, a Hendrick Motorsports-owned twin-engine aircraft transporting two pilots and eight passengers had gone down on a mountainside several miles from an airport near the race track.

Details of the accident and the names of the occupants had not yet been released. Only the horrifying news that there were no survivors.

*Rusty Wallace (2) tries for the lead on the outside of Jimmie Johnson (48) (above) just after the last restart with only a handful of laps left. Ryan Newman (12) took advantage of the situation and dove to the inside, slamming the door on teammate Wallace, and then ended up battling Jamie McMurray (below) for second place as they crossed the finish line while banging fenders.*

## Chase for the NASCAR NEXTEL Cup Standings
*(With 4 Races Remaining)*

| Pos. | Driver | Points | Behind | Change |
|---|---|---|---|---|
| 1 | **Kurt Busch** | **6015** | — | — |
| 2 | Jeff Gordon | 5919 | -96 | +1 |
| 3 | Dale Earnhardt Jr. | 5890 | -125 | -1 |
| 4 | Jimmie Johnson | 5808 | -207 | +4 |
| 5 | Mark Martin | 5791 | -224 | — |
| 6 | Tony Stewart | 5769 | -246 | — |
| 7 | Elliott Sadler | 5760 | -255 | -3 |
| 8 | Matt Kenseth | 5755 | -260 | -1 |
| 9 | Ryan Newman | 5749 | -266 | — |
| 10 | Jeremy Mayfield | 5651 | -364 | — |

## SUBWAY 500 *final race results*

| Fin. Pos. | Start Pos. | Car No. | Driver | Team |
|---|---|---|---|---|
| 1 | 18 | 48 | Jimmie Johnson | Lowe's Chevrolet |
| 2 | 8 | 42 | Jamie McMurray | Texaco/Havoline Dodge |
| 3 | 1 | 12 | Ryan Newman | ALLTEL Dodge |
| 4 | 16 | 40 | Sterling Marlin | Coors Light Dodge |
| 5 | 7 | 97 | Kurt Busch | IRWIN Industrial Tools Ford |
| 6 | 11 | 19 | Jeremy Mayfield | Dodge Dealers/UAW Dodge |
| 7 | 10 | 43 | Jeff Green | Cheerios/Betty Crocker Dodge |
| 8 | 19 | 29 | Kevin Harvick | GM Goodwrench Chevrolet |
| 9 | 15 | 24 | Jeff Gordon | DuPont Chevrolet |
| 10 | 2 | 2 | Rusty Wallace | Miller Lite Dodge |
| 11 | 12 | 30 | Jeff Burton | America Online Chevrolet |
| 12 | 23 | 6 | Mark Martin | Viagra Ford |
| 13 | 38 | 9 | Kasey Kahne | Dodge Dealers/UAW Dodge |
| 14 | 9 | 21 | Ricky Rudd | Motorcraft Ford |
| 15 | 13 | 20 | Tony Stewart | The Home Depot Chevrolet |
| 16 | 25 | 17 | Matt Kenseth | DeWalt Power Tools Ford |
| 17 | 21 | 16 | Greg Biffle | Subway/National Guard Ford |
| 18 | 17 | 18 | Bobby Labonte | Interstate Batteries Chevrolet |
| 19 | 30 | 15 | Michael Waltrip | NAPA Chevrolet |
| 20 | 24 | 22 | Scott Wimmer | Caterpillar Dodge |
| 21 | 5 | 06 | Travis Kvapil | Mobil 1/Jasper Engines Dodge |
| 22 | 26 | 45 | Kyle Petty | Georgia-Pacific/Brawny Dodge |
| 23 | 36 | 31 | Robby Gordon | Cingular Wireless Chevrolet |
| 24 | 22 | 99 | Carl Edwards | Roush Racing Ford |
| 25 | 27 | 5 | Terry Labonte | Kellogg's Chevrolet |
| 26 | 6 | 10 | Scott Riggs | Valvoline Chevrolet |
| 27 | 34 | 25 | Brian Vickers | GMAC Chevrolet |
| 28 | 4 | 0 | Ward Burton | NetZero Chevrolet |
| 29 | 28 | 41 | Casey Mears | Target Dodge |
| 30 | 29 | 01 | Joe Nemechek | U.S. Army Chevrolet |
| 31 | 20 | 49 | Ken Schrader | Schwan's Home Service Dodge |
| 32 | 33 | 38 | Elliott Sadler | M&M's Ford |
| 33 | 3 | 8 | Dale Earnhardt Jr. | Budweiser Chevrolet |
| 34 | 14 | 77 | Brendan Gaughan | Kodak/Jasper Eng. & Trans. Dodge |
| 35 | 39 | 4 | Jimmy Spencer | Lucas Oil Chevrolet |
| 36 | 35 | 32 | Bobby Hamilton Jr. | Tide Chevrolet |
| 37 | 32 | 88 | Dale Jarrett | UPS Ford |
| 38 | 31 | 02 | Hermie Sadler | SCORE Motorsports Chevrolet |
| 39 | 37 | 98 | Chad Chaffin | Mach 1 Inc. Ford |
| 40 | 41 | 72 | Kirk Shelmerdine | Vote for Bush Ford |
| 41 | 42 | 80 | Mario Gosselin | Hover Racing Ford |
| 42 | 43 | 37 | Kevin Lepage | Carter Racing Dodge |
| 43 | 40 | 50 | Todd Bodine | Arnold Development Co. Dodge |

# BASS PRO SHOPS
# MBNA 500

In the days between the Subway 500 at Martinsville, Va., and the Bass Pro Shops MBNA 500 at Atlanta, the entire racing community was overcome with sadness that stemmed from the news of a downed aircraft owned by Hendrick Motorsports. The private plane had crashed into a mountain near a small airfield while en route to Martinsville Speedway.

Ten people were aboard, it was learned in the hours following the Martinsville race, and among the fatalities were team owner Rick Hendrick's son, Ricky; his brother, John; two nieces; Hendrick Motorsports' engine department director, Randy Dorton; the organization's general manager, Jeff Turner and Joe Jackson, DuPont's motorsports manager.

"The thoughts and prayers of the entire NASCAR family go out to all the families affected by this accident," said NASCAR CEO Brian France. "As a family-oriented sport, we are all feeling a very personal loss at this time."

Indeed, the blow was devastating. And with barely enough time to comprehend the loss, those involved in the NASCAR NEXTEL Cup Series gathered themselves, as they had done on other such occasions in the past, and returned to the task at hand. This time, it would be the 33rd event of the 2004 season, and a championship still lay in the balance.

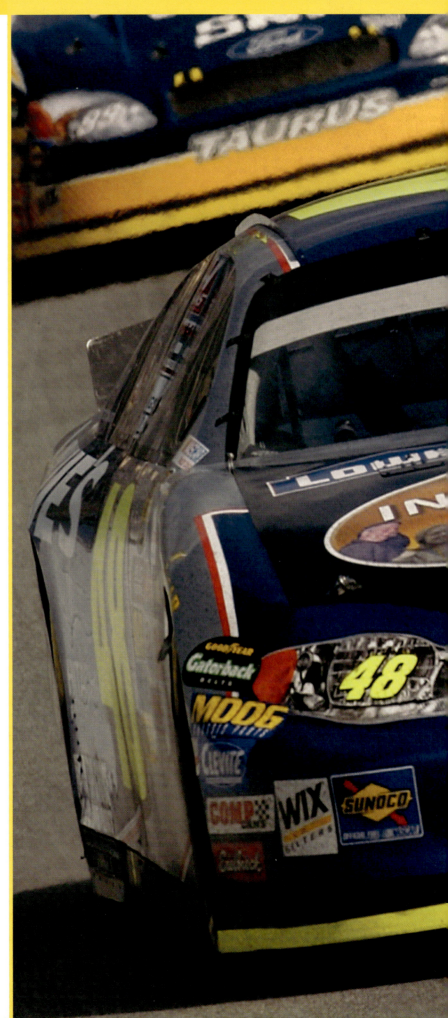

(Left) Good medicine. Smiles abound for Hendrick competitors (from left) Jimmie Johnson, Brian Vickers, Chad Knaus, Jeff Gordon and Terry Labonte, as all joined the winner's celebration after an emotionally draining week.

Jimmie Johnson's Lowe's Chevrolet sails through the tri-oval at Atlanta Motor Speedway ahead of Carl Edwards in the Roush Racing Ford. Johnson's win made him the first driver to score three straight victories since Jeff Gordon, who did it with a win in the 1999 Daytona 500 after sweeping the final two two events of 1998.

*(Right) Jeff Burton prepares for his day in the No. 30 AOL Chevrolet one day after team owner Richard Childress announced that Burton would take over the wheel of the No. 31 car, currently driven by Robby Gordon.*

*(Opposite Page, Top) Ryan Newman (12) and Joe Nemechek (01) pace the field before the start of the Bass Pro Shops MBNA 500. Newman's Bud Pole run gave him a series-leading seven for the year, while Nemechek was starting on the front row for the third time in the last five events.*

*(Opposite Page, Middle) Point leader Kurt Busch's day ends with his Sharpie Ford being loaded on the truck with a blown motor after completing just 51 laps. Even so, he left Atlanta still No. 1 in the standings.*

*(Below) Jeff Burton (30), Michael Waltrip (15) and Carl Edwards (99) race three wide ahead of Joe Nemechek (01) and Mark Martin (6). Edwards finished third (behind Martin) in his best performance to date, while Nemechek took fourth ahead of Burton in sixth.*

Kurt Busch arrived at Atlanta Motor Speedway with a distinct advantage in the Chase for the NASCAR NEXTEL Cup. He had gone into the previous week's event first in points, finished fifth in the Subway 500 and emerged still the leader with 6,015 points. That was 96 more than Jeff Gordon, who ended up

ninth at Martinsville and moved from third to second in the standings.

Dale Earnhardt Jr. simply had no good luck at Martinsville. He was swept into an accident, finished 33rd and dropped from second to third in points. With 5,890 markers, he headed to Atlanta 29 points behind Gordon but 82 in front of Jimmie Johnson.

"The car was awful," Earnhardt said following the event in southern Virginia. "It fell apart — went right out from under us today."

Though it was shrouded in sorrow, Johnson had a remarkable day at Martinsville. He backed up a win at Lowe's Motor Speedway with another victory and leaped from eighth to fourth in points. His 17th finish of fifth or better this year raised his point total to 5,808, but he had to keep an eye on fifth-place Mark Martin, who ran 12th in the Subway 500 and raised his own total to 5,791.

Tony Stewart paced the Martinsville field for 18 laps but ended up with a mediocre finish of 15th. He did, however, hold onto the sixth spot in points and left the track with 5,769, just nine more than seventh-place Elliott Sadler. It was also a frustrating event for Ford-driving Sadler, who was involved in two incidents, one a debilitating accident that put him out of the race and saw him fall from fourth to seventh in points.

Matt Kenseth also took a hit in points at Martinsville. He started 25th but could get no

higher than 16th and fell to eighth in the standings from seventh. Both Ryan Newman and Jeremy Mayfield remained static in the points at ninth and 10th, respectively, despite good runs at Martinsville. Newman started on the pole and finished third, while Mayfield advanced from an 11th-place start to a sixth-place finish.

Newman approached the Atlanta event with 5,749 points, 266 behind leader Busch, and with his championship hopes fading. But he apparently put that out of his mind, at least as far as Bud Pole qualifying for the Bass Pro Shops MBNA 500 was concerned. Newman recorded a lap speed of 191.575 mph, notching the No. 1 starting spot for the fourth consecutive Atlanta race. It was also his third straight Bud Pole and his eighth of the year.

"We've proven we're the fastest car on one lap. Now we have to do it for 60 laps in a row," Newman said. "We have to work on our car and keep the back end underneath (us) for the long runs."

Joe Nemechek was second quickest at 191.318 mph, Sadler was third (191.080), Carl Edwards fourth (190.988) and Greg Biffle fifth (190.561). Completing the top 10 qualifiers were Earnhardt, Martin, Johnson, Kevin Harvick and Gordon.

Fifty-eight drivers made qualifying laps, which meant that 15 failed to make the cut.

*(Right) Ryan Newman (12), Jeff Burton (30) and Bill Elliott in the McDonalds Dodge, demonstrate how to race while using all of Atlanta's 24-degree banking. The well-seasoned track allowed plenty of racing room, even with the speedway's newly-installed SAFER barriers.*

*(Middle Right) The day ends abruptly for the Budweiser Chevrolet just 15 laps from the finish. Dale Earnhardt Jr. was firmly in the top five and racing for third with Carl Edwards when the two cars touched, which sent Earnhardt Jr. into the backstretch wall.*

*(Below) Mark Martin (6), who dominated the event by leading four times for 227 laps, is left to chase Jimmie Johnson (48) in the closing laps. Johnson, with fresher tires after a late-race caution, moved around the Roush driver and held onto the top spot, while Martin could only watch from second place.*

*(Opposite Page) Jimmie Johnson motors quietly down pit road, checkered flag in hand, on his way to an emotional victory celebration for the entire Hendrick Motorsports organization.*

Among them were Raybestos Rookie of the Year contenders Scott Riggs and Scott Wimmer. Two drivers who did make the field, though, were Jeff Burton and Robby Gordon, both driving for Richard Childress Racing. Gordon had recently let it be known he'd be winding up his third full season with RCR and would field his own team in 2005.

Team owner Childress noted that Burton, who joined the organization in August, would fill the slot in the No. 31 Cingular Wireless

Chevrolet vacated by Gordon, while a driver and sponsor for the No. 30 car, now driven by Burton, would be announced later in the year. Childress' third driver, Harvick, would remain in the No. 29 GM Goodwrench Chevrolet, a ride he'd been in since early 2001.

In a race filled with drama, Johnson, who started eighth, led four times for just 17 of the event's 325 laps. Included though, were the all-important final 10 around the 1.54-mile track.

Johnson passed Martin's No. 6 Roush Racing Ford to lead laps 116-119 and then passed Martin again to pace lap 237. He was running strong, but it looked as if Martin, who had dominated the event by leading four times for 227 laps, would emerge as the victor.

Then when the fifth of six caution-flag periods began on lap 301, Johnson pitted and got four new tires. Martin, caught in a dilemma (if

he pitted, his competition wouldn't and vice versa) elected to stay on the track and in the lead. The race went green on lap 306, and four circuits later Johnson shot by Martin for the lead. One lap after that, Earnhardt, while battling Carl Edwards for third place, tapped Edward's Ford, then spun, crashed out of the race and finished 33rd.

Kasey Kahne paced the field during the ensuing caution (laps 312-315) while the leaders all pitted for fresh rubber, but he was no match for Johnson once the field returned to green. He passed Kahne on the 316th circuit, while all Martin (also with fresh Goodyears) could do was try to run down Johnson. At the finish, he came up 0.293 second short.

Edwards, Nemechek and Kahne completed the top five, while Jeff Burton, Brian Vickers, Jamie McMurray, Stewart and Biffle were sixth through 10th, respectively.

Busch's day came to an end on lap 52 because of a blown engine. He, however, retained the points lead, only because a rear-end gear on Gordon's Chevrolet broke, relegating him to a 34th-place finish.

After taking a ceremonial backwards lap with checkered flag in hand, Johnson went to victory circle, which was already jam-packed with as many members of the Hendrick Motorsports family as could find a spot to stand, all there to congratulate the winner.

With their racing caps on backwards in honor of Ricky Hendrick, who drove his father to distraction by wearing his cap with the bill in the back, crewmen from all four Hendrick Motorsports teams crowded around Jimmie Johnson. They were there not just to congratulate him on his third straight win and seventh of the season, but also to partake of a joyful occasion. In a way, it made up for the week before when Johnson forewent any celebration in Martinsville and instead joined everyone in sorrow and grief.

Now, at Atlanta, the tragedy could momentarily but put aside. "This is medicine," Johnson said. "Maybe this will put a smile on the faces of some of our family at Hendrick Motorsports. I don't think they've smiled all week."

Circumstances that had worked against contenders Busch, Gordon, Martin and Earnhardt in the Chase for the NASCAR NEXTEL Cup all contributed to Johnson's win and a jump in the point standings from fourth to second place. Once again, it now appeared that the driver of the No. 48 Lowe's Chevrolet had, with three races left, a real shot at the title.

## Chase for the NASCAR NEXTEL Cup Standings
*(With 3 Races Remaining)*

| Pos. | Driver | Points | Behind | Change |
|------|--------|--------|--------|--------|
| 1 | **Kurt Busch** | **6052** | — | — |
| 2 | Jimmie Johnson | 5993 | -59 | +2 |
| 3 | Jeff Gordon | 5980 | -72 | -1 |
| 4 | Mark Martin | 5971 | -81 | +1 |
| 5 | Dale Earnhardt Jr. | 5954 | -98 | -2 |
| 6 | Tony Stewart | 5907 | -145 | — |
| 7 | Ryan Newman | 5866 | -186 | +2 |
| 8 | Elliott Sadler | 5815 | -237 | -1 |
| 9 | Matt Kenseth | 5795 | -257 | -1 |
| 10 | Jeremy Mayfield | 5736 | -316 | — |

## BASS PRO SHOPS MBNA 500 *final race results*

| Fin. Pos. | Start Pos. | Car No. | Driver | Team |
|-----------|-----------|---------|--------|------|
| 1 | 8 | 48 | Jimmie Johnson | Lowe's Chevrolet |
| 2 | 7 | 6 | Mark Martin | Viagra Ford |
| 3 | 4 | 99 | Carl Edwards | World Financial Group Ford |
| 4 | 2 | 01 | Joe Nemechek | U.S. Army Chevrolet |
| 5 | 32 | 9 | Kasey Kahne | Dodge Dealers/UAW Dodge |
| 6 | 21 | 30 | Jeff Burton | America Online Chevrolet |
| 7 | 13 | 25 | Brian Vickers | GMAC Chevrolet |
| 8 | 29 | 42 | Jamie McMurray | Texaco/Havoline Dodge |
| 9 | 15 | 20 | Tony Stewart | Home Depot Chevrolet |
| 10 | 5 | 16 | Greg Biffle | National Guard/Subway Ford |
| 11 | 12 | 2 | Rusty Wallace | Miller Lite Dodge |
| 12 | 43 | 21 | Ricky Rudd | Rent-a-Center Motorcraft Ford |
| 13 | 16 | 41 | Casey Mears | Target Dodge |
| 14 | 40 | 15 | Michael Waltrip | NAPA Chevrolet |
| 15 | 20 | 88 | Dale Jarrett | UPS Ford |
| 16 | 14 | 31 | Robby Gordon | Cingular Wireless Chevrolet |
| 17 | 1 | 12 | Ryan Newman | Mobil 1/ALLTEL Dodge |
| 18 | 25 | 77 | Brendan Gaughan | Jasper Eng. & Trans./Kodak Dodge |
| 19 | 41 | 40 | Sterling Marlin | Coors Light Dodge |
| 20 | 19 | 18 | Bobby Labonte | Wellbutrin XL(tm) Chevrolet |
| 21 | 35 | 43 | Jeff Green | Bugles Dodge |
| 22 | 38 | 98 | Bill Elliott | McDonald's Dodge |
| 23 | 37 | 49 | Ken Schrader | Red Baron Frozen Pizza Dodge |
| 24 | 31 | 23 | Shane Hmiel | CAT Dodge |
| 25 | 17 | 14 | John Andretti | VB/APlus at Sunoco Ford |
| 26 | 11 | 19 | Jeremy Mayfield | Dodge Dealers/UAW Dodge |
| 27 | 36 | 11 | J.J. Yeley | MBNA Chevrolet |
| 28 | 23 | 37 | Kevin Lepage | Carter Racing Dodge |
| 29 | 18 | 45 | Kyle Petty | Georgia-Pacific/Brawny Dodge |
| 30 | 34 | 0 | Ward Burton | NetZero Chevrolet |
| 31 | 42 | 5 | Terry Labonte | Kellogg's Chevrolet |
| 32 | 26 | 06 | Travis Kvapil | Mobil 1 Dodge |
| 33 | 6 | 8 | Dale Earnhardt Jr. | Budweiser Chevrolet |
| 34 | 10 | 24 | Jeff Gordon | DuPont Chevrolet |
| 35 | 9 | 29 | Kevin Harvick | GM Goodwrench Chevrolet |
| 36 | 3 | 38 | Elliott Sadler | M&M's Ford |
| 37 | 33 | 1 | Martin Truex Jr. | Bass Pro Shops Chevrolet |
| 38 | 27 | 32 | Bobby Hamilton Jr. | Tide Chevrolet |
| 39 | 24 | 50 | Todd Bodine | U.S. Micro Dodge |
| 40 | 30 | 51 | Tony Raines | Universal/Marathon Oil Products Chev. |
| 41 | 39 | 17 | Matt Kenseth | DeWalt Power Tools Ford |
| 42 | 22 | 97 | Kurt Busch | Sharpie Ford |
| 43 | 28 | 84 | Kyle Busch | CarQuest Chevrolet |

# CHECKER
# AUTO PARTS 500

Although Phoenix International Raceway is located in one of the nation's most arid areas, precipitation does sometimes dampen the desert.

Rain soaked the area the night before the start of the year's 34th stop on the NASCAR NEXTEL Cup Series tour. By race time, though, it was dry enough for an on-time start of the scheduled 500-kilometer, 312-mile event.

And as the race got underway, Dale Earnhardt Jr. was determined to make up for his previous week's performance at Atlanta Motor Speedway, where, after a very competitive run that could have vaulted him to the top of the standings, he was involved in a late-race accident and instead finished 33rd. Third in the standings going in, Earnhardt left the track fifth, 98 points out of the lead.

Kurt Busch's day at Atlanta was as tough as Earnhardt's. The engine in his Ford blew and he finished 42nd, but an odd turn of events left him still first in the Chase for the NASCAR NEXTEL Cup with 6,052 points.

Jimmie Johnson's seventh win of the season boosted him from fourth to second in the standings, where he now stood 59 points away from the top slot, while his teammate, Jeff Gordon, salvaged what could have been a disastrous race.

(Left) Crew chief Tony Eury Sr. (left) and driver Dale Earnhardt Jr. seem pleased with car preparations leading up to the Checker Auto Parts 500. Indeed, they had reason to smile; the Budweiser Chevrolet proved fastest in the field on its way to victory lane.

Ryan Newman's ALLTEL Dodge leads the way ahead of Dale Earnhardt Jr.'s Budweiser Chevrolet and Kasey Kahne's Dodge Dealers Dodge, while Robby Gordon looks for an opening on the outside in his Cingular Chevrolet. Newman, who led the first 59 laps, stayed among the leaders for most of the race and wound up runner-up to Earnhardt Jr. at the finish.

Atlanta was another "near miss" for Mark Martin. He ran strong, but after dicing with Roush Racing teammates Greg Biffle and Carl Edwards late in the event, he came home second to Johnson. Martin's ninth top-five finish of the year allowed him to advance one spot in the standings, from fifth to fourth, and he arrived in Phoenix just nine points behind Gordon and 17 up on Earnhardt Jr., who fell from third to fifth.

"I told you guys they weren't my teammates," Martin joked, referring to Biffle and Edwards. "If they were ... they'd only be on the race track to make sure I won."

A workmanlike ninth-place run by Home Depot Chevrolet driver Tony Stewart at Atlanta got him nowhere in the battle for the title. He went into the event sixth in points and emerged in the same spot with 5,907 markers. That put him 47 behind Earnhardt Jr. and 41 ahead of Ryan Newman, who started on the pole but ended up finishing 17th. Newman had decided to "play it safe" when he re-pitted after a scheduled stop because of a tire vibration, a move that likely cost him a spot in the top 10.

The victim of a freak pit-road accident — he collided with another car — Elliott Sadler saw a third-place start turn into a 36th-place finish. His Ford never really recovered, and the Robert Yates Racing driver fell from seventh to eighth in the standings, leaving Atlanta with 5,815 points, 237 behind Busch.

Matt Kenseth also took a one-position dive in points, falling to ninth from eighth, because of a blown engine that resulted in a 41st-place finish. He left Atlanta just 59 markers up on 10th-place Jeremy Mayfield.

Jamie McMurray, who finished eighth at Atlanta, seemed to have a lock on 11th place in

*(Above) Observers take advantage of the great view atop the infield bridge to watch competitors leave the garage and head out to the track during practice. Rains during the weekend wetted the asphalt, but not enough to cancel practice and qualifying.*

*(Right) Ryan Newman (12) leads the field toward the initial green flag with second-fastest qualifier Brian Vickers (25) on his right followed by third-quickest Joe Nemechek in the U.S. Army Chevrolet. Newman's track record qualifying run was his fourth consecutive first-place start and locked up the annual Bud Pole Award for the second straight year.*

A rear-end gear on Gordon's car broke while he was in the pits, and he ended up in the garage for emergency repairs. He got back into the event, finished 34th and lost just one spot in the points. He headed to Arizona in the No. 3 position with 5,980 markers, just 13 in back of Johnson and 72 behind Busch.

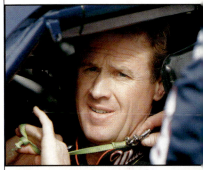

(Left) The Interstate Batteries crew falls to work to refresh the tires and add fuel for driver Bobby Labonte, who drove to the point from his 27th-place starting position and then settled in for a top-10 finish.

(Below) Rusty Wallace, a Phoenix winner in 1998, straps in for a good run on one of his favorite tracks. Wallace had a solid run to seventh place, his third straight finish of 11th of better.

(Bottom) Jeff Gordon (24) feels the heat from Kevin Harvick (29) with Elliott Sadler (38) applying pressure from behind in their early-race fight for position. Harvick posted his fifth top five of the year in fourth. Sadler, who led once for 16 laps, wasn't as lucky and fell out of contention after hitting the turn-one wall.

the points, a spot he had now held for nine consecutive weeks. The driver who finishes 11th overall is in line for a sizeable bonus and a trip to New York for the NASCAR NEXTEL Cup Series Awards Ceremony, and McMurray seemed destined to fill the position, leaving Atlanta with 4,195 points, 221 more than 12th-pace Dale Jarrett.

Maybe they should call it the "Newman/Bud Pole Award." The Penske Racing South Dodge pilot zipped around the one-mile Phoenix track in a record 26.499 seconds at 135.854 mph to record his ninth No. 1 start of the year and his fourth in a row. Oddly enough, though, Newman had yet in 2004 to score a victory from a No. 1 starting position.

*(Below) Mark Martin (6) finds himself in the thick of things as the field sorts out after a restart. Martin, who has a win and 13 top 10s in his 16 Phoenix starts, was hoping for better than his 15th-place finish in his bid to gain ground on the point leaders.*

*(Right) Kasey Kahne waits for fresh rubber under caution while other lead-lap cars head toward their pits. Although he did not lead in the race, Kahne had another good showing in his second consecutive fifth-place effort.*

"I've always said that whoever is on the pole, whether it's us or not, has no excuse," Newman noted. "You've proved you have the fastest car, but you have to be consistent for the length of the race."

Raybestos Brakes Rookie of the Year contender Brian Vickers, in the No. 25 Hendrick Motorsports Chevrolet, recorded the second-fastest time and speed of 26.890 seconds at 133.879 mph, while Joe Nemechek, Kasey Kahne and Kevin Harvick were third through fifth quickest.

"Today (Newman) beat us by almost four-tenths (of a second)," Vickers said. "We had a great car. ... I don't know where he got that speed."

No one in attendance was seen doing a "rain dance" on the hillside overlooking the third and fourth turns. Yet the race was red-flagged on the 106th lap (the start of the second of 11 caution-flag periods for 63 laps) when it began drizzling. The interruption lasted about 22 minutes, and when the green flag waved again on lap 115, Elliott Sadler had emerged from the pits first and taken the lead.

Lurking in the shadows, however, was Dale Earnhardt Jr., who had already paced the field for 48 circuits, from laps 60 to 107.

The day's final yellow flag flew on lap 308 because of Casey Mears' accident in turn two, and when another car's blown engine spread oil on the track, the red flag came out again.

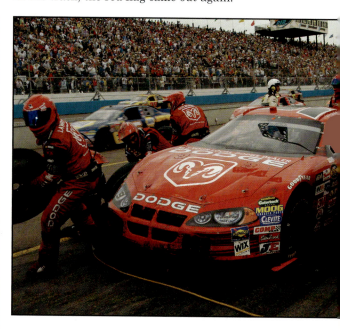

The event got the nod for the final time one lap after it's scheduled distance had been completed, and under the green-white-checkered rule, the fans were treated to a 315-lap event.

None of this mattered to Earnhardt Jr., as he'd taken the lead from Jeff Gordon with a pass on the 304th lap. Earnhardt's dominant Budweiser Chevrolet sped to the checkered flag, while Gordon's faltering DuPont Monte Carlo fell victim to Ryan Newman's Dodge. Newman was 1.431 seconds behind Earnhardt Jr. at the finish, while Gordon, Kevin Harvick and Kasey Kahne rounded out the top five.

"I got chills having a car that fast," Earnhardt Jr. said following his sixth win of the season. "I was gobbling up ground on those guys in the center of the corner. I just couldn't believe they couldn't get their cars driving as good as mine was.

(Above) Everybody scatters coming off the fourth turn in an incident before the halfway point that ultimately affected seven cars, including championship contenders Kurt Busch (97) and Mark Martin (6).

(Below) Dale Earnhardt Jr. (8) makes his presence known to Jeff Gordon (24) while challenging for the lead. Gordon had led a 76-lap stint until, with 11 laps remaining, "Junior" motored past on his way to the win.

"Gordon was a sitting duck at the end. His car was terrible. He was lucky just to get what he got."

"Junior had a dominant car all day long. We needed (the race) to go green the whole way to have any chance," said Gordon, who watched Earnhardt pick up two spots in the Chase for the NASCAR NEXTEL Cup, while he advanced from third to second in points.

Had not "Junior" lost an argument with crew chief Tony Eury Sr., he might not have won. When the ninth yellow flag waved on lap 282, Earnhardt Jr., who was running third, wanted to pit for tires. Eury Sr. told him to stay on the track and keep his position. The driver grudgingly complied, and Eury's strategy proved to be a winner.

Earnhardt Jr. paced the field three times for 118 laps, Gordon led three times for 100 laps, while Newman, Sadler, Busch, Kenseth and Bobby Labonte also picked up five bonus points each for leading at some point in the race.

Earnhardt completed the event in 3 hours, 19 minutes and 16 seconds at an average speed of 94.848 mph and won $274,503.

Also during the weekend at Phoenix, NASCAR announced that it would probably change qualifying procedures in 2005 to reduce costs for the teams and reduce time spent at the track. In addition, the top 35 teams in this year's car owner points would be guaranteed starting spots in races. The remaining eight spots would be determined by qualifying speeds and by provisionals.

## Chase for the NASCAR NEXTEL Cup Standings
*(With 2 Races Remaining)*

| Pos. | Driver | Points | Behind | Change |
|------|--------|--------|--------|--------|
| 1 | **Kurt Busch** | **6191** | — | — |
| 2 | Jeff Gordon | 6150 | -41 | +1 |
| 3 | Dale Earnhardt Jr. | 6144 | -47 | +2 |
| 4 | Jimmie Johnson | 6143 | -48 | -2 |
| 5 | Mark Martin | 6089 | -102 | -1 |
| 6 | Tony Stewart | 6049 | -142 | — |
| 7 | Ryan Newman | 6041 | -150 | — |
| 8 | Elliott Sadler | 5869 | -322 | — |
| 9 | Matt Kenseth | 5855 | -336 | — |
| 10 | Jeremy Mayfield | 5836 | -355 | — |

## CHECKER AUTO PARTS 500   *final race results*

| Fin. Pos. | Start Pos. | Car No. | Driver | Team |
|-----------|-----------|---------|--------|------|
| 1 | 14 | 8 | Dale Earnhardt Jr. | Budweiser Chevrolet |
| 2 | 1 | 12 | Ryan Newman | ALLTEL Dodge |
| 3 | 8 | 24 | Jeff Gordon | DuPont Chevrolet |
| 4 | 5 | 29 | Kevin Harvick | GM Goodwrench Chevrolet |
| 5 | 4 | 9 | Kasey Kahne | Dodge Dealers/UAW Dodge |
| 6 | 13 | 48 | Jimmie Johnson | Lowe's Chevrolet |
| 7 | 15 | 2 | Rusty Wallace | Miller Lite Dodge |
| 8 | 6 | 20 | Tony Stewart | The Home Depot Chevrolet |
| 9 | 27 | 18 | Bobby Labonte | Interstate Batteries Chevrolet |
| 10 | 28 | 97 | Kurt Busch | IRWIN Industrial Tools Ford |
| 11 | 20 | 30 | Jeff Burton | America Online Chevrolet |
| 12 | 3 | 01 | Joe Nemechek | U.S. Army Chevrolet |
| 13 | 23 | 16 | Greg Biffle | National Guard Ford |
| 14 | 11 | 10 | Scott Riggs | Valvoline Chevrolet |
| 15 | 22 | 6 | Mark Martin | Viagra Ford |
| 16 | 32 | 32 | Bobby Hamilton Jr. | Tide Chevrolet |
| 17 | 19 | 15 | Michael Waltrip | NAPA Chevrolet |
| 18 | 2 | 25 | Brian Vickers | GMAC Chevrolet |
| 19 | 25 | 21 | Ricky Rudd | Motorcraft Ford |
| 20 | 18 | 49 | Ken Schrader | Schwan's Home Service Dodge |
| 21 | 24 | 19 | Jeremy Mayfield | Dodge Dealers/UAW Dodge |
| 22 | 26 | 88 | Dale Jarrett | UPS Ford |
| 23 | 12 | 43 | Jeff Green | Cheerios/Betty Crocker Dodge |
| 24 | 10 | 42 | Jamie McMurray | Texaco/Havoline Dodge |
| 25 | 35 | 40 | Sterling Marlin | Coors Light Dodge |
| 26 | 38 | 22 | Scott Wimmer | Caterpillar Dodge |
| 27 | 37 | 37 | Kevin Lepage | Carter Racing Dodge |
| 28 | 34 | 45 | Kyle Petty | Georgia-Pacific/Brawny Dodge |
| 29 | 33 | 4 | Mike Wallace | Lucas Oil Chevrolet |
| 30 | 40 | 77 | Brendan Gaughan | Kodak/Jasper Eng. & Trans. Dodge |
| 31 | 21 | 14 | John Andretti | VB/APlus at Sunoco Ford |
| 32 | 31 | 5 | Terry Labonte | "The Incredibles"/Kellogg's Chevrolet |
| 33 | 42 | 02 | Hermie Sadler | Treasue Island-Las Vegas Chevrolet |
| 34 | 7 | 41 | Casey Mears | Target Dodge |
| 35 | 17 | 31 | Robby Gordon | Cingular Wireless Chevrolet |
| 36 | 16 | 17 | Matt Kenseth | DeWalt Power Tools Ford |
| 37 | 29 | 99 | Carl Edwards | Roush Racing Ford |
| 38 | 9 | 38 | Elliott Sadler | Pedigree Ford |
| 39 | 30 | 09 | Johnny Sauter | Miccosukee Resort Dodge |
| 40 | 39 | 0 | Ward Burton | NetZero Chevrolet |
| 41 | 43 | 89 | Morgan Shepherd | Racing with Jesus/Red Line Oil Dodge |
| 42 | 41 | 98 | Randy LaJoie | Airaid Premium Filters Ford |
| 43 | 36 | 50 | Todd Bodine | Arnold Development Co. Dodge |

# MOUNTAIN DEW SOUTHERN 500

— RACE NO.9 —
## DARLINGTON RACEWAY
### NOVEMBER 14, 2004

There were just two NASCAR NEXTEL Cup Series races left in a season that had begun 10 months ago in Daytona Beach, Fla. What's more, a mere 48 points separated the leader from the fourth-place runner in the Chase for the NASCAR NEXTEL Cup. So, all bets were off going into the 55th and final edition of the Mountain Dew Southern 500.

As far as the leaders were concerned, however, there was just one game plan — victory!

"We all really have the same stake here. We all know we've got to win," Jeff Gordon, driver of the DuPont Chevrolet said. "We've got to run up front and finish ahead of those guys. It's not about getting a top 10; it's about getting wins."

Gordon's teammate, Jimmie Johnson, concurred. With three victories in the past four outings, as well as a win in the 400-mile race at Darlington in late March, the pilot of the Lowe's Chevrolet was fourth in points. He, however, knew this was no time to back off and cruise.

"The best thing this team can do is act and feel like we did three weeks ago," he noted. "That's to say, 'we don't have a shot at it, and we just need to go out there and win races.'

(Left) Jimmie Johnson and crew chief Chad Knaus (right) hoist the winning hardware at Darlington. Five weeks earlier, the Lowe's team appeared to be all but out of the title hunt, mired in ninth place and 247 points out of the lead. Now, after four wins in five events, Johnson was a mere 18 points down with one race remaining.

Rusty Wallace is a picture of intensity while he prepares to roll off the line, his focus purely on winning his first race at venerable Darlington. This, his 42nd career start on the egg-shaped track, would result in a disappointing 18th place.

"When we play offense, we do a lot better job than when we play defense."

Johnson meant what he said and played a superb offensive game. He led 107 of the first 195 laps, overcame a potentially disastrous problem while in the pits, took the lead away from Jamie McMurray with nine laps to go and held off Mark Martin's Roush Racing Ford by 0.959 second to score a series-leading eighth victory.

Point leader Kurt Busch, on the strength of a 10th-place run in the Checker Auto Parts 500 at Phoenix the week before, arrived in Darlington for the Southern 500

with 6,191 points. Gordon, however, came away with a third-place run at Phoenix, moved from third to second in points and now trailed Busch by just 41 markers.

Dale Earnhardt Jr. captured the win at Phoenix, his sixth of the year, and leapt from fifth to third in points, where he was how just six in arrears of Gordon and only 47 out of the lead.

Johnson started 13th at Phoenix and came away with a sixth-place finish. While he gained 11 points on Busch, he slipped from second to fourth in points but was just one in back of Earnhardt Jr. and only 48 behind Busch.

"We had a good car (and) once we got going, we were fine," Johnson noted. "We just ran out of laps."

Martin recovered from a mid-race spinout in Arizona, but the mishap was costly. He finished 15th, dropped from fourth to fifth in points and headed to South Carolina 102 markers in back of Busch.

Positions six through 10 in the standings remained unchanged in the week between the Bass Pro Shops 500 at Atlanta and the 312-mile run in Arizona. Although Tony Stewart "backed up" a bit in Phoenix (he started sixth and finished eighth), he was pleased that his Home Depot team was able to adjust his Chevrolet during the event and come out with a top-10 finish. With 6,049 points, he headed to Darlington 40 behind Martin but only eight in front of Ryan Newman.

Newman, the Bud Pole leader in 2004 with nine, started first at Phoenix, ran well and ended up finishing second to Earnhardt Jr., but his 11th top-five finish of the year wasn't enough to edge him out of seventh in points going into the Southern 500.

Newman, however, did have a healthy lead over eighth-place Elliott Sadler, who stumbled at Phoenix and ended up 38th in the final order. Sadler came away with 5,869 points — 172 behind Newman and 322 out of first place — and with ninth-running Matt Kenseth nipping at his heels, 14 points back. Kenseth bid a not-so-fond adieu to Phoenix after suffering a blown engine and finishing 36th.

(Opposite Page) Stress test. The pressure of a championship fight spreads throughout the team, including crew members, whose race consists of waiting around, interrupted by 15-second bursts of adrenaline. For points leader Kurt Busch their job was invaluable; his crew helped him turn mid-race struggles into a top-10 finish to stay atop the standings.

(Above) Jeff Gordon streaks over the start/finish line, vying for his seventh Southern 500 crown in the event's final chapter. Although he led three times for 155 circuits and took the lap-leader bonus, his bid to win fell two places short.

(Below) Casey Mears (41) and Mike Bliss, driving the NetZero car for the first time, go fender-to-fender in front of the Darlington crowd. Bliss fought his way up from 30th place to a very respectable top-10 finish in just his third start of the season.

(Right) Pit crews wait anxiously for their cars to report under caution. Their jobs played large parts in the outcome of the race, as there were eight yellow flags spread rather evenly over the 367-lap affair.

(Far Right) Kurt Busch blasts away from the No. 1 pit stall at the end of pit road, edging out Dale Earnhardt Jr. for position on the restart. Both contenders struggled with ill-handling cars, but both were able to salvage lead-lap finishes.

(Below) Jeff Gordon leads (in order) Jimmie Johnson, Mark Martin and Jamie McMurray behind the pace truck while daylight fades into a beautiful sunset behind the frontstretch grandstands.

"We just broke something in the motor. I don't know why or what, we just broke something." Kenseth said.

Although mired in 10th place with 5,836 points following Phoenix, Jeremy Mayfield left on an optimistic note, saying, "We made a lot of gains and got a lot better today."

The wet weather that skewed things a bit a Phoenix seemed to follow the competitors back across the United States, as Bud Pole qualifying for the Mountain Dew Southern 500 was washed out. That meant the field was set by car owner points, which put Busch first on the starting grid.

"That was a heck of a lap for us," quipped Busch, who hadn't taken a pole in almost two years. "It's definitely a great opportunity for us, but having all of the drivers in the Chase (for the NASCAR NEXTEL Cup) right up front, everybody's going to want to lead a lap quickly."

"It's risk versus gain," Gordon added. "If it's not a super risky move to do it, I'd love to have those five bonus points. But I'll have nine other guys around me who want those points."

As it turned out, Busch led the race's first lap, while Gordon paced laps two through 19. Busch then paced laps 20-26, but eventual winner Johnson showed his strength early on by going to the front for the first time on lap 27 and leading through the 61st circuit on the egg-shaped oval.

Johnson, though, did have one scary moment. After taking the No. 1 spot on lap 147, he ran up front until pitting under the fourth caution period (laps 195-201). It was then that a lug nut got hung up between a brake rotor and wheel

hub, and Johnson lost valuable time while the problem was fixed. He re-entered the event running 11th and watched teammate Gordon lead 135 of the next 140 laps.

Johnson, however, was not to be denied. A superb pit stop on the day's seventh caution put the Lowe's Chevrolet back up front. Jamie McMurray took over the point during the eighth and final caution of the race, but once under green, it took Johnson just nine laps to track down the Texaco/Havoline Dodge at take over for good.

With the win, Johnson gained two spots in points, moving from fourth to second, and tightened up the Chase for the NASCAR NEXTEL Cup even more with one race remaining. And, too, he helped continue the healing process at Hendrick Motorsports after the tragedy involving the downed place near Martinsville three weeks earlier.

"I can't believe it," Johnson said. "Fighting our way back into this championship with what took place with the airplane, I just can't believe it.

"The void inside me isn't filled, but this certainly helps. This is good medicine."

Gordon, who led more than anyone else (155 laps on three occasions), finished third. McMurray faltered but finished fourth, Raybestos Rookie of the Year points leader Kasey Kahne was fifth and Kurt Busch finished sixth and retained his No. 1 spot in the standings.

"We felt like we dodged a bullet today," said Busch. Early in the event his car was hit by Kahne's Dodge, and while he continued on, it was with an ill-handling Ford.

Johnson took the win in 4 hours and 33 seconds at an average speed of 125.044 mph and won $269.675.

Four days before the race, NASCAR officials announced that the sanctioning body had lifted its long-standing ban on hard-liquor sponsorship of race teams and would now permit it. Although brewed beverages such as beer had long been a part of the sport, the liquor prohibition had dated back to the start of the "modern era" (1972 forward) when the top NASCAR circuit was revamped.

"We felt the time was right," said NASCAR President Mike Helton. "Attitudes have changed, and spirits companies have a long record of responsible advertising."

*Carl Edwards (99) looks for an opening on Jimmie Johnson's inside, while Matt Kenseth tries to gain ground near the wall. Edwards battled hard in the race before taking seventh place, his fifth top 10 in 12 career starts.*

## Chase for the NASCAR NEXTEL Cup Standings
*(With 1 Race Remaining)*

| Pos. | Driver | Points | Behind | Change |
|------|--------|--------|--------|--------|
| **1** | **Kurt Busch** | **6346** | — | — |
| 2 | Jimmie Johnson | 6328 | -18 | +2 |
| 3 | Jeff Gordon | 6325 | -21 | -1 |
| 4 | Dale Earnhardt Jr. | 6274 | -72 | -1 |
| 5 | Mark Martin | 6264 | -82 | — |
| 6 | Tony Stewart | 6161 | -185 | — |
| 7 | Ryan Newman | 6102 | -244 | — |
| 8 | Matt Kenseth | 5963 | -383 | +1 |
| 9 | Elliott Sadler | 5963 | -383 | -1 |
| 10 | Jeremy Mayfield | 5942 | -404 | — |

## MOUNTAIN DEW SOUTHERN 500 *final race results*

| Fin. Pos. | Start Pos. | Car No. | Driver | Team |
|------|------|------|--------|------|
| 1 | 4 | 48 | Jimmie Johnson | Lowe's Chevrolet |
| 2 | 5 | 6 | Mark Martin | Viagra Ford |
| 3 | 2 | 24 | Jeff Gordon | DuPont Chevrolet |
| 4 | 11 | 42 | Jamie McMurray | Texaco/Havoline Dodge |
| 5 | 13 | 9 | Kasey Kahne | Dodge Dealers/UAW Dodge |
| 6 | 1 | 97 | Kurt Busch | Smirnoff Ice/Sharpie Ford |
| 7 | 24 | 99 | Carl Edwards | World Financial Group Ford |
| 8 | 18 | 01 | Joe Nemechek | USG Sheetrock Chevrolet |
| 9 | 15 | 18 | Bobby Labonte | Interstate Batteries Chevrolet |
| 10 | 30 | 0 | Mike Bliss | NetZero Chevrolet |
| 11 | 3 | 8 | Dale Earnhardt Jr. | Budweiser Chevrolet |
| 12 | 20 | 40 | Sterling Marlin | Coors Light Dodge |
| 13 | 21 | 30 | Jeff Burton | America Online Chevrolet |
| 14 | 32 | 43 | Jeff Green | Cheerios/Betty Crocker Dodge |
| 15 | 23 | 31 | Robby Gordon | Cingular Wireless Chevrolet |
| 16 | 26 | 21 | Ricky Rudd | Motorcraft Ford |
| 17 | 6 | 20 | Tony Stewart | Home Depot Chevrolet |
| 18 | 16 | 2 | Rusty Wallace | Miller Lite Dodge |
| 19 | 10 | 19 | Jeremy Mayfield | Dodge Dealers/UAW Dodge |
| 20 | 9 | 17 | Matt Kenseth | DeWalt Power Tools Ford |
| 21 | 27 | 25 | Brian Vickers | GMAC Chevrolet |
| 22 | 28 | 22 | Scott Wimmer | Caterpillar Dodge |
| 23 | 8 | 38 | Elliott Sadler | M&M's Ford |
| 24 | 19 | 16 | Greg Biffle | National Guard/Subway Ford |
| 25 | 31 | 10 | Scott Riggs | Valvoline Chevrolet |
| 26 | 22 | 41 | Casey Mears | Target Dodge |
| 27 | 29 | 77 | Brendan Gaughan | Kodak/Jasper Eng. & Trans. Dodge |
| 28 | 25 | 5 | Terry Labonte | Kellogg's Chevrolet |
| 29 | 42 | 09 | Johnny Sauter | Miccosukee Resort Dodge |
| 30 | 33 | 49 | Ken Schrader | Schwan's Home Service Dodge |
| 31 | 35 | 32 | Bobby Hamilton Jr. | Tide Chevrolet |
| 32 | 14 | 29 | Kevin Harvick | GM Goodwrench Chevrolet |
| 33 | 17 | 15 | Michael Waltrip | NAPA Chevrolet |
| 34 | 7 | 12 | Ryan Newman | ALLTEL/Mobil 1 Dodge |
| 35 | 34 | 45 | Kyle Petty | Georgia-Pacific/Brawny Dodge |
| 36 | 39 | 98 | Randy LaJoie | Mach 1 Inc. Ford |
| 37 | 12 | 88 | Dale Jarrett | UPS Ford |
| 38 | 37 | 4 | Mike Wallace | Lucas Oil Chevrolet |
| 39 | 38 | 50 | Todd Bodine | Mesco Building Solutions Dodge |
| 40 | 41 | 02 | Hermie Sadler | East Tennessee Trailers Chevrolet |
| 41 | 43 | 80 | Mario Gosselin | Adesa Impact Ford |
| 42 | 36 | 72 | Kirk Shelmerdine | Freddie B's Ford |
| 43 | 40 | 89 | Morgan Shepherd | Racing with Jesus/Red Line Oil Dodge |

# FORD **400**

---

There should be little argument that the Ford 400 turned out to be an almost perfect way to close out the 2004 NASCAR NEXTEL Cup Series season.

The event's loops, turns, circles and overall drama provided as many "oohs," "aahs" and dynamic moments of intrigue as the wildest roller coaster at any amusement park you might care to name. Homestead-Miami Speedway was covered with an aura of suspense from the race's first green flag forward and, almost fittingly, had to go into "overtime" before its outcome was decided.

When the dust finally settled 3 hours, 50 minutes and 55 seconds later, the event turned out to be a smash hit for the company that sponsored it, Roush Racing and its cerebral owner, Jack "Man in the Hat" Roush, and NASCAR itself.

It was a success for NASCAR and its officials because it showed that the revised points system with the 10-race Chase for the NASCAR NEXTEL Cup, introduced in February, worked. The season ended with the closest-ever margin of victory in points.

Ford Motor Co. sponsored the event and two of Roush's drivers emerged victorious. Greg Biffle, in the No. 16 National Guard Ford won the race and Kurt Busch, in the No. 97 Sharpie Ford, gave Roush his second consecutive NASCAR Cup Series championship.

(Left) Greg Biffle's National Guard Ford fronts the field for a restart ahead of second-place Kurt Busch (97) on the outside, with Robby Gordon (31) leading the lap-down cars on the inside. Biffle led off on four restarts, three of them during a 110-lap stretch at the front early in the race.

In a frightening moment for the Sharpie team, Kurt Busch slides his Ford into the waiting hands of his crew sans the right-front wheel. They recovered quickly and kept Busch on the lead lap, where he was able to save his championship hopes.

*(Above) Tony Stewart takes a peek on the inside of Kevin Harvick (29), while (in order) Jeff Gordon, Jeff Green, Rusty Wallace and Mike Wallace give chase. Harvick picked up another top-10 finish in the race, his third in the last five events and his 14th of the season.*

*(Right) Martin Truex Jr. prepares for his second career start, driving the No. 1 Chevrolet for Dale Earnhardt Inc. The day before, Truex put the final touches on the NASCAR Busch Series championship for the DEI-owned Chance2 Motorsports team.*

Busch had led in points since the running of the third of 10 races (at Talladega, Ala., in October) that would determine the championship. He, however, had to constantly keep an eye on Jimmie Johnson, Jeff Gordon and Dale Earnhardt Jr., who were never that far behind.

Following a sixth-place run in the previous week's Southern 500 at Darlington, S.C., Busch arrived at Homestead with 6,346 points, only 18 more than Johnson, 21 ahead of Gordon and 72 in front of Earnhardt. Fifth-place Mark Martin, with 6,264 points (10 less than Earnhardt) still had a remote shot at the first championship trophy carrying the Nextel name, but everyone else was out of the running.

Johnson had set himself up for a shot at Busch by winning the Southern 500. Gordon went into the Darlington event second in points, but fell to third after a pit-road mistake by one of his crewmen had him finishing third instead of potentially snaring the win. Martin kept his slim hopes for a championship alive by finishing second to Johnson, while Busch finished sixth and Earnhardt 11th.

Johnson didn't make things easy on himself with a terrible day in Bud Pole qualifying for the Ford 400. He was 39th quickest and had to take a provisional start for the race. On the

other hand, Busch set himself up perfectly by taking the No. 1 spot in qualifying. Busch, who hadn't won a pole since 2002, was the last of 56 drivers to make a run, and his lap at 171.379 mph put Biffle (179.307) on the outside of the starting grid's front row.

"I hope that people don't get too far ahead of themselves," Busch said after his run. "They do have to come chase us down, though. That's the mental side of it."

Newman clocked in third quickest at 179.053 mph, Raybestos Brakes Rookie of the Year points leader Kasey Kahne was fourth with a speed of 178.891mph, and Gordon took spot No. 5 at 178.719 mph.

A track record 14 caution-flags for 79 laps and 14 lead changes among seven drivers kept fans and competitors alike wondering just how the Ford 400 would all shake out. Finally, Busch, who could have easily lost his bid for a first championship, gutted out a fifth-place finish and came away with a total of 6,506 points, just eight up on runner-up Johnson and with 16 more than Johnson's teammate, Gordon.

"This is what a team does to win a championship. They persevere on a day such as this," said Busch. "All year long we've done things like this. ... I just can't believe we were able to overcome all that turmoil."

And there was enough "turmoil" to keep the pot on a constant boil, with Busch himself the cause of at least two heart-stopping moments. While running second on the 93rd lap, the entire right-front wheel detached itself from the Ford and went rolling down the track. Busch almost crashed into the end of the retaining

wall at the entrance to pit road, but made it in under the fourth caution for repairs.

He pitted a second time almost immediately, and less than 10 laps later the fifth caution came out when Jeremy Mayfield cut a tire and hit the wall. Busch made yet another stop and lost additional time and positions when his crew got its signals crossed.

"I basically screwed that one up," crew chief Jimmy Fennig said. "I called for two tires, (but) we went for four."

*(Above) Jeremy Mayfield finds the fence after cutting a tire on lap 113, bringing out the fifth of 14 cautions for 79 laps in the Ford 400. The mishap doused his chances of ending the season on a high note and solidified his 10th-place standing in the Chase for the NASCAR NEXTEL Cup.*

*(Left) Brendan Gaughan (77) puts the heat on the champ-to-be on the way to a strong sixth-place finish, one spot behind Kurt Busch. As the top-finishing rookie in the race, Gaughan bested his competition in an extremely tight battle for second place behind Kasey Kahne in the Raybestos Rookie of the Year battle.*

*(Above) Greg Biffle (16), Jeff Gordon (24) and Jimmie Johnson (48) stack up behind Tony Stewart's Home Depot Chevrolet in a four-way fight for the late-race lead. Stewart, who looked to be in position to take his third win of the year, unfortunately suffered a fuel pressure problem on the last restart and dropped to fourth at the finish.*

*(Right, Above) Greg Biffle (16) stretches his advantage over the field in his fleet-running Ford. Biffle, who started on the front row next to Kurt Busch, led on three occasions early in the event, and then was in position to take advantage of Stewart's bad luck to take the victory.*

*(Right, Below) Team owner Jack Roush shows off the winner's trophy flanked by driver Greg Biffle (right) and crew chief Dough Richert (left). This was the second such celebration for the "16" team in 2004, having also won at Michigan in August.*

*(Opposite Page) Sweet success. 2004 NASCAR NEXTEL Cup Series Champion Kurt Busch makes his feelings clear about taking ownership of the sport's new championship trophy. Busch finished the season with three wins, 10 top fives and 21 top 10s with just three DNFs to take the title by a mere eight points over Jimmie Johnson in the closest championship battle on record.*

While Johnson and Gordon took turns temporarily leading in points, Busch, who led just the first four laps, overcame the miscue, managed to avoid all the ensuing action and soldiered on to a fifth-place finish.

The man nobody could beat, however, was Biffle, who led four times for 117 laps en route to his second win of the season. He paced laps

5-114, 147-148 and 171-173. Then, while he was running third with just three laps of the scheduled 267 left, race leader Ryan Newman had a right-front tire go down, causing him to smack the wall.

The final yellow flag emerged, putting Stewart in the lead, and the event was forced into a green-white-checkered finish to ensure it would not end under caution. Biffle mashed the gas on the lap-270 restart and got by Stewart, whose Chevrolet experienced fuel-delivery problems. Johnson and Gordon got by Stewart, as well, to take second and third place, while Stewart finished fourth.

"It's unfortunate that Ryan had trouble today, but it was the determining factor in giving me the opportunity to win," Biffle said. "There was no way we were going to catch him."

While the Ford 400, with its myriad of interruptions for all sorts of reasons, smiled on the two Roush drivers, it was unkind to those who needed a good finish the most. Along with Newman's and Mayfield's poor luck, Martin ran strong at first but made an unscheduled pit stop and fell back to finish 11th. Earnhardt ran into the back of another car and also ran over a traffic-light cover that had blown loose and fallen onto the track. He nursed his ill-handling Chevrolet to a 23rd-place finish, while Kenseth had a mediocre run with a 19th-place result.

"We gave it a heck of an effort," Gordon noted. "We had a flat left-rear (tire) that got us really behind, and we fought all day long. We struggled a little bit there at the beginning and got better and better.

## Chase for the NASCAR NEXTEL Cup Standings
*(Final Standings)*

| Pos. | Driver | Points | Behind | Change |
|------|--------|--------|--------|--------|
| **1** | **Kurt Busch** | **6506** | **0** | — |
| 2 | Jimmie Johnson | 6498 | -8 | — |
| 3 | Jeff Gordon | 6490 | -16 | — |
| 4 | Mark Martin | 6399 | -107 | +1 |
| 5 | Dale Earnhardt Jr. | 6368 | -138 | -1 |
| 6 | Tony Stewart | 6326 | -180 | — |
| 7 | Ryan Newman | 6180 | -326 | — |
| 8 | Matt Kenseth | 6069 | -437 | — |
| 9 | Elliott Sadler | 6024 | -482 | — |
| 10 | Jeremy Mayfield | 6000 | -506 | — |

## FORD 400  *final race results*

| Fin. Pos. | Start Pos. | Car No. | Driver | Team |
|-----------|-----------|---------|--------|------|
| 1 | 2 | 16 | Greg Biffle | National Guard Ford |
| 2 | 39 | 48 | Jimmie Johnson | Lowe's Chevrolet |
| 3 | 5 | 24 | Jeff Gordon | DuPont Chevrolet |
| 4 | 8 | 20 | Tony Stewart | The Home Depot Chevrolet |
| 5 | 1 | 97 | Kurt Busch | Sharpie Ford |
| 6 | 17 | 77 | Brendan Gaughan | Kodak/Jasper Eng. & Trans. Dodge |
| 7 | 18 | 42 | Jamie McMurray | Texaco/Havoline Dodge |
| 8 | 10 | 2 | Rusty Wallace | Miller Lite Dodge |
| 9 | 7 | 21 | Ricky Rudd | Motorcraft Ford |
| 10 | 9 | 29 | Kevin Harvick | GM Goodwrench Chevrolet |
| 11 | 11 | 6 | Mark Martin | Viagra Ford |
| 12 | 6 | 18 | Bobby Labonte | Interstate Batteries Chevrolet |
| 13 | 21 | 22 | Scott Wimmer | Caterpillar Dodge |
| 14 | 22 | 99 | Carl Edwards | Roush Racing Ford |
| 15 | 25 | 10 | Scott Riggs | Valvoline Chevrolet |
| 16 | 38 | 40 | Sterling Marlin | Coors Light/LoneStar Steakhouse Dodge |
| 17 | 24 | 15 | Michael Waltrip | NAPA Chevrolet |
| 18 | 14 | 25 | Brian Vickers | GMAC Chevrolet |
| 19 | 30 | 17 | Matt Kenseth | DeWalt Power Tools Ford |
| 20 | 23 | 14 | John Andretti | VB/APlus at Sunoco Ford |
| 21 | 29 | 32 | Bobby Hamilton Jr. | Tide Chevrolet |
| 22 | 37 | 00 | Kenny Wallace | Aaron's Chevrolet |
| 23 | 16 | 8 | Dale Earnhardt Jr. | Budweiser Chevrolet |
| 24 | 27 | 88 | Dale Jarrett | UPS Ford |
| 25 | 43 | 49 | Ken Schrader | Schwan's Home Service Dodge |
| 26 | 41 | 41 | Casey Mears | Target Dodge |
| 27 | 19 | 01 | Joe Nemechek | U.S. Army Chevrolet |
| 28 | 32 | 36 | Boris Said | USG Durock Chevrolet |
| 29 | 33 | 31 | Robby Gordon | Cingular Wireless Chevrolet |
| 30 | 3 | 12 | Ryan Newman | ALLTEL Dodge |
| 31 | 42 | 5 | Terry Labonte | Kellogg's Chevrolet |
| 32 | 35 | 1 | Martin Truex Jr. | Enterprise Rental Car Chevrolet |
| 33 | 28 | 4 | Mike Wallace | Lucas Oil Chevrolet |
| 34 | 15 | 38 | Elliott Sadler | M&M's Ford |
| 35 | 20 | 19 | Jeremy Mayfield | Dodge Dealers/UAW Dodge |
| 36 | 40 | 30 | Jeff Burton | America Online Chevrolet |
| 37 | 31 | 43 | Jeff Green | Chex Party Mix Dodge |
| 38 | 4 | 9 | Kasey Kahne | Dodge Dealers/UAW Dodge |
| 39 | 26 | 06 | Travis Kvapil | Mobil 1 Dodge |
| 40 | 12 | 0 | Mike Bliss | NetZero Chevrolet |
| 41 | 13 | 23 | Shane Hmiel | Miccosukee Resorts Dodge |
| 42 | 34 | 13 | Greg Sacks | ARCDehooker/Vita Coco Dodge |
| 43 | 36 | 02 | Hermie Sadler | Drive for Diversity/Sam Bass Chevrolet |

"I wish we could have gotten the job done," added Johnson, who, like Gordon, never led a lap. "We can leave here knowing that we (did) everything we could. We just came up short."

At the finish, though, Biffle edged out Johnson by 0.342 second and headed to victory lane, where he received the winner's check for $314,850. Busch, meanwhile, headed toward a $5 million-plus payday as the first NASCAR NEXTEL Cup Series champion.

# Reflections

## 2004 NASCAR NEXTEL Cup Series

*Year of change. With new title sponsor Nextel Communications, venues throughout the series erected new signs reflecting the change (inset). The same was true for North Carolina Speedway when track personnel prepared for their event date in February. That race would be the last at the venerable old track, as it would not be returning to the schedule again. Between 1965 and 2004, "The Rock" hosted 78 NASCAR Cup Series events.*

(Above) Kyle Petty participates in a charity walk at Texas Motor Speedway to support the Victory Junction Gang Camp, surrounded by kids who are more than happy to join in with the extremely popular third-generation driver.

(Right) Although Kyle retains most of the responsibility for racing operations of his family-owned team, The King, Richard Petty, is still a fixture in the garage area wearing his trademark hat and famous Petty smile.

(Below) Veteran drivers Sterling Marlin (left) and Jimmy Spencer laugh it up at Bristol Motor Speedway in August. Spencer started 26 races during the season, most of those in the No. 4 car fielded by Morgan-McClure Motorsports.

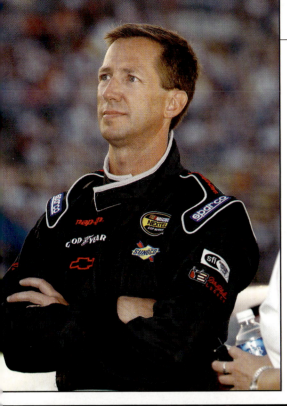

(Far Left) John Andretti made appearances in selected events in 2004 driving a Chevrolet fielded by Dale Earnhardt, Inc. His best performance came in February when he posted a 13th place in the Daytona 500.

(Left) Fighter jets make a low pass over California Speedway in May as part of pre-race ceremonies, a real treat for fans that has become a tradition before most NASCAR events.

(Below) The hardest ticket to get in all of NASCAR remains the summer-night 500-lapper at Bristol Motor Speedway. This year, 160,000 fans packed the Tennessee half-mile speedbowl and witnessed Dale Earnhardt Jr. winning there for the first time in his career.

(Above) "Hey, what's the big deal?" says Joe Nemechek. He might have been referring to his late-season surge that included strong qualifying runs and a couple of Bud Poles, a string of top 10s and a victory at Kansas.

(Above Right) Nemechek's MB2/MBV Motorsports teammate, Scott Riggs, persevered through the rigors of a rookie season. Like Nemechek's, his team came on strong late in the season and built momentum for Riggs' sophomore campaign.

(Right) Brothers Mike (left) and Kenny Wallace "discuss" a few things at Daytona in February. Both drivers competed full time in the NASCAR Busch Series with occasional starts in NASCAR NEXTEL Cup Series events.

(Below) These two fans are having a great time at Pocono Raceway while waiting for their favorite drivers to stop by to sign autographs.

(Above Left) Bobby Hamilton Jr. sports his new colors at California Speedway after taking over the wheel of the Tide Chevrolet. In all, he made 17 starts during the season in addition to competing in the NASCAR Busch Series and NASCAR Craftsman Truck Series.

(Above Right) It's true that Texans like to do things in a big way, as Jeff Gordon finds out by taking a gander at this little lady's show of devotion for her favorite driver. Jeff? ... Oh, Jeff?

(Left) Robbie Reiser guided his driver, Matt Kenseth, through a season-long defense of their NASCAR Cup Series title. Two straight wins early in the year got them off to a great start, but problems down the stretch thwarted their bid for two in a row.

(Below) California Speedway hosted two NASCAR Cup Series events for the first time since joining the schedule in 1997. This year, in addition to the annual spring/early summer race, the beautiful speedway in Fontana was the site of the Labor Day weekend event, for which nearly 100,000 fans showed up on a sunny Southern California afternoon.

(Above) Brothers Terry (left) and Bobby Labonte enjoy some time together before racing the road course at Watkins Glen. Terry, after 26 years in the series, announced that this would be his last season running a full schedule and would scale back to racing only in selected events in 2005 and 2006.

(Right) Rusty Wallace (below right) bangs fenders with Tony Stewart at Martinsville in April on the way to his 55th career victory, his seventh at the Virginia short track. Wallace, the 1989 NASCAR Cup Series champion, put rumors to rest during the summer by saying 2005 would be his final year of competition.

(Below) Joining Labonte and Wallace in planning for life after racing, Mark Martin unveiled his "Salute to You" campaign in Charlotte, N.C., signifying his final year of NASCAR NEXTEL Cup Series competition to take place in 2005.

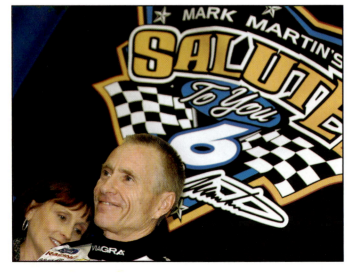

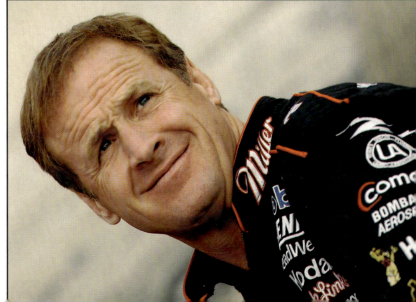

# Autographs
NASCAR NEXTEL Cup Series 2004